Urban Lowlands

Historical Studies of Urban America

EDITED BY LILIA FERNÁNDEZ, TIMOTHY J. GILFOYLE, BECKY M. NICOLAIDES,
AND AMANDA I. SELIGMAN, JAMES R. GROSSMAN, EDITOR EMERITUS

Recent titles in the series

Ann Durkin Keating, THE WORLD OF JULIETTE KINZIE: CHICAGO BEFORE THE FIRE

Jeffrey S. Adler, MURDER IN NEW ORLEANS: THE CREATION OF JIM CROW POLICING

David A. Gamson, THE IMPORTANCE OF BEING URBAN: DESIGNING THE PROGRESSIVE SCHOOL DISTRICT, 1890–1940

Kara Schlichting, NEW YORK RECENTERED: BUILDING THE METROPOLIS FROM THE SHORE

Mark Wild, RENEWAL: LIBERAL PROTESTANTS AND THE AMERICAN CITY AFTER WORLD WAR II

Meredith Oda, THE GATEWAY TO THE PACIFIC: JAPANESE AMERICANS AND THE REMAKING OF SAN FRANCISCO

Sean Dinces, BULLS MARKETS: CHICAGO'S BASKETBALL BUSINESS AND THE NEW INEQUALITY

Julia Guarneri, NEWSPRINT METROPOLIS: CITY PAPERS AND THE MAKING OF MODERN AMERICANS

Kyle B. Roberts, EVANGELICAL GOTHAM: RELIGION AND THE MAKING OF NEW YORK CITY, 1783–1860

Timothy Neary, CROSSING PARISH BOUNDARIES: RACE, SPORTS, AND CATHOLIC YOUTH IN CHICAGO, 1914–1954

Julia Rabig, THE FIXERS: DEVOLUTION, DEVELOPMENT, AND CIVIL SOCIETY IN NEWARK, 1960–1990

Amanda I. Seligman, CHICAGO'S BLOCK CLUBS: HOW NEIGHBORS SHAPE THE CITY

Aaron Shkuda, THE LOFTS OF SOHO: GENTRIFICATION, ART, AND INDUSTRY IN NEW YORK, 1950–1980

Mark Krasovic, THE NEWARK FRONTIER: COMMUNITY ACTION IN THE GREAT SOCIETY

Ansley T. Erickson, MAKING THE UNEQUAL METROPOLIS: SCHOOL DESEGREGATION AND ITS LIMITS

Andrew L. Slap and Frank Towers, Eds., CONFEDERATE CITIES: THE URBAN SOUTH DURING THE CIVIL WAR ERA

Evan Friss, THE CYCLING CITY: BICYCLES AND URBAN AMERICA IN THE 1890S

Ocean Howell, MAKING THE MISSION: PLANNING AND ETHNICITY IN SAN FRANCISCO

Benjamin Looker, A NATION OF NEIGHBORHOODS: IMAGINING CITIES, COMMUNITIES, AND DEMOCRACY IN POSTWAR AMERICA

Nancy H. Kwak, A WORLD OF HOMEOWNERS: AMERICAN POWER AND THE POLITICS OF HOUSING AID

Andrew R. Highsmith, DEMOLITION MEANS PROGRESS: FLINT, MICHIGAN, AND THE FATE OF THE AMERICAN METROPOLIS

Lila Corwin Berman, METROPOLITAN JEWS: POLITICS, RACE, AND RELIGION IN POSTWAR DETROIT

Gillian O'Brien, BLOOD RUNS GREEN: THE MURDER THAT TRANSFIXED GILDED AGE CHICAGO

Marta Gutman, A CITY FOR CHILDREN: WOMEN, ARCHITECTURE, AND THE CHARITABLE LANDSCAPES OF OAKLAND, 1850–1950

N. D. B. Connolly, A WORLD MORE CONCRETE: REAL ESTATE AND THE REMAKING OF JIM CROW SOUTH FLORIDA

Cindy R. Lobel, URBAN APPETITES: FOOD AND CULTURE IN NINETEENTH-CENTURY NEW YORK

Jeffrey Helgeson, CRUCIBLES OF BLACK EMPOWERMENT: CHICAGO'S NEIGHBORHOOD POLITICS FROM THE NEW DEAL TO HAROLD WASHINGTON

A complete list of series titles is available on the University of Chicago Press website.

Urban Lowlands

A History of Neighborhoods, Poverty, and Planning

STEVEN T. MOGA

The University of Chicago Press
Chicago and London

PUBLICATION OF THIS BOOK HAS BEEN AIDED BY A GRANT FROM THE BEVINGTON FUND.

The University of Chicago Press, Chicago 60637
The University of Chicago Press, Ltd., London
© 2020 by The University of Chicago
All rights reserved. No part of this book may be used or reproduced in any manner whatsoever without written permission, except in the case of brief quotations in critical articles and reviews. For more information, contact the University of Chicago Press, 1427 E. 60th St., Chicago, IL 60637.
Published 2020
Paperback edition 2024

33 32 31 30 29 28 27 26 25 24   1 2 3 4 5

ISBN-13: 978-0-226-71053-2 (cloth)
ISBN-13: 978-0-226-83333-0 (paper)
ISBN-13: 978-0-226-71067-9 (e-book)
DOI: https://doi.org/10.7208/chicago/9780226710679.001.0001

Library of Congress Cataloging-in-Publication Data

Names: Moga, Steven T., author.
Title: Urban lowlands : a history of neighborhoods, poverty, and planning / Steven T. Moga.
Other titles: Historical studies of urban America.
Description: Chicago ; London : The University of Chicago Press, 2020. | Series: Historical studies of urban America | Includes bibliographical references and index.
Identifiers: LCCN 2019052168 | ISBN 9780226710532 (cloth) | ISBN 9780226710679 (ebook)
Subjects: LCSH: City planning—United States—History—19th century. | City planning—United States—History—20th century. | City planning—Health aspects—United States. | Neighborhood planning—United States—History. | Neighborhood planning—United States—Case studies. | Urban poor—United States. | Urban health—United States. | Urban minorities—United States. | Urban ecology (Sociology)—United States. | Discrimination—United States—History.
Classification: LCC HT167 .M628 2020 | DDC 307.1/2160973—dc23
LC record available at https://lccn.loc.gov/2019052168

*For my parents, William and Dorothy
And for Leigh, Matthew, and Anders*

Contents

	Introduction: The Low Wards	1
1	From Bottomlands to Bottom Neighborhoods	11
2	Harlem Flats New York, New York	31
3	Black Bottom Nashville, Tennessee	55
4	Swede Hollow Saint Paul, Minnesota	85
5	The Flats Los Angeles, California	113
6	Landscapes of Poverty and Power	146
	Epilogue: Lowland Legacies	172

Acknowledgments 175
Notes 179
Index 211

INTRODUCTION

The Low Wards

On a Monday morning in the spring of 1898, Reverend James A. addressed a group of civic leaders to dedicate a new orphanage for African American children in Nashville. A pastor at Saint Paul's African Methodist Episcopal Church, Davis delivered a "forceful, practical and eloquent" address about the community's responsibilities and the need to save the two thousand "parentless and neglected" children living in run-down housing and on city streets. Reciting the names of the neighborhoods where these children lived, he said, "When I think of the hundreds that swarm in Black Bottom, Hell's Half Acre, Smoky Row, Ten Cup Alley, Crappy Chute, Wood Money Bottom, and many other low wards of the city, my soul staggers."[1]

Reverend Davis, whose church stood in the center of the Black Bottom neighborhood, understood the hardships faced by poor and orphaned children quite well. He recognized that Nashville's poor tended to live in flood-prone areas where dilapidated housing and disease threatened lives. He was not alone in his worries. In fact, these types of urban lowland neighborhoods extended far beyond Nashville and other southern cities. In cities around the United States, Davis's rhetorical connection between low ground, poverty, and urban social problems was apparent to many Americans. Doctors, business leaders, clergy, urban reformers, elected officials, and civic elites, both from within and outside immigrant and African American communities, actively debated what to do about these places and the people who lived there. The story of "low down" places provides a unique perspective on the history of city planning in the United States, from its nineteenth-century beginnings in public health, engineering, landscape, and architecture to the implementation of zoning, public housing, and urban renewal in the twentieth century.

Urban lowland neighborhoods signified the bottom of the social hierarchy because they were commonly understood to be unhealthy, ugly, and hazardous. And they were frequently unpleasant and dangerous to the people that lived there, due to water and sanitation problems. Located close to the old city and proximate to industrial jobs, they became places for the working (and walking) poor. These topographically bounded neighborhood spaces became visually and mentally associated with the environmental conditions of industrialized creeks, streams, and rivers and the class, race, or ethnicity of the residents.

Elected officials, religious leaders, and journalists commonly blamed lowland residents for sanitation problems, and urban lowland neighborhoods were stigmatized as "slums." Health and housing experts legitimized racial disease fears and xenophobic contempt for "foreign colonies" through purportedly objective municipal surveys and reports. This marginalization of people according to place naturalized inequities. In contrast, in the partly real and partly imagined social construction of residence and altitude, native-born upper-class white residents lived on highland sites with fresh breezes, quiet streets, and substantial homes in exclusive residential enclaves. From the 1870s onward, the title "the Heights" was used in multiple cities and became synonymous with suburban amenities and physical separation from the old city. Higher elevations were also promoted as healthy. The perceived quality of any residential location was directly tied to one's relative vertical position in the landscape of river cities especially, where streetcars facilitated residential development away from the old walking city and its noisy waterfront and up into the forested hills.[2] While inaccessible or rugged hills were sometimes marginal locations, too, these land uses and cultural associations became seen as the exception. In Kansas City, one fashionable and exclusive hilltop neighborhood was called Quality Hill, while below laid the West Bottoms. These economic and geographic patterns, and cultural practices of place naming, inscribed class into the landscape of the late nineteenth-century American city. To many Americans the urban landscape of topography-by-class seemed normal.

Urban lowland neighborhoods like Nashville's Black Bottom tell an American story about immigration, race, and social mobility in society. Some forgotten, some celebrated, urban lowland neighborhoods reflect the American experience: how freedom from slavery led into life under Jim Crow in urban neighborhoods; how emigration from Europe, Asia, and Latin America transformed cities; how poverty and limited economic opportunity shaped the lives of working people under industrial capitalism; how Americans' ideas about class and race mutated and shifted in the context of mass immigration; how assumptions about assimilation and heterogeneity influenced attitudes about immigrant and black neighborhoods; and how the legacies of Progressive Era reform, New Deal policies, and urban renewal shaped the American city.

Urban Lowlands provides an alternative interpretive framework for studying poverty and the urban environment, arguing that urban lowland neighborhoods represent a distinct historical phenomenon with contemporary implications for the American city. It tells the story of how urban lowland neighborhoods became common and familiar features of the American urban landscape between 1870 and 1940.

The Lowland Neighborhood Paradox

In the late nineteenth and early twentieth centuries, Americans knew urban lowland neighborhoods as "plague spots" and dangerous threats to the city as a whole. They gave them pejorative names like the Flats, Bohemian Flats, Harlem Flats, Mud Flats, Black Bottom, Crawfish Bottom, the Bottoms, West Bottoms, Frog Hollow, Kalb Hollow, Skunk Hollow, and Swede Hollow. They read about them in the newspapers, and they heard elected officials tout plans to clean them up. But they were paradoxical: urban lowland neighborhoods facilitated the spatial containment of the poor while simultaneously arousing fears of contamination and precipitating calls for charitable outreach and social reform.

Containment prevailed over dispersal until federal intervention in urban policy and planning in the 1930s and 1940s tipped the balance in favor of neighborhood demolition and resident displacement. A combination of municipal neglect, limited use of condemnation powers and demolition, and targeted infrastructure projects typified the response. Nineteenth-century American city builders espoused the superiority of privately based charitable or volunteer solutions as a response to city problems and touted laissez-faire capitalism as an ideal economic system. But disorderly and dangerous cities, beset with health problems and outbreaks of deadly disease, alarmed city dwellers. Sanitary engineers, physicians, and other urban reformers successfully rallied support for a wide range of policy innovations and physical interventions, including new governmental powers, debt finance mechanisms, and infrastructure projects in the 1870s and 1880s.

In many cities, voters mounted political resistance to public health–related evictions or "slum clearance" initiatives because they feared that displaced residents would move closer to them. The containment approach generally favored limiting government costs and maintaining boundaries, but this opposition was contingent, not absolute, and projects that caused limited displacement were often celebrated for accomplishing multiple municipal goals simultaneously. In 1880s Nashville, for example, public health officials promoted a major sewer project in the Black Bottom neighborhood as an opportunity to demolish the houses of poor African Americans.

Fear of disease reinforced the desire to keep lowland residents in their place, but it could also be invoked to support physical alterations of the urban landscape, from chemical treatments to landfilling to sewer construction. Cholera particularly terrorized Americans due to its dramatic and sudden onset of debilitating and deadly symptoms. In the 1870s and 1880s, the causes of diseases like yellow fever, malaria, typhoid, and cholera were not widely known. Even after major scientific discoveries, anxieties about poverty, environment, and disease lingered and public understanding lagged significantly behind medical knowledge. In his masterful history of cholera and public health in the United States, historian Charles Rosenberg describes how American physicians, health officers, and religious leaders had primarily understood the disease as the "scourge of the sinful" in the 1820s, but by the 1860s many viewed it as a problem of sanitation.[3] Many urban experts associated urban topography with disease and death well into the 1890s. Librarian and surgeon John S. Billings examined the connection between altitude, population density, and death rates in the nation's cities with populations over fifty thousand in his analysis of 1890 US Census data.[4]

Newspaper journalists and elected officials frequently blamed residents for environmental conditions, often in racist and xenophobic terms. In San Francisco, whites demonized Chinese residents as a menace to the city.[5] In Los Angeles, Anglos painted Mexican residents as diseased and dangerous.[6] In Nashville, whites blamed African Americans for the deadly cholera outbreak of 1873. In Saint Paul and in dozens of other cities around the country, city leaders pointed to immigrants and their "foreign" ways of life as threats to the citizenry. Proposed physical interventions and housing inspection efforts claimed to improve both residents' moral behavior and neighborhood environmental conditions.[7]

Public health interventions and improvements in the quality of the water supply and implementation of sanitary engineering systems, notably sewers, decreased urban morbidity and conquered cholera in the United States. But as fears of cholera and other so-called miasmatic diseases ebbed, housing concerns became central to environmentally based definitions of urban poverty. During the Progressive Era, reformers identified dilapidated, crowded, or substandard housing conditions as the major urban problem of the early twentieth century. Simultaneously, engineers, landscape architects, architects, housing reformers, and sanitarians convened to create a formally organized profession of city planning.[8] Reformers and housing inspectors scrutinized everything from the spatial arrangement of buildings and shared open spaces to the internal organization of household belongings and services.

By the 1920s, officials, business leaders, and planners began to identify urban lowland neighborhoods as potential redevelopment sites such as parks and single-use industrial districts. In subsequent decades, many of these sites would also be targeted for slum clearance projects that purged poor residents for the construction of public housing developments. Often planners and elected officials justified resident removal as an end in itself, as it removed people who were considered to be problems and allowed land to be put to other uses. Commercial and industrial redevelopment received formal and legal public backing after cities adopted zoning. Many lowland neighborhoods were zoned for industrial use.

During these seven decades, spanning from Reconstruction to the New Deal, urban lowland neighborhoods and their negative reputations persisted despite significant changes in urban society from transportation to medicine to social thought. Land speculators, industrialists, and railroad companies made "the bottoms." They created a new type of place by overlaying the city's river flats and valley bottoms with factories, railroads, and houses. The poor people, immigrants, and African Americans who lived there were not helpless or passive victims of circumstance. Residents invested in these neighborhoods by constructing homes and building communities. They planted small gardens, opened businesses, and created gathering places. Meanwhile, newspaper journalists and urban reformers invoked the unusual and pejorative neighborhood names, sensationalizing and occasionally romanticizing life there, through paternalistic depictions and colorful stories. Health officials and planners surveyed, inspected, and documented them. Policy and planning debates caricatured the complexity of lowland neighborhoods and their human communities. Federal government policies led to the dismantling of many urban lowland communities, as the American metropolis decentralized, railroads declined, and the automobile dominated transportation and land use planning.[9]

Despite their negative reputations and ascribed racial-ethnic identities, urban lowland neighborhoods were socially and culturally heterogeneous. Swede Hollow in Saint Paul, Minnesota, for example, began as a Swedish immigrant community in the 1880s, became mixed Swedish, Irish, and Italian by 1900, then mostly Italian through the 1920s, and finally Italian and Mexican in the 1930s. Black Bottom in Nashville, although it was racially identified as an African American neighborhood, was also home to foreign-born immigrants from Ireland, Germany, Russia, and Poland in the 1870s and 1880s, and native-born white migrants from the surrounding countryside of middle Tennessee from the 1890s to the 1930s.

Pejorative place names linked people and environment and carried with them the assumption that such neighborhoods existed in the city because of the moral behavior of the inhabitants. However, residents' experiences did not match the ways that photographers, health officials, housing inspectors, planners, or journalists depicted them. Together with allies and supporters, they built neighborhood-based and citywide institutions to provide education, to worship together, to extend charity, and to organize businesses. Lowland residents knew their neighborhoods neither as the newspaper sensationalized them nor as surveyors described them through quantitative data, maps, or field reports by social scientists. They understood them through their experiences with their neighbors and with the places themselves.

Writing and Telling Lowland Neighborhood Histories

Local histories of urban lowland neighborhoods are variously told with a tone of disgust about slums, outrage at environmental injustice, or nostalgia for the past. While many older accounts lean toward moral judgment or pity, local historical projects since 1970 tend to emphasize aspects of community life as seen by their residents. An early example is *Bohemian Flats*, a Works Progress Administration Writers' Project monograph profiling an immigrant community on the banks of the Mississippi River in Minneapolis.[10] Around the US, hundreds of scholars, community residents, museum professionals, public historians, and archivists have been involved in efforts to recover community histories. In cities like Cleveland and Saint Paul, archeologists have excavated the sites of former urban lowland neighborhoods to unearth evidence of how nineteenth-century Americans lived. Public historians at the National Park Service and museum curators at immigrant heritage museums have interpreted the history of urban lowland communities such as the Upper Levee Little Italy in Saint Paul. Oral historians have recorded former African American residents' memories of lowland communities from Frankfort, Kentucky, to Battle Creek, Michigan.[11] These projects add up to a significant compendium of historical data about urban lowland neighborhoods that documents urban lowland neighborhoods as a national phenomenon.

The catastrophic flooding of New Orleans following Hurricane Katrina in August 2005 spurred further research. Urban scholars, geographers, and environmental justice researchers investigated the connections between topography, flood risk, and neighborhood location within the urban landscape.[12] Employing GIS, regression analysis, and other quantitative and spatial methodologies, these investigators probed contemporary spatial patterns of poverty and environment in the American city. These scholars found that the historical connection between lowland topography, class, and race/ethnicity persists, albeit in new forms. Historians, anthropologists, artists, and preservationists, among many other researchers from around the US, both professional and amateur, have newly examined microscale local histories, community memories, and the history of the built environment in flooded neighborhoods of New Orleans. These projects have catalyzed similar research efforts in many other cities.

Urban geographers, notably William Meyer, have published nuanced historical analyses of topography in cities over several decades and their work has informed new research efforts using historical GIS. Meyer writes: "The sorting of different income groups by altitude is an important process contributing to American city form."[13] He reminds us that the study of topography and class in cities is not new, pointing out in "The Other Burgess Model" that the famous University of Chicago sociologist published an analysis of the topic in 1929.[14] Meyer urges geographers to reexamine Burgess's largely forgotten vertical hypothesis of urban spatial structure. Unlike Meyer's work, *Urban Lowlands* focuses at the neighborhood rather than the citywide scale to examine the political and social context for urban planning and policy debates. This book examines the trajectories of individual lowland neighborhoods like Nashville's Black Bottom with particular attention to the period 1870–1940, when bottoms, hollows, and flats were most common.

Historically urban lowland neighborhoods imposed environmental hazards and class-based segregation on their residents, but, for some, they also served as starting places or "stepping-stones" for individuals who later found success. In local African American communities, one hears stories of perseverance, triumphs, and struggles in the pursuit of a better life, remembrance, and tribute. In immigrant histories, one encounters stories of ethnic heritage and pride, community building in urban neighborhoods, and the American Dream. Common metaphors of upward social mobility often align closely with landscape metaphors that link one's relative spatial location in the city with one's position in the social hierarchy. In this narrative, immigrants move up from "lowly status" to the "lofty plateaus of the American mainstream." But, as historians of American immigration have shown, most immigrants did not achieve improved occupational status within their own lifetimes.[15] Horizontal movement in occupational status and geographic relocation in the hope of improving one's opportunities were more common. Immigrants, African Americans, and working-class people frequently moved, while neighborhood reputations, especially for low-lying "slum" areas, remained relatively fixed.[16] For these reasons and more, urban lowland neighborhoods are a part of the ideology of immigration history in American life and broad themes in American history.

Urban reformers and city planners framed urban problems of poverty and environment using the concept of "slum."[17] The label rhetorically collapsed any nuanced understanding of human communities in the urban landscape as it injected a moral charge, implicit judgment, and call for intervention into public debate. In studies of the twentieth-century American city, particularly public housing and urban renewal, the term is ubiquitous. But as sociologist Herbert Gans pointed out in his 1962 classic *The Urban Villagers*, "slum" is a deeply problematic term. Planners, he argued, identified slums based primarily upon social and cultural factors, while they simultaneously pursued physically based solutions rooted in environmental determinism.[18] In 1971 planner Charles Abrams wrote in *The Language of Cities* that the term "reveals its meaning the moment it is uttered. Abhorrence of slums has often led to reckless destruction and more than once contributed to severe housing shortages."[19] In *Slums: The History of a Global Injustice*, historian Alan Mayne considers the term in international perspective and over two centuries, concluding that it is time to delete the word from the world's vocabulary. He argues that "slum" as an intellectual construct is "unhelpful," "deceitful," and misleading.[20] It would be impossible to write the history of urban lowland neighborhoods without the word and reference to its multiple meanings and uses. *Urban Lowlands* highlights how the imagined and real qualities of urban lowland places have influenced the American definition of "slum."

A Comparative History

Harlem Flats in New York City, Black Bottom in Nashville, Swede Hollow in Saint Paul, and the Flats in Los Angeles are the four urban lowland neighborhoods examined in this book. Chapter 1 describes how urban lowland neighborhoods were created, examining their physical and social construction up to the 1870s. Chapters 2 through 5 describe the four urban lowland neighborhood cases. Chapter 6 compares these case histories to establish the significance of the lowland neighborhood pattern in the history of the American city. The epilogue offers reflections on how and why these histories are relevant to planners and designers in the twenty-first century.

Urban lowland neighborhoods in New York, Nashville, Saint Paul, and Los Angeles differ in their ecological and historical contexts. The ethnicity and race of residents, total city population size, neighborhood land area, city land area, period of historical development, economic geographies, and local physiographic conditions are different. But the cases also exhibit significant commonalities related to water problems and disease fears, housing and city building issues, and policy and planning debates about "slum" areas. Similarly, the cultural construction of these neighborhoods exhibits both commonalities and important local differences. Place names and the metaphorical use of "low" are consistent themes throughout. Class bias and moral judgment of residents are common. At the same time, African Americans and the places where they lived, often side by side with immigrants from European countries, were subject to a distinctly racialized and frequently harsher and more violent set of spatial practices.

Compared to other neighborhoods, it is the relative position in the landscape that was important. Bottoms, hollows, and flats were typically built into floodplains and valley bottoms, they were proximate to downtowns, and they were highly visible. Compared to other poor neighborhoods, they were more physically varied in terms of building types, street patterns, and landforms. They included shacks, flats, tenements, house courts, duplexes, and cottages. They were defined by their uneasy and putatively dangerous relationship between land and water. They were considered distinct enough from other poor neighborhoods to garner their own pejorative labels identifying them as a unique type of urban landscape. Some cities like Nashville had several lowland neighborhoods during the period from 1870 to 1940: Black Bottom and Hell's Half Acre on either side of downtown, but also, further from the city center, Trimble Bottom, Kalb Hollow, and Mud Flats. Each urban lowland neighborhood is unique, but together these examples demonstrate a significant spatial and temporal pattern.

The cases are arranged in a loose chronological order, and they move from east to west. While each case includes historical analysis of the period 1870 to 1940, the chapters highlight key events based on the timing of the physical development in each place, from the filling of New York City's Harlem Flats in the 1870s to the sewer projects and real estate development in the Flats in Los Angeles between 1900 and 1910.

Bottoms, hollows, and flats were not the inevitable result of processes of industrial capitalism. An alternative trajectory based on rehabilitation and incremental change, a third option that was neither containment nor dispersal, received little political support during the period from 1870 to 1940, but gained force as a response to urban renewal after 1960. The planning conflicts and political contestation over urban lowland neighborhoods are not over. The issues of poverty and environment continue to be urgent societal problems and sources of political conflict in an era of increased economic polarization. The challenges of advancing environmental justice and social equity through fair housing and lending, inclusionary zoning, affordable housing construction, community development, and equitable planning practices continue in the twenty-first century.

Urban Lowlands draws from city planning history, environmental history, and landscape studies to examine connections between poverty and environment by looking at a particular kind of neighborhood in historical perspective. Throughout, it emphasizes both the social and physical construction of urban lowland neighborhoods to examine spatial and environmental thinking about urban poverty, race, and ethnicity over seven decades of American urban history. The story begins in the bottomlands.

1

From Bottomlands to Bottom Neighborhoods

In the 1830s, newly arrived settlers planted the bottomlands of the Los Angeles River with orchards and vineyards. Decades before the Northern California counties of Napa and Sonoma became synonymous with wine, the industry centered on Los Angeles, where vintners and distillers produced a variety of wines and brandies for export. Citrus groves, particularly oranges, filled the floodplain, along with plantings of corn and grain and vegetable gardens.[1] By 1910, it was gone. A new urban landscape of railroad lines, freight yards, houses, tenements, stores, churches, wholesale markets, and warehouses rose in its place. On the east side of the river, the built-over lowlands became known as the Flats.

Ripping out orange groves for industrial development in the Los Angeles lowlands was not unique. Landowners plowed under crops, cut down bottomland forests, and filled in marshlands in cities across the country to facilitate industrial development. In the process, railroad magnates, industrial capitalists, and government officials deliberately and systematically created urban lowland neighborhoods. Engineers, real estate speculators, land subdividers, municipal officials, urban elites, public health officers, railroad workers, and builders facilitated their construction.

Urban lowlands morphed into railroad-industrial neighborhoods with residential populations during the last three decades of the nineteenth century. The underlying geology of these urban locations varied significantly, as did the climatic and ecological conditions: cities built on karst landscapes with river valleys and limestone hills like Nashville; Atlantic seaboard cities built at the fall line where hard rock terrain met an outwash plain like Philadelphia and Baltimore; or southwestern cities built on alluvial washes in an arid, sandy basin surrounded by mountains like Los Angeles. New Orleans developed on a wet, marshy site with very little, but very significant, variation in elevation: the high ground created by sediment deposits along the banks of the Mississippi River sits above the rest of the city. In spite of these differences, the physical and social construction of low-lying, marginal places in the American cities during the period 1870–1940 followed a distinct and identifiable pattern. These low-lying neighborhoods were visible to the eye, and they were socially constructed through both vernacular speech and professional discourses on poverty and environment.[2]

In the two decades following the end of the Civil War, migrants from the countryside and around the world moved into urban lowland neighborhoods. As railroad engineers and factory builders pushed city development into the lowlands, reorienting economic processes and restructuring urban space around railroad-based movement of people and goods, they reshaped the American urban landscape. Where creeks and streams abutted railroad tracks or marshy spots sat below graded streets and built-up city districts, American built new communities in varied forms.

A hodgepodge of architectural forms and building sizes and types gave these new neighborhoods a motley character. Old wooden mills, new brick breweries and manufacturing houses, lumberyards, railroad spurs and sidings, and unpaved roads surrounded houses and stores. They spread out across bottomlands and river flats, clustered together in steep ravines, and sat on filled land in stream valleys. From atop bluffs and ridges, prosperous Americans looked down on their poor neighbors from Victorian homes and elaborately designed mansions. Around the edges of the new communities were middle-class homes. Located on marginally higher or drier land, they were a short distance from the shanties, cottages, and other modest homes in urban lowland neighborhoods. The new lowland communities became visual manifestations of growing inequality in American society and potent symbols of hierarchy and power in the urban landscape.

One explanation for the physical construction of urban lowland neighborhoods was that the best land in cities, which was relatively flat, accessible, and dry, was platted and built up with houses first, leaving the less desirable sites for later property developers. Lowland sites could be marshy, wet, or poorly drained. They might be difficult to access, or cut off from the main part of the city by bluffs or steep slopes. A second explanation was that rapid industrialization and population growth in the nineteenth century put pressure on existing housing, causing newcomers to seek out anything they could find in order to survive. This explanation, like the first, was reasonable, and partly true, as American cities were rapidly expanding in population during this era. But bottoms, hollows, and flats do not simply reflect the normal or typical processes of urban land use or migration during a period of industrial capitalism. They were intentionally built.

Lowlands, City Building, and Grids

Lowlands have always been a part of American cities. A waterfront is a lowland. Stream valleys are lowlands. Swamps and marshes are lowlands. But railroad building, industrialization, and water and sanitation problems changed urban lowland functions and land uses. The process of laying out the American city with streets and property lines began the sequence of events that led to bottoms, hollows, and flats.

The federal government established a national grid in the Land Ordinance of 1785, organizing all western territory into a regular geometric pattern of square townships. Land speculators and promoters used the gridiron plan to organize new cities linked by an expanding network of railroad lines across the western United States. The grid also proved a useful tool for promoting real estate speculation, property sales, and industrial capitalism in the form of the company town. Planning historian John Reps has argued that Americans have mostly ignored topography in laying out cities and the "gridiron plan stamped an identical brand of uniformity and mediocrity on American cities from coast to coast."[3] For critics of the grid, this regularity and repetition symbolized a rejection of nature.

Americans planned and constructed new towns along rivers and coastlines, especially at places of confluence where small tributaries flowed into rivers, a river met a lake, a major estuary linked freshwater and ocean water, or two rivers merged together. Highlands such as bluffs, close to the river but outside the floodplain, developed with clusters of houses and, later, churches, warehouses, taverns, hotels, and other buildings. Lowlands, on the other hand, were typically nonnavigable places where water would periodically collect or inconveniently flow: marshes, muddy shallows at the river's edge, rocky creeks or streams, swamps, fens, or poorly drained lands.[4] Americans were often not the first people to settle there. On existing sites, developed by Native Americans or Spanish, French, Dutch, or British colonial settlers, they imprinted a distinctly new American pattern of urban development on the land (see figure 1.1).[5]

Landscape historian John Stilgoe has argued that the regularity and predictability of an orderly geometry prevailed over early settlers' assumption "that topography indicated the best outlines for future towns and lots, and most tracts conformed to soil types, elevations, and water frontage."[6] As landscape writer and editor J. B. Jackson has eloquently described, the positive symbolic qualities of the square had a powerful appeal and offered many advantages in

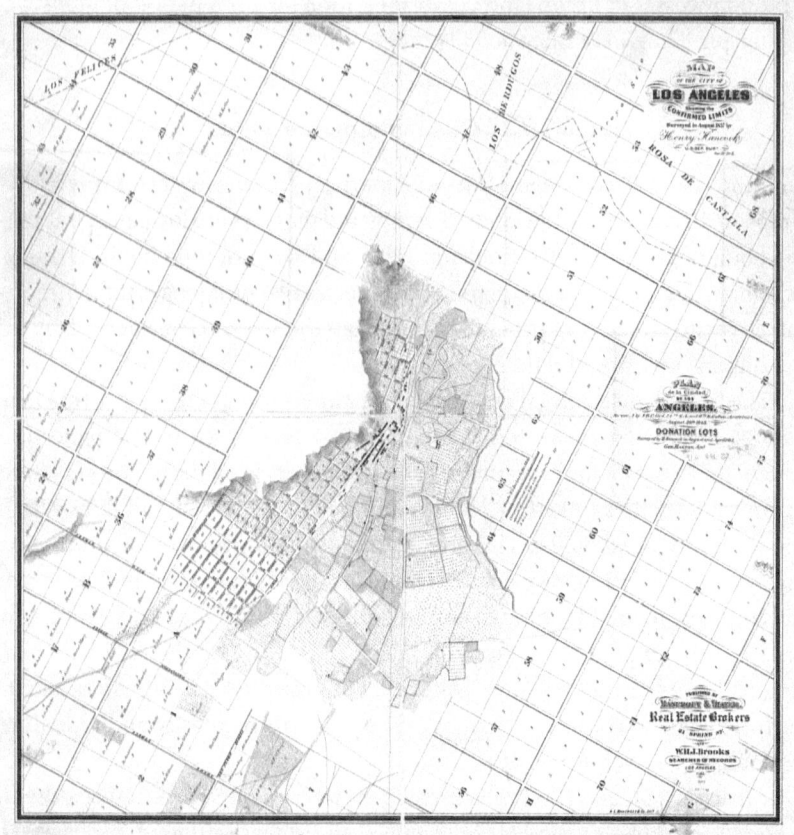

FIGURE 1.1. Spanish settlers founded the pueblo of Los Angeles on the site of a Yangna village along the Los Angeles River. This map juxtaposes the 1849 city survey by Edward O. C. Ord (*center*) with property boundaries identified by Henry Hancock and George Hansen. Note the delineation of agricultural fields in the bottomlands of the Los Angeles River at center. The composite illustration, created by the real estate firm Bancroft and Thayer to attract prospective buyers, visually disconnects the pueblo from its ecological context, allowing it to float in abstract geometric space. Hansen map, circa 1875. Collection of Los Angeles Public Library.

land organization and development.[7] Although square- and rectangle-based grid plans had been used for centuries in many parts of the world, Americans employed them on scale previously unseen.

Manhattan's 1811 street plan was both highly influential and exceptional; few cities applied the grid over such a large urban territory with such consistency.[8] More typical was a process of laying out "additions" to the original street plan by different land subdividers and developers over time. Where the tracts met, the result was unusual angles, triangular or odd-shaped parcels, and confusing intersections: what landscape journalist Grady Clay labeled as breaks, interfaces, and fracture zones.[9] They often correlated with hills or lowlands, obstacles to urban development.

Within each new plat or addition, multiple variations might be found from one area of the city to the next. The number and dimensions of urban lots could differ, as could the regularity of lot sizes, the width of streets and the use (or not) of alleys, or the presence of land set aside for open space such as parks or urban squares, not to mention the slope and character of streets as they traveled over flat, undulating, hilly, or steep terrain. Straight-line streets might ignore topography, creating steep inclines and descents. But in other cities, they could be accompanied by curving streets traveling around steep hills or following the toe of the slope, creating a lower-level street network that allowed traffic to circumnavigate higher elevations.[10] Some cities simply cut down these hills, or tried to, and used the material to build up lowlands or expand the city outward into a harbor, a practice known as landmaking. American city builders filled swamps, marshes, and coves; and they pushed out, straightened up, and hardened down shorelines.[11] They enlisted engineers to design and construct the city to modify natural environments for human purposes in the city.

As urban historians and historical geographers have documented, American cities founded along rivers or at the confluence of two waterways often grew extremely quickly. Urban boosters and land developers took advantage of all available land as "usable territory" in the pursuit of profit and "progress."[12] The use of the grid pattern to stimulate economic investment and to facilitate the ease of property transfer was a predominant factor in the organization of settlements, though town builders also arranged streets and planned for the future according to a wide range of economic factors and political, social, and cultural beliefs.[13]

As Americans built cities west of the Appalachian Mountains, state governments and territories established and enforced a legal system that turned Indian lands into private property defined as lots, blocks, and tracts. For the most part, the sites they identified were proximate to lowlands, but not in the lowest areas.[14] However, where lowlands had rich soils, productive for growing grains, vegetables, or fruits, towns and agriculture grew up together, in close relation to one another, as in pre-1870 Los Angeles. Fertile valleys and alluvial lands were the places where many ancient civilizations flourished. For instance, the extensive pre-Columbian city of Cahokia located in the "American Bottoms" was a low-lying region of nearly 175 square miles around the Mississippi River in southern Illinois. Defined by its constructed earthen mounds standing as tall as ten-story buildings, Cahokia reached a population of more than thirty thousand at its peak sometime between 1200 and 1300. Cahokia's builders developed sophisticated engineering approaches to create an urban settlement by building up in a lowland setting. By the time

French explorers reached the area, Cahokia's original inhabitants had long since abandoned the site.[15] The presence of ancient mounds and evidence of other settlements can be found throughout the vast expanse of the Mississippi and its tributaries, including in Saint Paul and Nashville. The Europeans who founded these new American towns, surveyed territory, and platted streets frequently built over Native American settlements, overlaying gridded plans for future development atop natural topography.

Urban Lowland Development

Surveyors and town planners attempted to anticipate future growth and expansion in their development schemes. The grid encouraged private property, facilitated land sales, provided a point of focus or concentration to a settlement, and allowed for extensions over time. In the capitalist economy of nineteenth-century America, land for town settlement would ideally be situated in close proximity to a major waterway, above the bottomlands on a bluff or plateau, with sufficient flat land for building purposes. Any hills in the immediate area should be accessible, without insurmountably steep slopes, and suitable as potential sites for prominent buildings or town features. The new town "fronted" the river, establishing a geometric matrix of streets. Within this framework, lowlands often defined the edges, sides, and back of town. They might be claimed by settlers or used in common by citizens, as grazing land, for example, but rarely were platted with streets. They were located at the vertical fringe at the near periphery. Ancillary and supporting uses, such as farms or water-powered mills, might occupy these sites to take advantage of creeks and streams. They could be close to the docks or the town landing. At the edges of the wharves and waterfronts, and particularly upland along either side of creeks and streams emptying into larger rivers, one could find tanneries, flour and textile mills, breweries, and other small-scale manufacturers.[16] Squatters, small-home builders, and real estate speculators often chose similar areas of available land to put up inexpensive housing for themselves or to rent to others within valleys, dales, ravines, and hollows. In many cities, however, by the mid-nineteenth century, increases in the scale of production and size of factories, technological advancements in power generation, and dense concentrations of industrial activity in geographically advantageous sites would transform these spatial relationships. Many urban lowland and waterfront sites became dominated by industry.

Waterways were the primary means of transport, serving as routes of cross-country travel and as major thoroughfares of trade and commerce. In an era when most goods arrived by water, waterfronts could be noisy and dangerous, associated with saloons and taverns, cheap lodging places for transients,

FROM BOTTOMLANDS TO BOTTOM NEIGHBORHOODS   17

and unsavory characters. But these working landscapes were also centrally located and highly visible. Only a short walk away, one could find respectable houses and prominent shops and hotels. Until the mid-nineteenth century, most urban residents walked to get around the city. The urban pattern was dense, with a mix of uses and activities located in mostly one-, two-, or three-story buildings dispersed throughout the city. The large homes of factory owners frequently overlooked their factory buildings and worker housing. Cities tended to be densely organized around a central core, and their extent was defined at the walking scale of approximately two to three miles.[17] Rich and poor lived close to one another.

Slavery, immigration, and labor conditions also shaped the built environment in powerful ways. Prior to emancipation, enslaved urban residents typically lived in small back houses and alley dwellings behind the prominent front-facing houses of slave owners. In southern cities, the enslaved population also constituted a significant percentage of the adult male workforce: between 50 and 60 percent in Charleston, Richmond, and Lynchburg and between 25 and 35 percent in Mobile, Baton Rouge, and Nashville. But after 1845, in cities across the country, including San Francisco, Boston, New York, Milwaukee, Cincinnati, and Nashville, an influx of German and Irish immigrant laborers altered the composition of the adult male workforce. In Boston and New York more than half of all residents were foreign born.[18] Before the Civil War, enslaved African Americans and immigrant laborers dug canals and built railroads, levees, roads, culverts, and drains. In some cases, workers rented houses, built shanties, or occupied worker housing adjacent to these projects. Along the Cuyahoga River in Cleveland, for example, a settlement of dozens of small wooden houses became known as Irishtown Bend by 1840, then, as the neighborhood expanded, the Flats.[19]

The location of prominent buildings on hilltops, such as the state capitol in Nashville, Tennessee, or the federal capitol in Washington, DC, oriented urban spaces around topographical high points. Engineers and architects employed elevation to define urban space. As architectural historian and urbanist Christine Kreyling points out in reference to Nashville, siting a temple for democracy atop a prominent hill allowed landscape allusions to the ancient Acropolis to reinforce the symbolic meaning of the choice of the Greek Revival architectural style for the building.[20]

Orientation to the riverfront meant that creeks and streams flowed "through" town, often on its immediate edges. The hydrological system was thus intertwined with urban form, with lowlands and waterways serving as points of reference for residents' image of the city, orienting and directing the character of town development.[21] Cities like Cincinnati were built on a series of low terraces, where the first

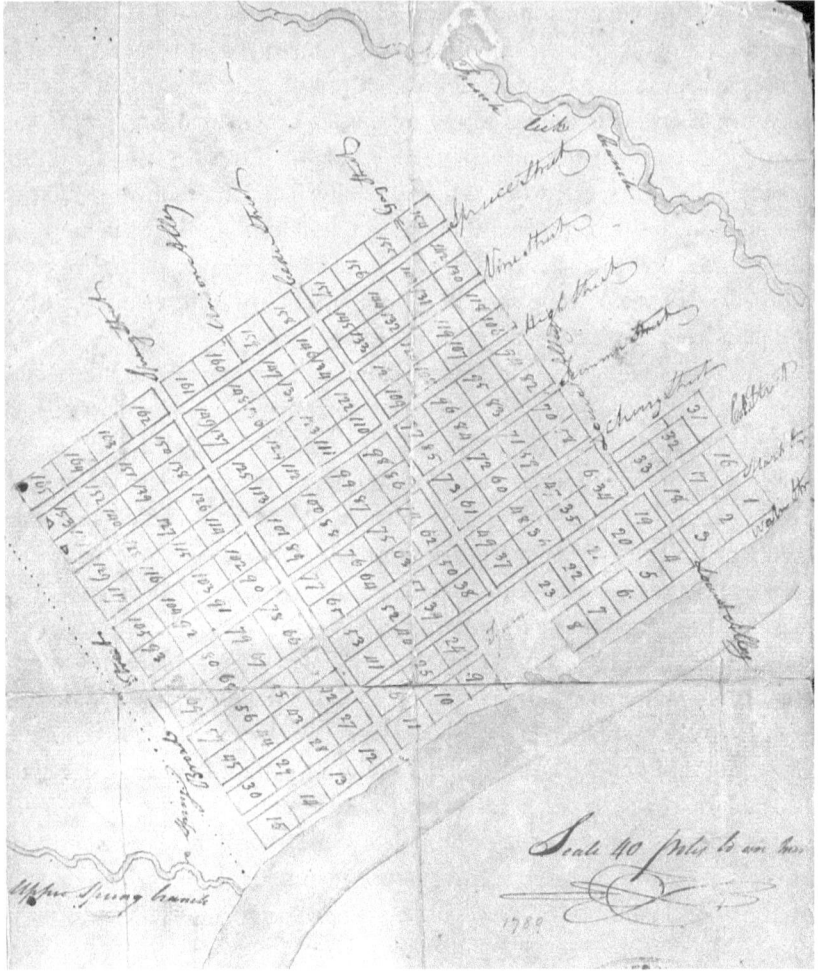

FIGURE 1.2. Thomas Molloy created the original plat for Nashville in 1784. Along the west bank of the Cumberland River, Molloy laid out a grid of one-acre lots on the high ground between stream valleys. The two waterways are shown here: Lick Branch (*upper right*) and Wilson's Spring Branch (*lower left*). Plan of Nashville, collection of Tennessee State Library and Archives.

and second "bottoms" at the edge of the Ohio River formed the lower section of a "natural amphitheater" surrounded by upland hills: a stage for city life.[22] New Orleans followed a reverse dynamic. The urban landscape descended as one moved away from the high ground of the Mississippi River toward the "back swamps."

Early town plans stopped at lowland edges, depicting marshes and swamps, creeks and streams as natural features of the landscape, resources for common use not private property (see figure 1.2).[23] By the mid-nineteenth century, however, lawmakers and city officials imagined a future in which city street

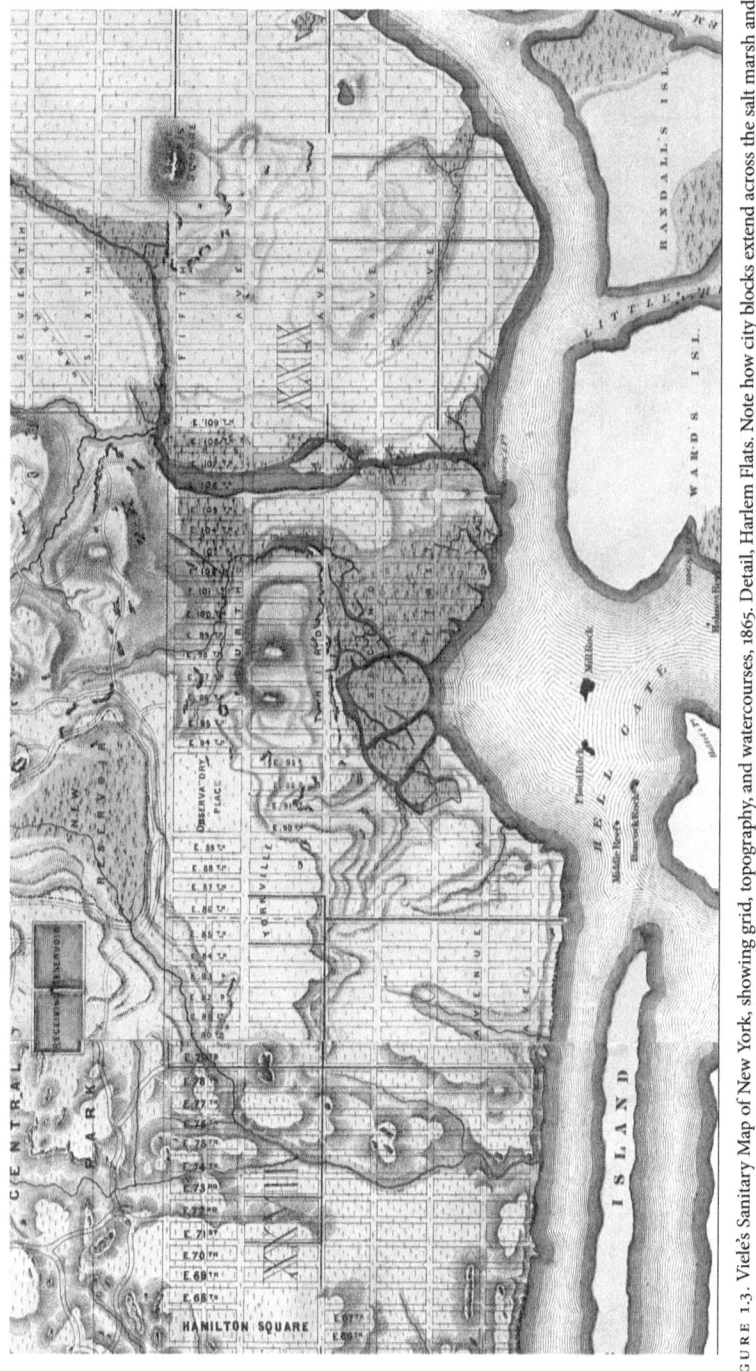

FIGURE 1.3. Viele's Sanitary Map of New York, showing grid, topography, and watercourses, 1865. Detail, Harlem Flats. Note how city blocks extend across the salt marsh and out into the East River. Collection of David Rumsey.

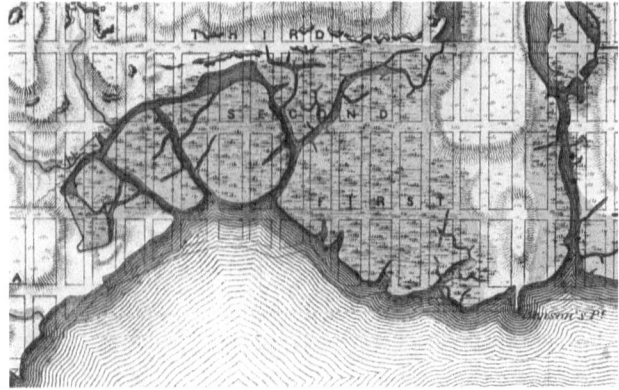

FIGURE 1.4. Detail, plans for the future city overlaid on Harlem Marsh and Harlem Creek. Viele map, 1865. Collection of David Rumsey.

systems and urban development would fill the lowlands. The sanitarian and civil engineer Egbert Viele famously mapped this transformation in process, showing how Manhattan's rectilinear street grid ran right over creeks and streams (see figures 1.3 and 1.4). In New York City and elsewhere, parcels partially or episodically submerged that were known as "water lots" became "made land" after they were filled. Previously viewed as an edge or an obstacle, urban lowlands were reimagined as new urban spaces. The process was fraught with danger and fear.

Water Problems and Disease Fears

Cities' troubled relationship with water, sanitation, and disease helped turn bottomlands into bottom neighborhoods. Swamps and marshes were often particularly feared and despised, associated with danger and ill health.[24] Lowlands collected water naturally, but when natural detention areas became filled with polluted and putrid waters, these urban areas became notorious for their offensive odors and bad air. Lowlands also flooded, which made them unstable and unpredictable. Freshets, back floods, and swollen streams delivered water into lowlands. Moving water eroded banks, carried away soil, and altered landforms.[25] Water collected in creeks, streams, marshes, fens, swamps, rivers, bays, coves, lakes, estuaries, and ponds. It could seep into basements and create muddy streets that were difficult to traverse. Standing water could be a menace. River flats, stream valleys, and salt marshes were dynamic environments that challenged nineteenth-century city builders.

Fire, drought, ice, and pollution further threatened urban dwellers. City dwellers pumped up water from wells, harvested and imported ice for refrigeration and cooling, and diverted water for gardens and farms. Water was needed to fight fires, and a frozen harbor could disrupt trade and increase fire risk. Freshwater supplies were threatened by drought and pollution. In lower Manhattan, New Yorkers dumped so much waste into Fresh Water Pond, a favored picnic and ice-skating spot of the eighteenth century, that it became known as the Collect Pond, an area so polluted that a nearby hill was cut down to fill it in. The process took eight years, from 1803 to 1811; by 1813 the pond had disappeared from the urban landscape.[26]

Poor drainage also led to standing stagnant water on streets and in houses and yards, producing unbearable stench. Problems with odors could be seasonal or weather dependent, with summers producing the worst smells; geographic, with some lowlands used for waste disposal while others were spared; or chronological, with some places, like the Collect Pond, mutating from idyllic and pastoral to dystopic and hellish over time. Flowing waters elicited praise and celebration, due in part to the commonly held belief that moving water purified itself, while murky waters prompted doubt and suspicion.[27] The detection and identification of odors was considered a necessary and fundamental skill for physicians.

Improperly filled lands suffered from poor drainage, impounded water, or rotting waste material that included household garbage, horse manure, coal ashes, and dead animals. Newly constructed sewers deposited human wastes from pipes into open creeks, streams, or riverfront harbors. Lowland-based tanneries, breweries, textile mills, and chemical factories expunged their waste products into city waters. Floods exacerbated all these problems.

These difficulties intensified as cities grew. Many cities relied upon the action of tides and adequate rainfall to flush waste away from the population. As larger groups of people clustered close together, greater amounts of waste and filth could accumulate, and when tides or rainfall did not cooperate, city residents would be subjected to the scent of wastes baking in mudflats or washing up around docks. Most American cities imported freshwater, constructing new infrastructural systems to pipe it in from miles away, before constructing sewer systems.[28] But until sewers could take away these imported waters after use, more water made the problem worse.

More than any other factor, fear of disease defined lowland reputations, and it was closely related to water problems. In the early nineteenth century, medical experts mistakenly believed that yellow fever, malaria, cholera, typhoid, and other diseases originated from miasmatic places, spreading to humans through dangerous emanations and vapors. In fact, many of these diseases were transmitted by water or mosquitoes. Relying upon leak- and overflow-prone privies and underground cisterns for the disposal of human wastes, American cities became very unhealthy places in the mid-nineteenth century. Contaminated wells and streams, damp basements, and inadequate drainage increased levels of human exposure to feces and transmitted deadly diseases.

A disease etiology based in environmental explanations led physicians and civic leaders to promote physically based solutions. Noting the dangers of yellow fever, and the potential threat it posed to cities such as New Orleans, President Thomas Jefferson proposed in an 1805 letter that street plans for new settlements employ a checkerboard pattern with half the squares left open in order to produce a healthful "atmosphere . . . like that of the country."[29] While Jefferson distrusted cities in their own right for reasons of political philosophy, and the dominant theories of disease of the time would later be proven incorrect, his concern about the possible negative health effects of crowded living conditions partly anticipated the public health and sanitation crises of the mid-nineteenth-century American city.

Urban reformers identified lowlands as soggy origination points of the miasmas that caused malaria, typhoid, fever, ague, and cholera, and they argued that the lowlands must be filled. Public health became linked to civil engineering and city building. Landfilling to eliminate low spots in the urban landscape turned out to be problematic in two ways: one, without adequate drainage, filled lowlands remained wet, and two, landfilling often required large volumes of material. The process of filling Harlem Flats in New York City dramatically illustrated all these problems. Foul odors exacerbated the fears of disease that motivated the filling in the first place.

Medical discoveries eventually led to a new scientific consensus around germ theory, discrediting topographically linked "bad air" explanations. But public acceptance was slow and lagged behind the discourse of epidemiological researchers. While so-called contagionists and anticontagionists debated disease etiology in public forums, many state and local elected officials clung to older explanations that were rooted in morality or hybrid theories that continued to see low places as inherently dangerous. In New York City and elsewhere, legislators, city councilors, and commissioners authorized lowland fill as a public health measure, adhering to an explanation that linked low ground to airborne transmission to human diseases. Mosquitoes and fecal-contaminated water would not come to be commonly accepted as disease vectors until the early twentieth century. Cholera in particular continued to terrify citizens due to its rapid onset and devastating effects on the body.[30]

Fears about miasmas reflected both cultural attitudes about low-lying places and material practices that concentrated unwanted and dangerous wastes. The former clearly influenced the latter: dirty, swampy, murky places became acceptable receptacles for filth and garbage. These place associations became attached to people, particularly immigrants and African Americans.

Railroads Remake the Lowlands

Railroad infrastructure and industrial development destroyed and displaced agricultural and water-supply uses in lowlands. Low areas provided the gradual grade changes and level terrain optimal for laying railroad lines, and railroad development made topography even more important to urban spatial structure. As urbanist Lewis Mumford explained, factories selected lowland sites because they required water in production processes, to supply steam boilers, to create chemical solutions, and for cooling.[31] In large cities like New York, which had concentrations of, and ready access to, capital, labor, and institutions, city builders could imagine and implement dramatic transformations of the city's natural setting, filling marshes, expanding factory development and wharf facilities, constructing parks, and building new neighborhoods. In smaller cities like Nashville, Saint Paul, or Los Angeles, industrialists were equally ambitious, albeit at smaller scales.

In 1840, the urban population totaled 1.845 million, or 10.8 percent of the United States population, and only four American cities exceeded one hundred thousand residents: New York, Philadelphia, Baltimore, and New Orleans. Reliance on water-based transportation reinforced the dominance of these port cities into the canal-building era, and the influence of the railroads was just beginning to be felt. By 1860, on the eve of the Civil War, the US urban population had jumped to 6.217 million, or 19.8 percent of the total, and five more cities had joined the one-hundred-thousand-plus club: Brooklyn, Boston, Cincinnati, Saint Louis, and Chicago.[32] Railroads quickly assumed dominance over other forms of transportation and, as they pushed into cities, developed new waterfront nodes, supply and distribution points, maintenance and repair facilities, freight yards and depots, sidings, and passenger stations. By 1870, a second major expansion of the nation's railroad network was underway. Nashville (16,988), Saint Paul (10,401), and Los Angeles (4,385) had been small cities before the Civil War, but grew rapidly after they linked up to a growing national railroad network.

Port connections and railroad-river linkages played a significant role in transporting crops, factory goods, manufacturing inputs, and freight to and from major markets. In the center of cities, these economic nodes were also the places where newcomers arrived by rail or by steamer. In Saint Paul and Nashville, railroads reworked waterfronts and set the stage for expanded

FIGURE 1.5. The City of Los Angeles granted a sixty-foot right-of-way along the east side of the Los Angeles River on the condition that the railroad company construct a levee. The Terminal Railway ran along this route, which connected downtown Los Angeles to the port at San Pedro, from 1888 to 1905. In 1905, the Salt Lake and Los Angeles Railroad took over the line. Salt Lake Station at First Street and the Los Angeles River, the Flats, Los Angeles, 1924. Security Pacific Collection, Los Angeles Public Library.

industrial development. But even in cities without steamboat wharves, railroads found their way to rivers. This phenomenon was particularly dramatic in Los Angeles, which lacked a consistently navigable river. The city gave away hundreds of acres of land around the Los Angeles River to facilitate railroad access (see figure 1.5).

Lowlands were extensively altered, transformed into a series of hybridized natural industrial corridors cutting through the city. Railroad engineers directed work crews as they pared back bluffs and hills, constructed embankments, and built bridges. Railroads created the new urban spatial relationships that defined urban lowland neighborhoods. In Saint Paul, Minnesota, for example, the Saint Paul and Duluth Railroad tracks formed the western boundary of a Swedish immigrant community located in the Phalen Creek Valley bottom (figures 1.6 and 1.7). A doubled-arched masonry bridge over the tracks marked the southern boundary of Swede Hollow.

The civic-commercial elite in these cities worked assiduously to expand

FIGURE 1.6 AND 1.7. Two views of the tracks at the north end of Swede Hollow, Saint Paul, circa 1910. The Lake Superior and Mississippi Railroad constructed the passage through Phalen Creek Valley in 1870. William Hamm's ornate mansion is visible in the distance. Photographs by Albert Charles Munson. Collection of the Minnesota Historical Society.

railroad connections, improve upon nature, promote the city, and achieve rapid economic growth. Speculative investments and boom-and-bust economic cycles created haphazard development in lowlands as continued foreign immigration and in-migration from the countryside fueled population growth. Overcrowding, sanitary problems, and low-quality housing quickly became major municipal problems.

Urban Lowlands Become Neighborhoods

Americans started calling urban lowland neighborhoods by the names bottoms, hollows, and flats because they pictured people living down by a river, near railroad tracks, below bluffs, or in a ravine. These landscapes were visually distinct and physically separated from other areas of the city by steep slopes and active railway lines. The presence of these boundaries, combined with the perceived homogeneity of neighborhood population, by class, ethnicity, race, or place of origin, led city dwellers to identify and label these neighborhoods as distinct places, and often as distinctly bad places. Once established, these neighborhood names and reputations assumed a life of their own.

Urban lowland neighborhoods with names like "the Bottoms" or "the Flats" were not confined to hilly cities like Pittsburgh, San Francisco, or Seattle. Instead the relative position of the neighborhood within the urban landscape was the key factor. In Columbus, Ohio, for example, the difference between the city's highest and lowest elevation is only 208 feet, yet the west side of Columbus has long been known as the Bottoms neighborhood. Atlanta's highest elevation is only 312 feet higher than its lowest point, yet it had lowland neighborhoods known as Tanyard Flats and Buttermilk Bottom.[33] Lowland neighborhoods were in both hilly and flat urban landscapes.

Native-born white Americans considered urban lowland neighborhoods to be undesirable places occupied by low-status and lower-class people. Beginning in the 1870s, Americans deployed what was once primarily geological language to negatively define neighborhood identity based on relative urban location and low topographical position. They also used these terms to discredit and undermine the people who lived there. More specific than "slum," a term that was also commonly employed, they made explicit reference to the environmental conditions of wet or poorly drained urban districts.[34]

Urban lowlands became populated places because they offered housing options. For migrants from the countryside, African Americans, and foreign immigrants, cities offered economic opportunity and the promise of political and religious freedom, but lacked quality housing. Like other neighborhoods, lowlands attracted residents based on proximity to workplaces, available land and materials, and migration networks. In cities like New York and Saint Paul, they tended to be European-born immigrants, while places like Nashville and Los Angeles became destinations for more African Americans and Mexican Americans, respectively.

Urban lowland neighborhoods were segregated by class, but heterogeneous in terms of race, ethnicity, and place of origin.[35] Not all Swedes lived in Swede Hollow; many lived in other neighborhoods throughout Saint Paul and Minneapolis. Nor was everyone who lived in Swede Hollow a Swedish immigrant. But, as Swedes became an increasingly significant percentage of the population of Saint Paul in the 1880s and 1890s, Swede Hollow meant something important. It was both a cultural symbol of Swedish ways of living and the presence of Swedish immigrants in the city. It also presented a challenge for Swedes outside the hollow: How would they deal with their countrymen and women? Was the path to success through assimilation and access to economic opportunity? What types of charity efforts or local government actions were required to help, or control, the poorer among them?

Likewise, not all African Americans lived in "the bottoms." In Nashville in the 1880s and 1890s, African Americans lived in Black Bottom, but also in Hell's Half Acre, Trimble Bottom, and other neighborhoods of the city. Nor was Black Bottom homogeneously black. In fact, the people who lived there came from many different backgrounds, immigrant and native white, Catholic and Jewish. But the neighborhood was a powerful symbol of black life in Nashville, and when civic elites and newspaper writers invoked its name and its associated reputation they painted a picture of all African American life in the city. Black professionals who lived outside the neighborhood confronted questions about their affiliation with and responsibility to lowland residents. A similar intra-ethnic and intra-racial dynamic factored into later political conflicts over what to do about lowland neighborhoods.

Newspaper reporters and urban observers frequently characterized urban lowlands in terms typically reserved for agricultural areas or animal habitats; "patches," "dens," "nests," and "rookeries" were commonly used, as were "bottoms," "hollows," and "flats." Or they were used in combination, such as in Frog Hollow, Skunk Hollow, or Goose Hollow. The new language reflected a new sociospatial understanding of the industrial city as an uneven physical landscape with "slums" in low places. Urban lowlands were clearly bounded and demarcated, frequently by natural features like hillsides, bluffs, or shorelines, and they were isolated. As urban districts they became associated with the characteristics of the people that lived there; city dwellers labeled them with ethnic and racial descriptors, animal names, or adjectives associated with poor air quality or other environmental conditions. The new names appeared in newspaper articles with increasing frequency beginning in the 1870s.[36]

Linguist George Lakoff and philosopher Mark Johnson argue that concepts of low position and low status are deeply intertwined. Or, as they say, "spatialization is so essential a part of a concept that is difficult for us to imagine any alternative metaphor that might structure the concept."[37] They provide several examples: "He has a *lofty* position. She'll *rise* to the *top*. He's at the *peak* of his career. He's *climbing* the ladder. He has little *upward* mobility. He's at the *bottom* of the social hierarchy. She *fell* in status."[38] When one "hits bottom," as recovering alcoholics and addicts frequently say, one has reached their lowest point in life.

In *Juba to Jive: A Dictionary of African-American Slang*, lexicographer Clarence Major dates the common usage of the phrase "the bottoms" to the period between the 1870s and the 1930s.[39] Like "other side of the tracks," bottoms, hollows, and flats expressed a sociospatial concept in memorable terms.[40] But while the "other side" suggested boundary lines and horizontally divided spaces, bottoms, hollows, and flats were "vertical metaphors" meant to establish "vertical classifications" of urban space.[41] Starting in the 1870s, as lowland slums became more common, city dwellers adopted this language, often adding an ethnic or racial modifier to mark the space as foreign or African American.

Black Bottoms

In southern cities, whites began to use the term "black bottom" to indicate the African American part of town in the 1870s. While the origins of the term have been debated, evidence from newspaper accounts and the observations of prominent African American sociologists suggests that the phrase was deliberately pejorative, one of many derogatory labels used by whites to denigrate blacks. The widespread use of the term was noted by sociologists George Edmund Hayes, W. E. B. DuBois, and Walter Chivers.[42] Southern whites used the phrase to imply that "low whites" and immigrants living in shared spaces with blacks were also suspect and marginal. Over several decades the term became commonplace, used by blacks and whites, and in northern and midwestern cities as well as southern ones.[43]

In rural and natural contexts, "black bottom" could be a landscape term and a place name without explicit racial connotations. It denoted alluvial black soil in floodplains, a condition frequently associated with richness, fecundity, or agricultural productivity. These associations are referenced in local histories of former "black bottom" communities, almost always now known by other names. In Jacksonville, Florida, for example, Black Bottom reportedly originated from muddy smells and swampy odors.[44] Some historians argue that Black Bottom neighborhoods in Detroit and Nashville were so labeled because of the soil conditions and that racial connotations were originally absent.[45] In Lakeland, Florida, local residents recall that Black Bottom got its name due to the "absence of streetlights."[46]

But, regardless of the multiple associations, the use of the term to stigmatize and denigrate is clear in the history of the Black Bottom neighborhood in Nashville. Thousands of freed slaves moved to Nashville during and after the Civil War. During Reconstruction, southern whites attempted to limit and restrict black freedom and to marginalize and discredit black people as voters, workers, and fellow citizens. The phrase "black bottom" racialized "the bottoms," emphasizing the presence of poor African Americans in urban lowland neighborhoods associated with environmental risk, unpleasant odors, inadequate sanitation, vice, immorality, and low social status. Beginning in the 1870s, Nashville newspaper stories used the term to invoke white fears of black crime, report on police activity, and urge removal of the creek-side shacks and small houses occupied by poor African Americans.

When whites began calling Nashville's Sixth Ward by the name "black bottom" in the 1870s, it was part of an intentional effort to both discredit and demean the middle-class African Americans who lived, worked, and worshipped there and a campaign to remove poor African Americans from the city. Although "black bottom" neighborhoods share many characteristics with other bottoms, hollows, and flats, the term originates in a specific historic context: the racial violence directed at African American communities during Reconstruction.

Conclusion: Bottom Neighborhoods as Urban Problems

No single factor was responsible for the new lowland neighborhoods, not capitalism or medical theory, technology or nature. They resulted from the interaction of these forces and their combined effect, aided by the direct efforts of industrialists, investors, engineers, and speculators. They created a new urban landscape for an increasingly stratified society.

The new urban lowland neighborhoods of the 1870s were almost immediately seen as urban problems. There were technical and logistical problems that needed to be addressed by engineers; development and planning problems that challenged city officials and courts; and environmental and medical problems that demanded action from physicians and public health officials.

But in the framing of urban lowland neighborhoods as urban problems, one question vexed urban communities unlike any other: what to do about the people. In New York's Harlem Flats, Nashville's Black Bottom, Saint Paul's Swede Hollow, and the Flats of Los Angeles, urban experts and city leaders wrestled with issues of poverty, environment, and planning. They debated whether it was best to leave residents where they were or forcibly displace them.

Newspaper journalists highlighted these problems and sensationalized them. They invoked the new derogatory place names of everyday speech to dramatize the social and physical transformations taking place in the city. They demonized, and occasionally romanticized or exoticized, immigrants and the neighborhood where they lived. They racialized places where any African Americans lived as black spaces and warned that the very presence of the African American poor was a threat to the whole city. They made the names bottoms, hollows, and flats resonate in the halls of the powerful and in debates over municipal policy and planning.

City officials, physicians, and planners responded with home inspections, surveys and reports, and targeted demolition and displacement, typically justified as needed infrastructure improvements. Landowners and developers pushed for commercial and industrial redevelopment. Residents suffered from drainage problems and floods. Notorious and neglected, urban lowland neighborhoods became a common feature of the late nineteenth-century American urban landscape.

2

Harlem Flats
New York, New York

The widow who lived in the marsh gathered rags, paper, and bones. She and her two children scavenged the refuse for anything that could be resold while cart-haulers busily dumped New York City's garbage around her small home at Ninety-Eighth Street and Second Avenue. They made startling discoveries, she told a newspaper reporter in June 1875, often finding dead animals and offal in the piles. The dumping had been going on for years. Her neighbor was "afraid to open the windows" of his house in summer due to the stench, constantly wishing for a strong breeze to lift the terrible smells away.[1]

The landfilling project on the Upper East Side of Manhattan had gone awry and something needed to be done. Immediately. Physicians and civil engineers sent to inspect the area reported that improper fill material and lack of coordination were impeding progress toward the ultimate goals of draining and filling the lowlands to prevent disease and create new land. In their reconnaissance visits, they relied upon their sense of smell, a key diagnostic tool in the medical profession before germ theory, to detect the source of the emanations, and they focused on "natural" swampy odors associated with low, wet ground, a known source of bad air.[2] But the problem they sensed was a conjoint concoction: environmental degradation produced by human action. In the summer months, ocean breezes carried the stench of rotting garbage, horse manure, and stagnant water across Manhattan. As the project dragged on, journalists expressed alarm and cited the odors as olfactory evidence of governmental corruption, inattention to the basic health needs of citizens, and the threat of deadly plagues, especially cholera. They dubbed the area Harlem Flats.

The scale of the project and the problem were immense. Harlem Marsh, the southern portion of the lowlands being filled, stretched over what would become thirty-six city blocks, the entire area east of Third Avenue from

Ninety-First Street to Harlem Creek (see figure 2.1). The creek in turn extended inland from the East River shoreline all the way to Central Park. Adjacent lowlands encompassed an additional forty-nine blocks between 102nd and 110th Streets. The freshwater creek, salt meadow, and tidal marshlands were "the largest wetland complex" in Manhattan prior to filling, totaling more than half a square mile in size.[3]

In the summer of 1875, dozens of shanties perched over the marsh while small older houses and substantial new apartment buildings dotted its edges. A *New York Times* reporter labeled the area a "quagmire village," lumping together the marshy natural environment, human residents, and garbage in a single pungent phrase. Residents actively protested the filling project, particularly people living on the south end of the marsh near the neighborhood of Yorkville, and they disputed the claims of city officials. After the police

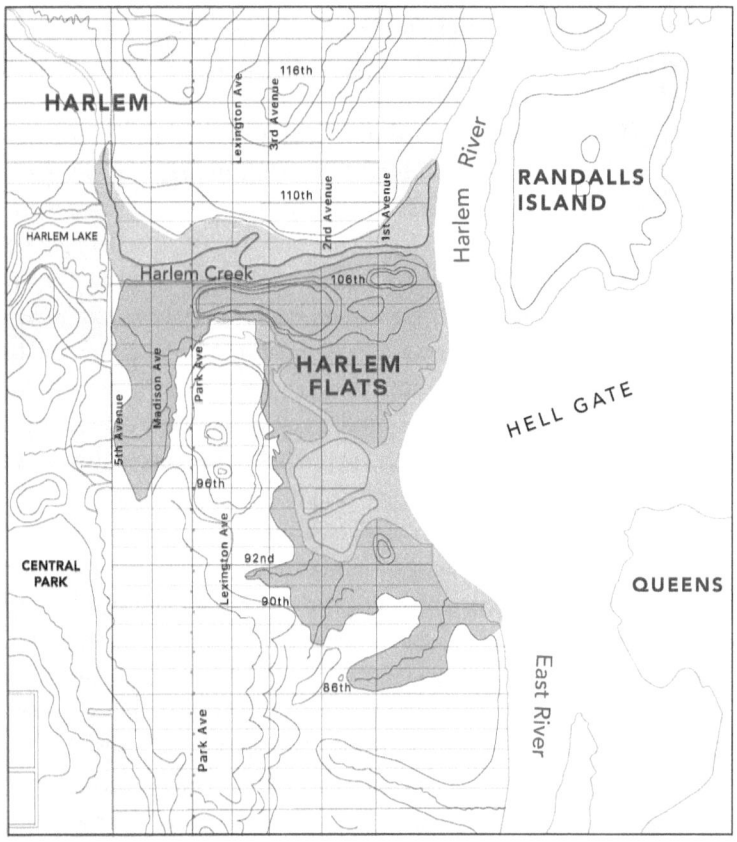

FIGURE 2.1. Harlem Flats, New York City, circa 1875. Map by Julie Kim.

department issued a report declaring that the refuse was "perfectly harmless," 136 property owners signed on to a dissenting report by three of the city's police surgeons. They argued that a high percentage of organic matter in the fill was making residents nauseated and sick.[4] It was only one of many political debates to follow.

The Harlem Flats estuary took more than a decade to fill. During this process, several thousand people lived in and among the muck and debris created by road grading, building construction, garbage hauling, and drainage projects. Within three decades, more than 150,000 people moved into the area. Almost all rented tenement apartments designed for the city's working-class residents. Five decades after filling, municipal planners and housing officials designated the neighborhood a slum and targeted it for demolition and redevelopment.

Viele's Crusade

As work crews busily filled New York City's largest wetland complex with garbage, one New Yorker repeatedly voiced his professional concerns about Harlem Flats: Egbert L. Viele. A West Point–trained civil engineer, cartographer, author, and sanitary reformer, Viele had mapped the topography and drainage of Manhattan. He was a long-standing rival of Frederick Law Olmsted Sr. and an unsuccessful entrant in the competition to design Central Park who nonetheless supervised the park's construction as chief engineer.[5] He also served as a city sanitary inspector, parks commissioner, and member of the US Congress in the 1870s and 1880s. It was Viele's maps, however, that gave him his claim to fame.

First issued in 1865, Viele's "Sanitary and Topographical Map of the City and Island of New York" was commissioned as part of a citywide sanitary survey directed by a group of medical professionals and prominent, wealthy New Yorkers who organized under the banner of the Citizens' Association.[6] They issued a 502-page report detailing inadequate street cleaning, disease mortality rates, sanitary engineering projects, overcrowding, and more. A doctor named Joseph O. Farrington and his team surveyed Harlem Flats, part of the Twelfth Ward. Upon inspecting the area, Farrington recommended filling, draining, and sewering the entire lowland, declaring confidently that "when this is done the district will compare in general healthfulness with any other on the Island."[7] Farrington's faith in filling was a commonly held view among physicians and sanitary experts. But, as Viele frequently observed during the 1860s, '70s, and '80s, landfilling projects often caused more problems than they alleviated.

Viele aimed to persuade city builders to take greater account of drainage and sanitation when laying out new blocks or constructing new buildings, but was only partially successful. He opposed many of the filling operations he witnessed around New York, calling the municipal government's inattention to proper drainage "inexcusable folly" that risked a major outbreak of disease.[8] The process, Viele repeatedly argued, was haphazard and uncoordinated. The Harlem Flats project in particular had many contradictions and unintended consequences.

Viele became city sanitary inspector just as the Harlem Flats controversy began in the autumn of 1872. He identified the problem as a failure to implement an integrated drainage solution to "take the place of the old-water courses extinguished by the filling." "Had it been possible to carry out this plan," he explained, "the subject of 'Harlem Flats' would long ago have ceased to possess any importance."[9] Viele excoriated his predecessors' inept work and described the site as a major civic failure and an example of professional negligence and incompetence. Unfortunately for Harlemites, the problem grew worse after 1872.

The tumultuous process by which legislators, medical experts, builders, and real estate speculators created East Harlem reveals formative decisions in the history of the American city. Harlem Flats was more than simply an obstacle to grid expansion, a challenge of nature to be overcome in a linear narrative of urban progress. It was a marginal lowland environment where the urban poor lived before, during, and after its chaotic development. In this urban lowland neighborhood, as in other cases around the country, fears of disease, poverty, and immigrants were deeply intertwined with environmental attitudes toward low-lying places. Terrible odors, corrupt practices, political disputes, and sensational reporting exacerbated the situation, influencing the neighborhood's trajectory for decades into the future.

Shanty Dwellers, Boaters, and "Fast Trotters"

By the time of the Harlem Flats crisis of the 1870s, speculators, builders, railroad companies, and engineers had pushed urban development up the East Side of Manhattan, as Yorkville and Harlem grew closer together. West of Fifth Avenue, teams of workers busily constructed the new Central Park. On the eastern edge, along the shoreline where the Harlem River flowed into the East River at Hell Gate, Irish railway laborers built shanties. Italian immigrant laborers would later join them, establishing a small village near 106th Street.[10] It was one of dozens of shantytowns north of Fifty-Seventh Street, a growing phenomenon that had begun decades earlier as poor New Yorkers and migrant laborers found ways to survive and adapt at the city's northern edge.[11] In 1864, the *New York Times* estimated that twenty thousand Manhattan residents paid "neither rent for the dwellings they occupy, nor municipal taxes as holders of real estate."[12] The Citizens' Association survey counted more than three hundred shanties in and around Harlem Flats.[13] Historian Catherine McNeur describes these communities of self-built housing as located along a "movable boundary between the city and its hinterland," an apt description of the agricultural and built environment of Harlem's marshy east side.[14]

Residents of these small communities often built their own housing on land at the city's near margin, just beyond the expanding street grid. Some shanty or cottage dwellers owned the land they lived on, such as the African American families at Seneca Village, a community that was demolished to create Central Park.[15] Some residents rented from the landowner, while squatters took residence without permission. But in the press words like "squatter" and "shanty" were often used loosely to denigrate poor people and their houses.[16] Viele, for one, expressed disgust. Of the residents of shanties in Central Park, he wrote that they resided in "rude huts of their own construction" and lived "off the refuse of the city, which they daily conveyed in small carts pulled by dogs from the lower part of the island."[17] The press depicted the settlements as "nests" of sickness and disease (see figure 2.2).

Rural in character and connected by pathways, the spatial arrangement of the houses in shantytowns provided a striking contrast to the orderly, geometric pattern established by adherence to the grid plan. Newspaper illustrations from the 1870s and 1880s depict scenes of shanty villages juxtaposed with new construction, often equating small wooden houses with the "old" city and masonry buildings on gridded streets with the "new" city (see figure 2.3). Characterizations of lowland houses as "old," "country," "rustic," or "primitive" became common tropes of journalistic writing about shantytowns and lowland neighborhoods.

Harlem Flats and its surroundings exhibited the striking contrasts of a rapidly changing urban landscape. To the north and west of the flats lay Central Harlem, where Dutch farmers had settled on the dry plain in the seventeenth and early eighteenth centuries.[18] Between the flats and the plain stood the high ground at the northeast corner of Central Park, where one could overlook the lowlands from a historic site: the strategic vantage point where Revolutionary War and the War of 1812 battles were fought. John Joseph Holland's 1814 painting of McGown's Pass depicts the view from this prospect, providing a glimpse of what the marshlands looked like before filling (see figure 2.4).[19] Andrew McGown's substantial two-story wooden house, built there in 1796, was a notable visual and historic landmark, and family members of McGown's

FIGURE 2.2. Depictions of shantytowns as diseased environments often conspicuously included goats and other animals. Source: "The Cholera and Fever Nests of New York City," *Frank Leslie's Illustrated*, September 15, 1866.

FIGURE 2.3. Juxtaposition of wooden shanties and new masonry construction. Source: "Squatter Life in New York," *Harper's New Monthly Magazine*, June 1880, 563.

FIGURE 2.4. *View at Fort Clinton, McGown's Pass, New York City*, John Joseph Holland, 1814, watercolor. Collection of New-York Historical Society.

FIGURE 2.5. Railroad trestle across Harlem Flats, stereograph, circa 1870. Collection of New York Public Library.

wife, Margaret Benson, were longtime property owners in the area (see "Benson's Point" in figure 1.4).[20]

Harlem's southeastern lowlands were divided into small farms, and sparsely populated. Railroad passengers whisked across the wet ground over a 658-foot timber viaduct, constructed by the New York and Harlem Railroad (see figure 2.5).[21] In the mid-nineteenth century, New Yorkers celebrated the upper stretches of Manhattan's East River shoreline as a natural and scenic landscape of fields and woodlands.[22] But urban development soon bordered the lowland on two sides. On the northern side of Harlem Creek, where Irish squatters took over several abandoned farms, real estate speculators purchased land for subdivision into urban lots and resale.[23] To the northwest, Central Harlem boomed.[24] In the summer of 1873, developers began construction on more than four hundred buildings there.[25] To the south, builders erected tenements, brownstones, luxury apartments, and two-story houses for the wealthy in the German village of Yorkville.[26] On all sides, property owners, city workers, and engineers were transforming Manhattan's terrain.

Immediately west of the flats was Central Park. At its extreme northeast corner was Harlem Lake, an artificially constructed, twelve-acre water feature rendered from lowland creeks and streams that previously had flowed into Harlem Flats.[27] Crews of workers reshaped land, redirected streams, planted tree groves and grassy meadows, and platted new carriage drives and paths to create the L-shaped lake, bracketing the park's corner at 110th Street and Fifth Avenue.[28] Frederick Law Olmsted Sr. and Calvert Vaux designed it to enhance natural beauty and impart a sense of calm to park visitors. Meanwhile, the nearby flats developed a reputation as a rowdy place for horse racing, an activity that attracted the attention of park planners.[29] Central Park's promoters argued that speed limits should be placed on riding horses, noting that a fast pace was better suited to the nearby lowland. "Fast trotters," they hoped, would be bored by "a public promenade pleasant for the general public" and therefore "confine their patronage to the Harlem Flats and the adjacent taverns."[30] Historian Jonathan Gill notes that boaters once watched the horse races from Harlem Creek.[31] The view from the water would be fleeting, however. Plans to bury the creek were underway.

Burying Harlem Creek

Harlem Creek was, according to one local historian, "one of the largest, most important, and most interesting" waterways to "penetrate the Island of Manhattan."[32] The creek flowed from the northwest, across Manhattan, as it collected the flows of several spring-fed freshwater streams and fed a deep tidal inlet.[33] Nearly a mile from north to south, the lowlands were interlaced with small freshwater streams and provided abundant habitat for flora and fauna, including the otters that had inspired the Dutch name Otterspoor.[34]

Initially surveyor John Randel omitted Harlem Creek from New York's grid plan, which stopped at the water's edge at 106th Street and resumed at 110th Street.[35] It was a notable exception to the otherwise uniform extension of the rectilinear framework over existing land holdings and natural features like hills and streams. Some historians have argued that the creek was considered "too daunting" a geographic obstacle. However, two decades later, in 1837, the New York State Legislature modified the original plan, erasing the creek from the map.[36] Engineering advances, pressure from land speculators, and a consensus favoring landfilling had triumphed over earlier concerns.[37]

Harlem Creek emptied out into Hell Gate, a section of swift, dangerous currents and rocky outcroppings in the East River. At the southern end of the flats, the Ninety-Second Street ferry shuttled passengers across the river to Astoria, Queens.[38] Across the river was Wards Island, site of the Emigrant and Refuge Hospital.

The early 1870s saw a bevy of new governmental measures to promote better sanitation. Across the city, new sewers were urgently needed, as documented in the Citizens' Association report. The new combined sewers were designed to address both drainage issues in lowland areas and the problem of increased wastewater, an unintended consequence of ready access to a freshwater supply made possible by the Croton Aqueduct project.[39] Privy vaults received human wastes prior to the development of the sewer system, and additional water led to overflowing vaults.[40] Water also leaked and drained into city streets, and runoff accumulated in low places.

The New York State Legislature authorized additional landfilling within the city and county of New York in April 1871, an important step in the transformation of Harlem Flats.[41] Then in 1872 city workers rerouted Harlem Creek into the new 110th Street sewer. One of the largest in the city, it was eight feet wide and twelve feet tall, and it drained an area of upper Manhattan comprising approximately seven hundred acres.[42] The previously unsurmountable natural barrier to grid expansion had been relegated to an underground pipe. Instead of flowing into the lowland, the springwater that fed the estuary went directly into the East River. It was the first major engineering intervention in the process of draining and filling the land.

Filling Harlem Flats with Waste

As sewer construction commenced, local politicians directed the police and the street-cleaning departments to oversee hundreds of workers filling Harlem Flats. New Yorkers began to complain of an unbearable stench permeating the city's air. This flow of waste material included street sweepings (of which horse manure constituted a major component, as horses remained a primary means of transporting people and goods), ashes (a common waste product, as most buildings were heated by wood or coal), garbage, privy wastes, animal carcasses (not an uncommon occurrence on city streets at the time), and other detritus. It was delivered largely by crews of men working on garbage scows and pushing carts (see figure 2.6). Local residents and property owners expressed alarm as crews unloaded and dumped more and more garbage, while the poorest of the shanty dwellers, like the woman and her two children who lived near Ninety-Eighth Street and Second Avenue, combed through the garbage in search of anything valuable that could be resold or repurposed. The press called them "ragpickers."

The fast-growing city concentrated both human activity and accumulations of waste, often dumped in creeks, marshes, or the harbor. These practices strained local ecology and polluted the water, destroying plant and animal life and preventing recreational or other uses. But, just as waste disposal was a problem for some, it was a potential benefit to others. The sheer volume of waste, its ready availability, and the urgent need to remove it attracted great interest from entrepreneurs interested in the potential of profitable by-products. Waste also stimulated public debate about who should clear the streets, empty the privies, cart away refuse, and remove ashes, and what

FIGURE 2.6. New York City garbage scows, undated photo, circa 1910. Collection of Municipal Archives, New York City.

the city should do with them. Proponents for burning, burying, or dumping waste in nearby waterways or at sea each argued their case.[43]

New Yorkers had buried or dumped various wastes at the immediate margins of the city, especially along shorelines and in lowlands, since the city's founding. As early as 1796, garbage disposal and landfilling practices elicited public health concerns, particularly the fear that "decaying organic material" emitted dangerous vapors. Physician Richard Bayley, who later became the city's first health commissioner, noted that to "dirt and filth . . . were occasionally added dead horses, dogs, cats, hogs" and other animals.[44] When Harlem Flats was filled, this same mix could be found, albeit in larger quantities and greater concentrations.

During the 1870s, political control of the city swung back and forth between Tammany Hall and various opponents and reformers. Forced from office and jailed in 1873, the infamous William M. "Boss" Tweed had left the scene, but his political machine endured.[45] Elected officials, waste haulers, and land speculators aimed to get rich through lucrative contracts and kickbacks or by buying and selling the newly made land, while sanitary reformers and political opponents cried foul. Building upon the results of the 1865 Citizens' Association report and the success of the Metropolitan Board of Health in combating the cholera outbreak of 1866, the reformers appealed to the public health apparatus to remedy the problems caused by the dumping. On full display in the coordinated and effective government response to cholera, the health board exercised significant power to fight disease, including the ability to seize and dispose of dangerous material, inspect dwellings, prevent ships from landing, and to quarantine residents. Their orders had forced the cleaning of city streets and yards, improving health conditions citywide. Without a current disease crisis, however, many of the city's problematic sanitary practices resumed. Reformers took to invoking the threat of another outbreak.

The Content of the Fill

One response to the Harlem Flats controversy involved greater scrutiny to what was being dumped and by whom. Surveys of environmental conditions and property inspections led by medical professionals and engineers continued. Their field observations reflect detailed attention to geographic location, landfilling activities, and odors. In a letter to Col. Emmons Clark, secretary to the board of health, dated May 10, 1872, City Sanitary Inspector Moreau Morris, MD, reported that a street-cleaning contractor was filling a six-block area of marshland with "street dirt, cellar excavations, and building refuse." In the course of the inspection, Morris and his team observed seven or eight garbage scows unloaded, as waste material was carted to the site, with "some offensive odor" similar in smell to garbage being removed from city streets.[46]

The medically trained sanitary surveyors took special note of the physical connections between land, water, and air. They also categorized smells as natural or unnatural, speculating about their causes and sources as they articulated in colorful language the intensity of odors and their potential danger. In an environmental report from the period, for example, the human nose was described as a particularly adept sensor, able to detect dangerous urban problems and threats to the city. "A wise Providence has made healthful odors pleasant to the senses and malarial ones disagreeable," the report declared. "The nose, like a friendly and watchful sentinel, alert both day and night, scents instantly in the air a dangerous smell, and gives warning of its approach as that of a deadly enemy."[47] Harlem Flats, they surmised, was sounding an olfactory alarm.

Both nature and human action represented potential causes of these threats. An 1872 report identified "a much more offensive odor proceeding from the untouched marshy land" than in the filling zone. In another section of the report, the inspectors suggest that the transfer process, specifically the "stirring and handling this rubbish and refuse" that allowed confined gases to escape, caused the offense to the nose. Some blocks in the flats, such as along 105th Street, were "found to have been filled in with good earth entirely, free from any admixture with street dirt." Mostly, they blamed the environment, concluding that the "peculiarly objectionable features of this region are due, in part, to the natural condition of the ground, and in part to the want of a comprehensive plan of improvement."[48]

As major landfilling operations entered their second and third years, the manner, scale, and effects of the fill became more contentious. Particularly in the summer months, the odor produced by heaping rotting, putrid garbage, horse manure, dirt, and offal in soggy ground, interspersed with stagnant ponds of impounded water and an incomplete sewer system, became unbearable. Repeatedly surveyors, reformers, journalists, and citizens called for the use of clean fill. In summer 1873, one editorialist noted that while "considerable areas in this region were filled" with the encouragement of the board of health, oversight was sporadic and uneven due to "its limited number of inspectors."[49] In November the *Times* reported that the board of health was investigating businessman Oliver Charlick, who apparently arranged to get paid both for the disposal of waste material and the filling of the flats.[50] That winter, the paper followed up with another story, observing that "the contractors, as well as private parties, became very careless in regard to the selection of the proper material."[51]

Complaints to the city board of health proliferated as the stench intensified. In response, the board of health demanded answers from the police department, who oversaw street-cleaning operations. Dumping must be "discontinued," argued the department head. Unsatisfied with the response, the board of health then adopted a resolution ordering the police department to arrest anyone found to be dumping "without a special written permit" from the board. On February 15, 1874, George M. Van Nort, commissioner of public works, weighed in. He defended his employees and the process. He wrote back to the health department claiming that "in no instance are the contractors allowed to use other material for filling than that allowed by the terms of the contract and the provisions of the Sanitary Code" while specifically noting that uncontaminated "coal ashes" were allowed by contract. Road grading, landfilling, and drain construction projects were underway all across Harlem Flats, from the river to Madison Avenue and from Ninety-Second Street up to 110th Street, and a massive brownstone railroad viaduct between Ninety-Eighth and 111th streets replaced the wooden structure in 1874.[52]

The problem according to Van Nort was created by private business interests, not the city, and it was geographically concentrated on private land east of Second Avenue, near the river. Unfortunately, he noted, the city had "no authority to stop the filling." By summer 1874, more complaints were lodged as some observers noted that the filling from east to west was causing water to pool and stagnate west of Fourth Avenue. These accusations, claims, and counterclaims would continue for several years. Public and private actors became entangled, with public officials abdicating responsibility and dodging questions about the fill. Multiple projects were taking place simultaneously across Harlem Flats, and tasks and responsibilities became increasingly unclear. Confusion spread about where and how the odors originated, suspicions regarding the marshes and wetlands grew, and little effort was made to coordinate or plan the sequence and process of filling. Viele's earlier complaint about the lack of a comprehensive plan rang true.

Goat Town

Road graders and filling operators surrounded the residents of the old farmhouses, new brownstones and tenements, and self-built wooden cottages and huts. As Harlem Flats' odors became the subject of public controversy, the hodgepodge character of the built environment inspired much commentary in the newspapers. An irregular pattern of newly filled lots, construction sites, and marshy zones of impounded, stagnant water stretched across the former wetlands. Local residents complained of the noise from construction, railroads, and shanty dwellers. Typical is one woman interviewed by the *Times* who lived south of the flats on Eighty-First Street near Madison Avenue. She explained that her block had only four houses, and might have been quiet and peaceful but for a shanty settlement nearby. Early each morning she awoke to a racket caused by chickens, ducks, and roosters, and the residents themselves.[53]

The presence of animals provoked many complaints. In the 1870s, one section of Harlem Flats briefly got the nickname Goat Town due to the number of free roaming animals.[54] In 1874 Harlem dairy farmer and Twelfth Ward Alderman John J. Morris proposed an ordinance to impose a three-dollar fine on any person who permitted goats to run free. After some mockery from other council members, the motion was adopted. It was widely regarded as unenforceable. A few years later, the paper reported that area around the new elevated train station at 111th Street was "in the midst of what is poetically known as 'the goat region.'"[55]

A common theme in descriptions of shanties was the rocky or swampy ground they rested upon, as journalists suggested that the residents who inhabited the city's margins and gaps lived like animals.[56] The newspapers described shanties found "among the rocks . . . scattered everywhere about uptown."[57] Another newspaper report described the wooden buildings as clinging to rock outcroppings. The anonymous author of an article entitled "Squatter Life in New York" in *Harper's Magazine* located the settlements "down in the hollows between the graded streets, and in spaces where no streets having been opened, the gray Laurentian rock stands with but a superficial layer of soil upon it." In addition to manual labor, ragpicking, garbage hauling, peddling, and other means to make a living, some shanty dwellers developed large gardens and sold vegetables in city markets. *Harper's* romanticized this landscape as "agriculture . . . with a primitive simplicity of life and . . . picturesqueness of condition."[58] As Harlem Flats was filled, property holders who had previously allowed shanties sold their land to speculators and builders who planned to put up brownstones and tenements. The January 17, 1880, edition of the *Real Estate Record*, for example, lists the sale of the lot at the northwest corner of Fourth Avenue and 110th Street containing "shanties," suggesting both the possibility of citizen concerns about a potential public nuisance and possible rental income.[59]

In public health discourse, however, the structures aroused disgust and suggested danger. Health inspectors saw shanty dwellers as "a careless, filthy class of people who ignore the commonest requirements of decency and cleanliness, living in intimate association with and proximity to dogs, horses, pigs, geese, and other [animals] whose habits they assimilate and whose filth comingles with their own."[60] Journalists largely followed suit. They raised alarms about the health threat represented by the shanty population. The *Times*, for instance, reminded readers that the first victim of the deadly 1866 cholera epidemic "lived in a shanty at 93rd and 3rd Avenue."[61] The shanty dweller was simultaneously portrayed as a part of the natural environment, living among animals and in animal-like habitats, and a morally degenerate human being responsible for his or her own fate.

Front-Page News

"Harlem Perfumery," "The Garbage Beds," "Beautiful Smells," "A City Plague Spot," "Harlem Flats Nuisance," "The Noisome Harlem Flats," and "A Nursery of Pestilence" read just a few of the dramatic and often sardonic newspaper headlines during the summer of 1875. Harlem Flats attracted the attention of the entire city. It was the front-page lead story of the June 9, 1875, *New York Tribune*, and on July 15, 1875, the *Daily Graphic* printed a map labeled "The Harlem Flats Nuisance Map Showing the Places to Be Filled and Those Which Will Remain Unfilled" (see figure 2.7). The paper noted that gray indicated areas being filled with "refuse and garbage" by private contractors and black showed where the "spasmodic effort" by the board of health was located, a tiny proportion of the total area. The city government had clearly failed to address the crisis, the authors contended. The board's response was

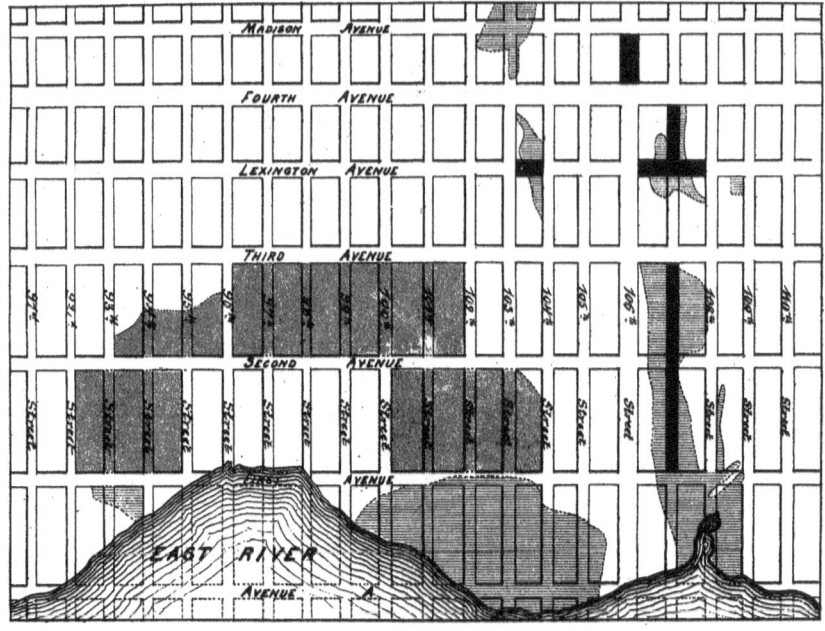

THE HARLEM FLATS NUISANCE.
MAP SHOWING THE PLACES TO BE FILLED AND THOSE WHICH WILL REMAIN UNFILLED.

FIGURE 2.7. A map to demand action. Source: "The Harlem Flats," *Daily Graphic*, July 15, 1875, 103.

like "blowing up one infected house" when a whole city was suffering from disease.[62]

Meanwhile, the board of health shifted tactics in an attempt to expedite filling. They acknowledged that the logistical challenges of inspecting and controlling the flows of fill material were beyond the board's control. They referenced the city's Sanitary Code, which defined three categories of material waste: manure and other street sweepings, ashes, and garbage. Ashes in particular were seen as a potential resource, valuable for filling "sunken lots."[63] The problem, according to the board of health's interpretation of the revised city code, was that the three types became mixed. Such mixed waste was not proper fill material and was "necessarily offensive . . . unless disinfectants are freely used or the material is speedily covered with several feet of good earth or gravel."[64] Going forward, they recommended two possible citywide strategies: either separate the material into three categories or dispose of everything in the combined waste collection stream to a location somewhere beyond the city limits.[65]

Harlem Flats, however, was a "peculiar district of the city" originally comprised "of low lands partly under water at high tide, intersected at several points by estuaries and creeks."[66] Filling with "pure earth only," they argued, was "practically impossible." Furthermore, the threatening natural condition of the salt marsh and the public's desire for action justified a looser inspection standard. In effect, they argued, the problem was so bad that not much could make it worse. "The natural and exposed surfaces of these tidal lands were so offensive, and the emanations arising from them so deleterious," they explained, "that hardly any material used as filling could render them any more obnoxious to the public." The board decided to allow "the use of ashes, street sweepings and cellar-earth for filling these lands," and while garbage should be kept out, they took the position that it would be "impossible to entirely exclude" it.[67]

In May 1875, the *Herald* reviewed police department records and reached the conclusion that more than 350,000 cubic yards of "putrid filth" had been dumped into the flats in the eleven-month period between February 1874 and January 1875.[68] "The filling up of these flats was a necessity; but it has been done in the most disgraceful way," the paper editorialized.[69] Many more newspaper articles in many different papers, each trumpeting the significance of their own investigative reports, followed.

In response, the board decided to adopt "an extensive system of disinfection" using dead oil, iron liquor, carbolic acid, and sawdust for remediation and odor reduction in an attempt to "afford temporary relief."[70] It reiterated that while the police department could use "the dirt and ashes collected by the Bureau of Street Cleaning" for fill, that power was subject to review and approval by the board of health.[71] In June 1875, they recommended the following additional actions: complete the filling process and the construction of streets and sewers, confront shanty dwellers and their privies, cover problematic areas, commission an engineering report, and insist on clean fill.

Conferences with New York City Mayor William H. Wickham, public works, and the board of health, and a presentation to the board of aldermen, followed. Under the leadership of Wickham, a reform Democrat, city leaders agreed upon a new coordinated approach: the city would take over in order to complete the filling process. The city issued a formal declaration under chapter 566 of the Laws of 1871, issued assessment bonds, and assessed property owners for the cost. Finally, it was hoped, the problems with this "peculiar" swampy district that produced "deleterious emanations" could be solved.

But some begged to differ. "Nobody called Harlem flats a nuisance" fifteen years ago, wrote a "Civil Engineer," possibly Viele himself, in a letter to the editor of the *Sun* newspaper. "On the contrary, being subject to the action of pure salt water and pure air alternately, they contributed greatly to the general salubrity of the neighborhood."[72] Echoing Viele's concerns from five years earlier, the writer focused on the sewer problem and the need for a deeper intercepting sewer line along First Avenue. The author also detailed problems in road construction, use of improper materials, and the absence of a culvert that impeded sewer hookups and led to impounded water in ponds. There was a lack of engineering supervision in the street department, he concluded. Nature, it seemed, had become a convenient excuse for graft, neglect, and shoddy construction.

Further complicating matters, in 1878, a dispute over assessments to property owners in the flats landed in the courts, and New York Supreme Court Justice Abraham R. Lawrence disallowed the assessments levied by the city to pay for the project, forcing the city to absorb the cost of the filling and draining work.[73] City government was not only implicated in the mess; taxpayers also paid the cost. For many observers, the episode represented another major civic failure.

Political critique and citizen anger infused newspaper reports, as journalists linked corrupt politicians to a degraded urban environment and bad smells. In August 1880, the satirical magazine *Puck* editorialized that Harlem Flats was overpowering New Yorkers with its "pestiferous nastiness."[74] An accompanying cartoon graphically depicted "The Seven Smells of New York": a bone boiling works; a bottle labeled "this is not cologne"; street filth; sewer gas; a garbage barrel that housed a cat inside and a broken broom that was "rotted for want of use" and had old shoe at its base; Tammany Hall, itself a metonym for New York City's Democratic Party; and Harlem Flats (see figure 2.8).[75] While garbage is located in the foreground as a present and visible concern, Harlem Flats appears in the distance, a peripheral but nonetheless potent source of odors. Tammany Hall, rotten with political corruption and responsible for producing the stench, visually frames and connects garbage and waste to the flats. The smell's impact is illustrated in the inset at upper left, which shows a man's face with his nostrils pinched shut with a clothespin. The short column heaps on one vivid and strenuous phrase after another, bemoaning the terrible sensory assault New Yorkers had to bear each summer. Harlem Flats was more than a local nuisance. It was, under the right wind conditions, emblematic of the urban environmental problems of the 1870s: one could smell in the air how corrupt, incompetent, and avaricious municipal management had put the lives of New Yorkers at risk.

Eventually, however, under city direction, the landfilling process concluded. Madison and Lexington Avenues, which were not part of the original grid, were inserted into the street plan, between Fifth and Park and between Park and Third, respectively.[76] The horse-drawn streetcars and a steamboat that had provided transportation from Harlem to the city were superseded in the 1880s by elevated railroads that extended their lines along Second and Third Avenues, and Fourth Avenue would be renamed Park Avenue in 1888.

HARLEM FLATS 49

FIGURE 2.8. Harlem Flats, one of "The Seven Smells of New York." Source: "Summer Luxuries," *Puck*, August 4, 1880, 394. Collection of New-York Historical Society.

Complaints about dangerous smells abated. Road, transit, sewer, drainage, and water projects to serve the neighborhood were completed. And on the "made land," a new neighborhood sprouted up. It quickly became home to tens of thousands of newcomers, mostly immigrants and their families.

The New East Side

The draining and filling of Harlem Flats permanently erased 40 percent of Manhattan's total wetland area.[77] Over a decade, citizens complained, journalists railed, elected officials dodged, speculators bet, lawyers litigated, and judges ruled while hundreds of laborers continued, year after year, to remake the landscape.[78] In the early 1880s, a wave of new building construction hit the neighborhood as tenements, factories, schools, churches, and shops went up everywhere, including on the filled land above Harlem Creek.[79] Residents of the newly constructed tenements were both foreign born, mostly from Prussia or Ireland, and native-born Americans, many of whom were born in New York City. At the neighborhood's edge, closer to the East River, industrial uses dominated: coal yards, lumberyards, gas tanks, stoneworks, stables, and storage facilities. The nickname Harlem Flats faded away.

By 1884, one real estate journalist confidently remarked that the neighborhood "formerly known as Harlem Flats" showed signs of great building activity.[80] By the mid-1880s, the "streets were lined with tenements . . . [housing] poor German, Irish, and Jewish immigrants."[81] Cigar-maker Louis Jaeger, for example, lived with his wife, five sons, three daughters, and brother-in-law on Third Avenue in 1880. While Louis, his wife, Theresa, and her brother Herman were born in the German state of Württemberg, all eight of their children were born in New York City. They were one of five families who lived in the building, a total of thirty-three people. The Jaegers' neighbors were born mostly in the US, including New York, Louisiana, and the Washington Territory. Three of the four were of Irish descent. The McKenna, Benard, and Farrell families all reported to census taker Alvaro Betancourt that they had Irish-born parents.[82]

The old McGown family house built in 1796 burned to the ground in January 1881. Reportedly one of the oldest structures in the city, the Sisters of Charity of the Roman Catholic Church used it as part of Mount Saint Vincent convent before it was converted to a restaurant and museum as part of Central Park.[83] Samson B. McGown, who was born in the house and lived only a few blocks away on Lexington Avenue, died shortly thereafter in 1884.[84] More than two dozen building lots owned by the family were offered in an executor's sale the next year.[85] By 1889 tenement buildings were built on all of them.[86]

In the last two decades of the nineteenth century, Jews and Italians, as well as other ethnic groups, moved into the neighborhood. On Third Avenue, for example, the Poholsky family moved into the former Jaeger home: Philipp, a painter; his wife, Rebecca; and young sons, Herman (aged two years) and Samuel (ten months). Census taker Emil Brettheimer recorded an additional two families (a total of seven) and twenty-nine people of Russian, German, English, and Irish heritage living in the building. None of the residents had lived in the building twenty years earlier.[87]

Tenement construction continued for decades and the neighborhood's population soon surpassed one hundred thousand residents. One study reported that sixty-five thousand apartments were constructed in East Harlem between 1870 and 1910.[88] Overall, the Twelfth Ward increased from 245,046, or 17.0 percent of Manhattan's total population in 1890 to 806,674, or 34.6 percent by 1910. Within the boundaries of the former Harlem Flats, an area of eighty-five city blocks, the US Census of 1910 recorded 138,200 people, an average of approximately 1,625 persons per city block.[89]

Buried below the new streets, Harlem Creek flowed through sewer pipes. But it didn't always stay there. In 1902, when Inspector George Colvin visited a five-story brick building on East 109th Street, for example, he stepped into "a cold stream" running across the cellar floor.[90] Inspector Alexander Gazzola found that every cellar from 213 to 220 East 108th Street was flooded and the buildings were in poor condition.[91]

Colvin and Gazzola worked as inspectors for the city's tenement commission, visiting tenements in all parts of the neighborhood and the city. It is notable, however, that the city's 1902–3 report highlighted two buildings constructed above the former path of Harlem Creek. Water and sanitation problems, documented in the 1865 Citizens' Association report as a public health concern, reappeared as housing issues four decades later. Inept and corrupt landfilling practices and speculative building led to poor-quality construction that accelerated the pace of neighborhood deterioration in the early twentieth century.

The four-story tenement that Gazzola had inspected at 213 East 108th Street housed sixty-nine residents, all of Italian heritage.[92] Many of the men worked as day laborers, stonecutters, and stone masons, some of the them likely employed by the stoneworks one block away. Tailor Paolo Casoto, who immigrated to the US from Italy in 1890, lived there with his wife, Jennie, three sons, and one daughter-in-law. The Casotos' neighbors, Santi and Guiseppina Mairche, both emigrated from Italy just three years earlier in 1897. Their seven-month-old daughter Lucia was born in New York City. The Mairches took in two boarders, the Rizzos, also recent immigrants from Italy. By the early twentieth century, as Italian immigrants became the dominant ethnic group, the neighborhood would come to be known as Italian Harlem.[93]

In 1904 the *Times* profiled the neighborhood built on "low ground," calling it the "New East Side." Nearly a quarter million people lived on the former "swampy land" transformed into "miles of dreary tenements."[94] Once the "territory of a lonely squatter and his faithful goat," the new urban landscape was "a characterless mass of buildings." The squatter who had inspired fear and disgust in previous decades became an object of nostalgia. Journalists defined the New East Side by its social problems, poor housing conditions, and Italian immigrant population. Other newspaper reports of the period focused specifically on the threat of violent crime, particularly the activities of the Black Hand organization.

Oral histories and community archives record a different story. In his classic study of the Italian immigrant community, public space, and Catholic religious practice, *The Madonna of 115th Street* (1985), Robert Orsi wrote that the streets of Italian Harlem were "crowded, filthy, and dangerous." At the end of the nineteenth century, the neighborhood included garbage transfer yards, a gasworks, and stockyards. It was noisy with train traffic and vehicle-crowded streets.⁹⁵ But while the descriptions of the physical fabric of the neighborhood are similar in these accounts, they diverge in their characterization of the community. Orsi's urban social history of religious life in East Harlem subtly details the meanings of the built environment and neighborhood spaces to residents themselves. In the rapid transition from Harlem Flats, with an approximate population of three thousand residents, to Italian Harlem, with a population of nearly 140,000 people, the recent history of the creek and the marsh, shantytowns and cholera, landfilling and political corruption was quickly fading from memory.

Lowland Trajectories: Public Housing

A second major transformation in the physical environment of the former Harlem Flats unfolded in the mid-twentieth century. More than fifty years after Gazzola and Colvin surveyed the tenements built over Harlem Creek, a photographer for the New York City Housing Authority (NYCHA) visited the same section of the same block. His purpose was to document existing conditions in the neighborhood prior to construction of a new housing complex. In April 1956, he accompanied NYCHA representatives who interviewed Mrs. Patsy Pesca and her family inside her home at 216 East 108th Street.⁹⁶ Soon thereafter the housing authority demolished Mrs. Pesca's home and dozens of buildings in the surrounding blocks to make way for the new Franklin Homes that opened in November 1962. Converted to co-op three years later and renamed Franklin Plaza, the planned development consolidated five city blocks into two new "superblocks." Fourteen twenty-story buildings with 1,635 apartments surrounded by open space replaced the old neighborhood. Where the Casoto, Mairche, and Rizzo families had lived in 1900 and the Pescas in 1956, the city parks department constructed a new playground.⁹⁷

In the preceding decades, sanitation campaigns and political organizing by residents had highlighted the need for improved living conditions and better city services. The public housing cause initially brought together housing reformers focused on "slum clearance" and progressives interested in low-income housing construction.⁹⁸ Targeted by the Slum Clearance Committee and then implemented by NYCHA, wide-scale demolition and reconstruction created one of the densest concentrations of public housing in the five boroughs of New York City. In total, between 1941 and 1965, NYCHA built twelve public housing complexes in the neighborhood. Historian Samuel Zipp recorded the immense scale of urban transformation: "164 acres of the nineteenth century speculative city grid" demolished and replaced by "a new superblocked landscape of 141 modern housing towers."⁹⁹ The extent of earthmoving, roadwork, and infrastructure development was equivalent in scale to the fill operations of the nineteenth century. The lowland was remade again.

The long history of East Harlem shows how immigrants and poor and working-class people were blamed for environmental problems created by both municipal government and private companies. The physical fabric of the neighborhood and the persistence of neighborhood stigma stemmed directly from decisions made in the 1870s and 1880s. Elected officials, waste haulers, real estate speculators, and civil engineers obliterated nearly all traces of the estuarine environment of Harlem Flats, save the artificial lake created at Harlem Meer and a few quasi-wild, industrialized stretches of the East River shoreline. Acrimonious political battles repeatedly delayed and complicated the filling of the lowland marsh. Yet, throughout the decade-long controversy, a diverse set of actors found consensus in the need for filling as a public health measure and the template of the grid as an organizing scheme for human settlement. Few questioned the form that urban expansion should take.

This viewpoint was supported by an environmentally based explanation of so-called zymotic diseases like cholera, and public officials viewed poor people as both victims and causes of "plague spots." "Flats" tied these ideas together. It suggested marshlands and shanties, disease threats and odors, haphazard development and marginality. The medical profession, civil engineers, landscape experts, nascent city designers, and proto-urban planners all focused on wet, low-lying places. As one reformer editorialized in 1866: "The remedy of all evils in great cities must be topographical."[100] Rapid population growth and expanded economic activity fueled this morally charged and environmentally focused city making. Removing suspect lowland spaces and their residents, replacing them with an orderly matrix of rectangular buildings on rectangular lots and blocks, was supposed to represent a symbolic triumph over disorder and disease.

The Harlem Flats of shanties and old farmhouses was rather short-lived, but the city's (and state's) response to a purportedly diseased environment has had long-lasting effects. The massive landfilling project removed valuable wetlands and significantly altered the island's hydrological pattern. But it also structured urban form, and future planning debates, by facilitating speculative apartment development for working-class residents on low-lying land. The pace of urban change, intensity of sociophysical transitions, and extent of territory were greater in New York than in other American cities, and, partly as a result, few observers have examined the historical connections between topography, sanitation, garbage, landfilling, poverty, "slum" environments, and public housing neighborhoods. In the voluminous scholarship on the history of the city, even in the specialized domains of sanitary history, medical history, and tenement history, lowlands received relatively little attention during the twentieth century. That is rapidly changing in the twenty-first century as cities begin to confront the ecological crisis of climate change.

The lasting impact of these historical events on city form is evident in the location of public housing and the disappearance of creeks, streams, and marshes. The built environment, despite near constant change, manifests the historical response to an estuarial landscape. The environmental modifications that erased Harlem Creek and Harlem Marsh, and created Harlem Meer, are unknown to many current city residents. Central Park attracts millions of visitors from around the world while a submerged Harlem Creek flows below city streets to the East River and New York harbor. East Harlem remains low-lying land today—a topographical fact clearly illustrated during Hurricane Sandy flooding in 2012.

3

Black Bottom
Nashville, Tennessee

The fight over Black Bottom lasted seven decades. From the 1870s to the 1930s, Nashville city leaders agreed that the neighborhood was a mess: flood prone, ramshackle, and unsanitary. Yet they repeatedly disagreed about what they should do. Formerly known as the Sixth Ward, Black Bottom stood at the southern edge of Nashville, near the bustling riverfront wharves and warehouses, in a low-lying, bowl-shaped depression in the land.[1] Stables, warehouses, churches, lumberyards, small houses, and tenements stood on either side of a creek called Wilson's Spring Branch (see figure 3.1). African Americans, native-born whites, and German, Irish, and Jewish immigrants called this urban lowland neighborhood home in the 1870s.

While the exact origins of the Black Bottom name remain unknown, conflicts over the neighborhood's social character and environmental conditions reveal that it was a racially coded synonym for "slum."[2] White business leaders, elected officials, and journalists used the name Black Bottom as part of a campaign to racialize and stigmatize both people and place. African Americans used the name to recognize and call attention to environmental and social conditions in the community, disagreeing at times about the neighborhood's physical development and what direction it should take. In the 1870s, for example, African American lawyer and investor James C. Napier argued that the poorest African Americans, unemployed freedmen living in dilapidated housing, would be better off migrating west in search of new opportunities.[3] In the 1880s, organized groups of white vigilantes attempted to terrorize and forcibly remove poor African Americans living in Black Bottom.[4] Neither the western exodus nor violent threats caused the neighborhood's end, however. Black Bottom residents persevered.

Black Bottom was not the center of African American life in Nashville, but

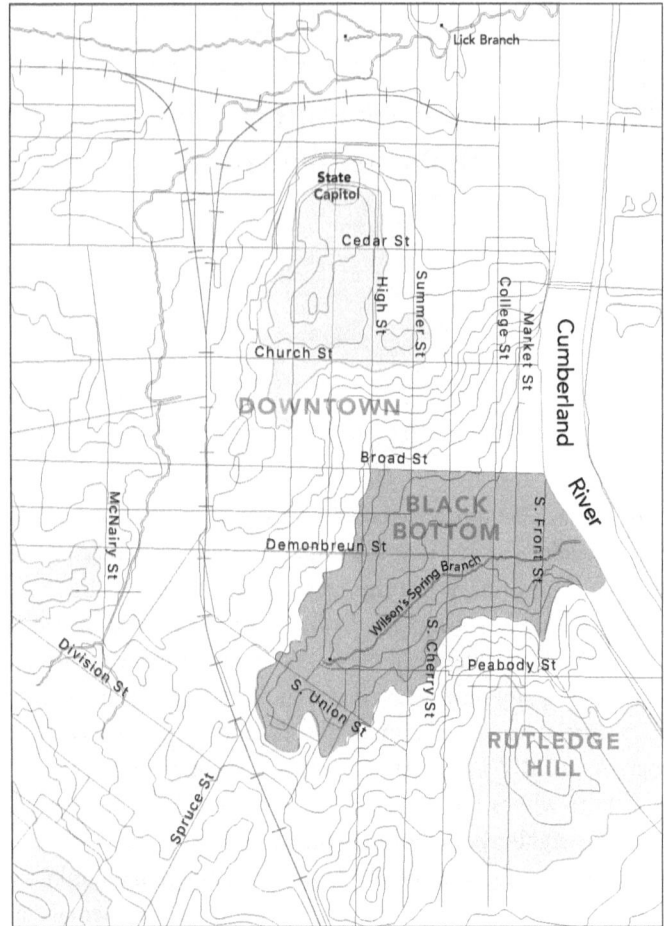

FIGURE 3.1. Black Bottom, Nashville, circa 1870. Map by Julie Kim.

one of several neighborhoods where African Americans lived after the Civil War. Nevertheless, two significant African American institutions located in the neighborhood in the 1870s: a segregated black-only public school and the city's second African Methodist Episcopal (AME) church. Black Nashvillians fought for better education, city services, economic opportunity, and political rights. They accumulated economic capital and built political and social institutions in the face of discrimination and violence. Black Bottom was a site for these struggles.

The term Black Bottom was not unique to Nashville. The use of a pejorative and racialized place label, a slang term to describe a social and physical phenomenon of urban life in cities throughout the South during Reconstruction, begins simultaneously with the end of slavery.[5] Emancipation, freedom, and the possibilities of black citizenship coexisted and were conflated with environmental and health hazards and poor living conditions in restricted space. Whites employed a vernacular politics of place naming to demean and marginalize by associating black life and black spaces with disease, odors, and immorality. Urban lowland residences simultaneously carried a powerful cultural stigma and subjected residents to environmental hazards: muddy streets and dirty spaces, risk of injury or death in floods, exposure to diseases, dangerous and unsanitary health conditions, and odors. Nashville's political leaders and civic elites inscribed race into the postbellum urban landscape through language.[6]

Journalists and elected officials claimed these spaces threatened the city as a whole, but municipal governments abetted their creation. The unhealthy living conditions made possible by floods, inadequate drainage, and "filth" stemmed from municipal neglect, particularly in the provision of infrastructure and city services. By the 1910s, "black bottom" had become a generic descriptor of a poor or low neighborhood where African Americans lived, a common rhetorical and physical phenomenon.

In the history of Nashville's Black Bottom, white decision makers were repeatedly challenged by the mere presence of the poor, and especially poor African Americans. They argued over whether segregated containment or forcible dispersal offered the best approach to dealing with them. In the racialized space of Black Bottom, generations of residents, black and white, foreign born and native born, lived, worked, worshipped, played, and struggled. Repeated attempts to remove the black population all at once failed, but eventually commercial and industrial development prevailed. By the 1940s, only a few hundred residents remained.

The Valley of Wilson's Spring Branch and the Epidemic of 1873

Black Bottom's early history is closely linked to the pollution of Wilson's Spring Branch. One nineteenth-century observer remarked that "the finger of nature" had divided Nashville into "distinct districts" separated by "the valleys of Lick Branch and Wilson's Spring Branch, two small streams which take their rise in the chain of hills south of the city, and flow northeastward to the Cumberland, their mouths being about one mile apart" (see figures 1.2 and 3.1). He described the "valley of Wilson's Spring Branch" (later Black Bottom) as "about one-quarter of a mile wide a short distance above its mouth, and one hundred yards wide a half mile from the river," noting that it "rises gradually from an elevation of thirty-nine feet above low water at its widest point, to fifty-seven feet above low water half a mile from the river."[7] Early Nashville maps, as well as recollections from contemporary residents, clearly identify the two creeks as settlement boundaries at the "edges" of town, with the town facing "front" toward the Cumberland. Broad Street would later serve as a dividing line between parts of town, but in this early period the city's divisions were understood in terms of the distance between creeks, and Wilson's Spring Branch was considered the southern border of Central Nashville (see figure 1.1).

Originating from a spring in a hillside near Fort Negley, Wilson's Spring Branch dropped more than forty feet in elevation as it traveled across the Sixth Ward toward the Cumberland River.[8] On either side lay the bowl-shaped valley of the bottom. Tanner George Wilson had owned the property where the water emerged from underground. A local historian explained that downstream from Wilson's five acres, the valley was "heavily wooded and thick with cane." In "Wilson's time," the author notes, "the large spring supplied water for Wilson's tannery, the tannery of Peter Bass lower down on the Branch, and other factories. Then, and for many years afterwards, it furnished cool, wholesome drinking water for the residents of that vicinity."[9] A second source, known as Hackberry Spring also located in the Sixth Ward, fed into the creek on its descent toward the Cumberland River.

Although Wilson's Spring Branch was once a "beautiful creek," it was permanently altered in the decades following the Civil War, overwhelmed by sanitary pressures as it was used for both water supply and waste disposal.[10] As steamboat activity at the wharves increased, property owners cleared the land around the creek and built up the Sixth Ward. After the Civil War, hundreds of emancipated slaves built their own small houses in Nashville's lowlands. The poorest people lived in shacks and huts, simple structures constructed using whatever materials they could scavenge. In the Sixth Ward, they placed their modest homes close to Wilson's Spring Branch.

By the early 1870s, the Sixth Ward had developed into a densely built, mixed-use urban neighborhood where one could find houses and tenements interspersed among stables, mills, lumberyards, and tobacco warehouses (see figures 3.2 and 3.3). Unskilled black laborers regularly gathered at Lower Broad Street near the wharves in hope of finding work.[11] Both the density of the residential population and the intensity of manufacturing processes increased, as the neighborhood south of Broad became home to nearly 3,500 people. The neighborhood got dirtier and smellier as it also became a place where poor blacks looking for work lived and gathered.

BLACK BOTTOM   59

Nashvillians started calling the Sixth Ward "Black Bottom" in the 1870s. Surprisingly, the name did not imply that only blacks lived there nor that Black Bottom was the only area of black residence within the city. Yet even within the scope of black neighborhoods, Black Bottom referred to something specific: a connection between low-lying topography, race, and disease. A cholera epidemic reinforced the Sixth Ward's reputation and fomented fear in the city's population as it struck hundreds dead in the summer of 1873. Nashville's poor sanitary condition became national news.

The polluted water in Wilson's Spring Branch directly contributed to the spread of cholera. In the early days of the crisis, the *Nashville Banner* identified the source of the outbreak "in the old locality known as the Wilson Spring

FIGURE 3.2. Black Bottom prior to the sewer project that buried Wilson's Spring Branch, circa 1890. The city's opening of the new Hay Market on Demonbreun Street (between Cherry and College Streets) coincided with the completion of the sewer in 1893. Map by Clelie Fielding.

FIGURE 3.3. A view across Black Bottom from Rutledge Hill toward the Tennessee State Capitol, circa 1890. The Cumberland River is visible at upper right. Collection of Tennessee State Library and Archives.

neighborhood, a hot-bed for all epidemics that reach Nashville."[12] A June 13 report stated that "the cholera, so far, has been mostly confined to the Wilson Spring Branch Bottom, which is the most sickly portion of the city. The branch is nothing more nor less than an open sewer, emitting foul and pestilential odors."[13] Physicians and health officials cited the Lick Branch, a stream on the north side of downtown, as an additional area of concern. Notably, these reports do not use the phrase Black Bottom. Its first known appearance in print came only a few years later.

At least thirty-five people died from the disease each day for nine consecutive days that summer, and approximately two-thirds of them were African Americans. Between June 7 and July 1, 1873, a total of 244 whites and 403 African Americans died. Neither the geographic location of the outbreak nor the race of the majority of the victims surprised observers. As one newspaper reported, "The disease has followed the 'old cholera track' in its former visits to this city and its greatest mortality this year has been in the belt in which the largest mortality resulted in previous visits, showing conclusively that there must be something local which invites pestilence to revel in the lower portions of the city, where the water is unquestionably bad, and the sewerage of such inferior character as scarcely to deserve the name."[14] The "something local" was in reality a tainted drinking water supply, the primary vector of infection, although the author clearly alludes to the presence of hundreds of poor black people as a cause. The author neglected to mention that raw sewage, transported by pipe under Broad Street, was being dumped directly into Wilson's Spring Branch.[15]

As was common during disease outbreaks in nineteenth-century cities in the US, many residents who had sufficient means fled the city for summer country retreats and safer destinations, to wait out the crisis from afar.[16] According to newspaper accounts, nearly one-quarter of the population left Nashville, and nearly all local businesses and government offices closed their doors. Meanwhile, city boosters protested journalists' reporting, arguing that only a few businesses shut down (mostly fruit sellers, they claimed), that schools were on vacation, and that many Nashvillians stayed.[17] For the three-quarters of the population that remained in place, avoiding the lowlands may have helped them avoid sickness or death. New York City physician John C. Peters, who studied and mapped the spread of cholera epidemics, reported to the board of health in New York City in July 1873: "Comparatively few deaths occurred in the highest, cleanest, best-ventilated, best-drained, and best-paved portions of the city. The best residence and business portion of Nashville during the whole of the terrible epidemic which raged on the outskirts was almost perfectly safe to live in."[18] For many Nashvillians, the crisis confirmed their beliefs about the connection between race, topography, and disease.

Peters continued his assessment of the situation in Nashville by quoting another physician, Dr. Jones, who asserted that along the Lick Branch and Wilson's Spring Branch, "there has been a rapid and progressive crowding of houses, or rather huts and shanties, either clustered together in narrow streets and alleys, or more frequently huddled together without system, and crowded with a careless and filthy population, wholly deficient in ventilation, without any facilities for the enforcement of hygienic regulations, forming a most favorable field for the lodgment and spread of a disease like cholera, and rendering it difficult if not wholly impossible, to devise any efficient measures for the arrest of communicable diseases in them." Jones was not alone in his view that the disease was the fault of black and poor people, residents who were labeled as "careless and filthy." Moral pronouncements about individual behavior, and the persistent belief that the poor lacked the desire to work, to keep clean, or to improve themselves, abound in the reports from the crisis. While household cleanliness and bodily hygiene received significant emphasis from health officials, so too did diet. Newspaper reports often focused on what the victims ate before becoming sick, noting vegetables and fruits in particular. The connection between the disease and diet reflected epidemiological concepts during the period, but it also raised further questions about poverty, including access to clean water for washing and preparing the food and the practice of growing and eating fruits and vegetables within the city.

Following the crisis, the Nashville Board of Health issued a series of annual reports examining and analyzing the outbreak's causes and recommending possible remedies (as well as a host of other public health issues). The reports included repeated calls for improved sanitation, citing the need for sewer construction along Lick Branch and Wilson's Spring Branch. The board of health explained that Nashville had made progress in providing clean water to its citizens, but had given "no systematic attention to drainage."[19] In addition, the board noted, the poor tended to take their water from springs and wells due to the high cost of the municipal water supply.[20] At the same time, Nashvillians were using large amounts of water (1,986,025.5 gallons daily, according to the board), and wasted water from spills, leaks, or frivolous uses was greatly contributing to sanitary problems due to inadequate drainage.[21]

The report provides a useful lens into the sanitary conditions of the city in general. Local and national authorities characterized the city as a whole as "filthy," a problem that was believed to be the result of environmental characteristics such as geological structure, behavioral characteristics such as idleness, and public health and engineering characteristics such as the sources of drinking water and the state of sewer systems. Newspapers across the country took note, including the *New York Times*, which labeled the conditions "frightful," drawing attention to the city's limestone foundation and poor people's use of springwater for drinking and cooking. They commented on the high rate of death in the "colored population" and the urgent need for a comprehensive sewer system. At least eight hundred people had died from the outbreak by mid-July 1873.[22] Nashville's disease crisis exposed major problems in the engineering and planning of its urban infrastructure and its inability to support a large and growing population. An entire chapter of the 1879 report was devoted to the topic of "sanitary geology" and examined interconnections between geology, engineering, and public health practices.

Drainage problems dominated the board of health's analysis. No element or characteristic related to the movement of water—whether in, atop, under, or through the city—was too minor. Even building downspouts received scrutiny. As the city wrestled with infrastructure questions, including how to pay for necessary improvements that were based on best engineering practices, the tension between public management and private approaches to shared problems became evident. Legal challenges slowed many potential advancements in public health and city planning. In one example, local residents protested the construction of sidewalks and related improvements key to better drainage and sanitation. Only in 1878 did the state supreme court uphold the so-called Sidewalk Law, allowing for the construction of curbs and gutters throughout the city, which was largely unpaved and without sidewalks.

The report's concerns included waste disposal, animal control, and public hygiene. In Nashville, as in other cities, scavengers removed garbage, and "night soil" men disposed of accumulated human wastes collected in privy vaults or other containers. The report described how the city might better regulate these trades, citing an 1877 committee report on the topic, noting that only two of the authorized four sanitary inspector positions were filled due to "stringent times." Regarding animals in the city, the report cited "considerable improvement as to hogs," while "cattle still roam at large." Other topics included the need for clean sidewalks and backyards, "the ventilation of private grounds," "widening of alleys," the need for "pure air," the benefits of trees in the city, the problem of "mantraps," "loss of life from fires and panics," smallpox, and keeping records of various social and medical statistics such as marriages and deaths. An appendix to the health officer's report described water testing at various locations, stating that public springs, including Wilson's Spring, were in "very bad condition."[23]

While the report made the need to remedy the conditions of the lowland branches clear, it also made evident that like the sidewalks issue, state action was required. An 1879 report recommended converting Wilson's Spring Branch into a "main first class sewer, by opening, straightening and covering it . . . [with work] to be done in whole or in part by the State."[24] In a combined sewer system, an underground conduit could, in theory, also remedy potential flooding problems. At the federal level, the US Supervising Surgeon's (now called the Surgeon General) 1875 report on the cholera epidemic noted that in Nashville the Wilson's Spring Branch was "subjected to annual overflows, which extended backward about half a mile with a width of about one-fourth of a mile" from the Cumberland River.[25]

Meanwhile, city officials attempted to improve sanitation by speeding stream flow and applying chemical treatments. That is, rather than addressing the problem of poverty or how people used water, they focused their efforts on treating the waterway itself. The response reflected officials' attitudes about environmental conditions as a potential threat to the entire city and signaled how solutions rooted in engineering, or in this case chemistry, were compatible with a social-political response of containment and segregation.

The city's 1879 report noted how the two streams "were disencumbered of all obstructions and the water allowed the free flow . . . a very necessary yet ticklish work." The report emphasized miasmatic theory, the idea that harmful vapors and emanations of bad air caused disease. The authors described the potential risks involved in intervention: "There could be no possibility of pure air with these streams in a befouled condition. Yet to stir up any mud, or expose fresh malarial surfaces was, in the opinion of all authorities upon yellow fever, from Merrill and Barton to the newspaper writer of the day, certain destruction." Therefore, chemicals were also needed. "The streams were cleansed and malaria avoided by the simple expedient of coating before nightfall every square inch of newly exposed surface with quicklime. The wet rocks were painted with coal tar. The water of the foul streams were purified by barrels of quicklime."[26] The treatment did nothing to help provide access to clean drinking water for residents or reduce the risk of transmission from the ingestion of the cholera bacteria, typically spread from person to person through contact with human feces or feces-contaminated water.

Still, sewer construction stalled. The creek continued in its filthy condition, and the spring continued to be used for drinking water. Fortunately, the city did not suffer another major cholera outbreak, but in 1890, the board of health renewed its call for improved sewerage and other sanitary measures—a recommendation it had urged for more than a decade.[27]

Only in 1893 did the city complete the lowland sewer projects at Lick Branch and Wilson's Spring Branch. In Black Bottom, the downtown pipe that had discharged effluent into the creek was connected to a buried sewer line that channeled the stream's flow underground to the Cumberland River. The plan to bury Wilson's Spring Branch underground had first been publicly announced nine years earlier.[28] For some public officials, sewer construction had an added benefit: it facilitated demolition of creek-side shacks and shanties. Above the pipe, fill and grading allowed speculators and builders to construct new warehouses, stores, and tenements on the new land atop the former stream course: a "buried floodplain."[29]

Building Black Bottom

In Nashville and cities throughout the South, whites abused and terrorized African Americans while the new pejorative label "black bottom" rhetorically marked certain urban living spaces as poor, black, and undesirable. The first known reference to Black Bottom in a Nashville newspaper was in the *Nashville Union and American* in 1874. The newspaper immediately linked the neighborhood's poverty with skin color while highlighting the city's intention to racially cleanse the space. The *Union and American* reported on June 2: "The colored vagrants who shelter themselves at night in the huts in what is known as 'Black Bottom,' lying just south of Broad, between Cherry and Market have been notified by Capt. Yater to move out by next Saturday."[30] This theme is repeated throughout the neighborhood's history: official actions, backed by force, intended to disperse the population, focused especially on African Americans. It also reflected national trends. By the mid-1870s, "the alliance between African Americans and northern white political leaders that had made the period's rapid and dramatic changes possible . . . began to unravel."[31] The disintegration of the relationship between black people and the US government ensued on a local level in Nashville.

With the removal of national protections, violence against African Americans quickly escalated. The lynching of Jo Reed on the night of April 30, 1875, illustrated the brutality of antiblack violence in Nashville. Reed, who lived on the north side of Nashville, not in Black Bottom, reportedly shot a white policeman named Robert Frazier who attempted to arrest Reed in his home on a charge of domestic violence. Reed fled the scene only to be captured, pistol-whipped, and then transported by a horse-drawn vehicle to the jail. A growing crowd threatened death to the two black police officers along the route, assuming they were the suspects. The mayor and a judge urged the crowd to disperse, but that night a mob of white men entered the jail, forcibly removed Reed from his locked cell, put a rope around his neck, shot him twice in the head, dragged him to the bridge, and threw Reed into the Cumberland River.[32] The perpetrators were never charged.

Whites not only targeted individual black people in Black Bottom; they also targeted the neighborhood as a whole. In 1886 the *Atlanta Constitution* reported from Nashville that Black Bottom was "a noted resort for thieves, thugs and vagrants" complaining that "the authorities failed to break it up." It continued: "Citizens of South Nashville, who have to pass Black Bottom to reach town, held an immense mass meeting tonight and formed a law and order league with the avowed intent of cleansing Black Bottom."[33] Characterizations of vagrancy and crime, which were common rhetorical devices for marginalizing African American participation in civic life, were applied first to a cluster of "huts" then a "section" of the city by 1886, implying that the whole area was dangerous. These early newspaper references indicate how the public health crisis caused by the deadly 1873 cholera outbreak and the ongoing disaster of insanitary conditions in the city produced more antipathy than empathy toward poor African Americans. They also make explicit the connection between the presence of "colored" people and the creation of a racially marked urban space.

Nashvillians disagreed about what, if anything, should be done about the "problem" of Black Bottom. While white residents of South Nashville attempted to purge poor African Americans from the city through intimidation and violence, civic elites and elected officials attempted to quarantine the population in place. Both groups relied upon derogatory speech to marginalize the neighborhood. But African American residents and their neighbors refused to be pushed out.

Despite this constant harassment and violence, African American leaders developed strong community institutions in the neighborhood. They were aided by national networks, too. Leaders of the AME church sought to expand their presence in the urban south during this period, planning to draw black parishioners away from the white-run Methodist Episcopal Church (MEC).[34] Under the leadership of Jordan W. Early, sent from Missouri to assist Nashville's congregations, Saint Paul's AME Church purchased a former Union Army building called Liberty Hall, and its number of churchgoers rapidly increased. In 1874, a group of churchgoers paraded from Liberty Hall to the corner of Franklin and South Cherry where they lay the cornerstone for a new building. They constructed an impressive new masonry church, which would serve as a visual landmark in the neighborhood for decades (see figure 3.4). It became a symbol of architectural permanence and a projection of strength and perseverance in response to continuing hostility. By 1880, Saint Paul's claimed nearly eight hundred church members.[35]

Carpenters, drivers, laborers, porters, sawyers, steamboat men, and their families lived in the neighborhood during this period. Several black businesses operated along a five-block stretch of South Cherry Street, including barbershops, general stores, a grocery, a physician's office, and shoemakers' stores.[36] Many black business owners lived outside the neighborhood, but one of the barbers, Charles Harris, and a shoemaker named J. L. Watkins lived nearby. Several dozen white-owned business also located on the street, including an attorney's office, carriage manufacturers, coal sellers, a confectioner, retail grocers, lumberyards, a purveyor of oysters, saloons, a steam engine manufacturer, and two wagon makers.

A complex built environment resulted from the decisions of a diverse group of property owners, white and black, native born and foreign born, who pursued varied economic and social ends, constructing industrial, agricultural, residential, religious, institutional, and commercial buildings, often side by side. Nashville remained a "walking city" in this era, as streetcar suburbs were just beginning to develop, and most of Nashville's population lived less than a mile from the public square.[37] Across the city, African Americans lived together with whites. Historian Don Doyle, for example, counted 158 people living in a downtown block that bordered Black Bottom in 1880. Located in a wholesale district near the waterfront, that single block included both

FIGURE 3.4. Saint Paul's AME Church, constructed 1874; photograph 1916. Source: *Centennial Encyclopaedia of the African Methodist Episcopal Church*.

"wealthy lumber merchants" and "transient riverboatmen" and three dozen black Nashvillians living next to whites.[38]

In 1876, white missionaries founded a black medical school, a part of Central Tennessee University known as Meharry Medical College located just south of the Black Bottom neighborhood, "one of two comprehensive, predominantly black colleges of medicine, dentistry, and health science in the United States."[39] Meharry developed into a significant institution for the city, region, and nation, training thousands of black physicians. African American community leaders also pushed for better public education at the elementary and secondary level. In 1883, Pearl School, a public black-only segregated high school opened at Demonbreun Street and Summer (Fifth Avenue South), one street over from Saint Paul's Church.[40]

The sacred and the profane shared neighborhood space. Saloons, brothels, and gambling rooms, a continuing presence in the neighborhood since the 1850s, were joined by dance halls and other commercial entertainment spaces, which were frequented by both blacks and whites. So-called red light districts were common in the nineteenth-century American city, frequently located in neighborhoods where African Americans lived. They often yielded significant profits, some of which were funneled as bribes to elected officials, police, and gangsters. City officials publicly disavowed "vice" and bribery, but the practices were tacitly allowed, and they provided rhetorical ammunition for politicians and city decision makers who wished to segregate blacks and associate them with immoral behavior.

As Nashville's African American population grew, real estate interests, elected officials, and civic elites built Black Bottom into a segregated low zone that could simultaneously function as a quasi-sanctioned commercial sex district, profitable site for landlords, and operating location for manufacturing and nuisance uses. Many Irish who could afford to move relocated to "an area west of the railroad gulch that by the 1880s came to be known as 'Little Ireland.'"[41] Nevertheless, Black Bottom remained racially mixed, despite being racially marked as black in vernacular speech and in Nashvillians' image of the city. Some white residents stayed in the neighborhood, and the neighborhood was never homogeneous in its land use, economic activities, housing stock, or elevation. The social mixing of the races, especially at dance halls and saloons, raised concerns among many white Nashvillians, and as such, labeling the neighborhood black could also describe a segregated zone where whites might be forced to interact with blacks, and particularly poor blacks.

Two major thoroughfares cut through the Bottom, connecting downtown to South Nashville, with street railroads running along College (later renamed Third Avenue South) and Cherry (later renamed Fourth Avenue South) Streets. By the end of the 1880s, real estate developers, speculators, landlords, and industrial interests had built out Black Bottom in a patchwork pattern with a concentration of cheap housing courts, tenements, and flats available to blacks, noisy or odiferous businesses, and drinking and gambling establishments. Behind the stores on Broad Street, which separated Black Bottom from downtown, and along the Cumberland River, they built wagon shops, a distillery, livery and feed companies, stables, a lime and cement warehouse, tobacco and cotton warehouses, junkyards, lumberyards, and machine shops. At the base of Demonbreun Street, where Wilson's Spring Branch once flowed, the Cumberland Lumber Company established a huge complex of buildings, including a sawmill and box factory.[42] In the lowest lying areas, landlords built "Negro tenements" as rental properties.[43] One became known as Freedman Flats.[44]

In March 1884, a Cumberland River flood inundated Black Bottom, a powerful reminder that polluted water could "back up" into the neighborhood and overflow stream banks. Flooding and sewerage posed interrelated health and safety threats. One reporter noted that "much suffering is being endured by the poor people whose homes are in low places. Many families have been driven from their homes by the water . . . [which is] washing the lower end of Broad-street, while in black bottom it is nearly up to Summer-street."[45] Five blocks inland, Summer Street was at the western edge of the neighborhood. The 1884 flood would be one among many to afflict Nashville's waterfront, and the Black Bottom lowland was particularly vulnerable.[46] Just three years later, the *Atlanta Constitution* reported of another Nashville flood that "hundreds of the wretched poor, who will be driven from their cheap homes in the lowlands, will suffer, if not helped by the citizens."[47] While expressions of sympathy or pity, and relief efforts in the name of Christian charity, were extended to residents, city officials framed floods and poor sanitation as problems best addressed by projects and investments that would also rid the Bottom of its tenements and poor black residents. It was time to "clean up" the neighborhood.

By the 1880s and early 1890s, city leaders began to discuss and implement specific removal projects that were publicly celebrated as municipal improvements for the public good. In May 1888, for example, the city's health officer argued that draining the bottom through improved sewerage would allow for redevelopment "and relieve that part of the city of the small shanties that exist there, because the property would become too valuable to be held by such an indifferent class of people."[48] In July of the same year, a *Daily American* editorialist imagined the future of Nashville with Black Bottom and its counterpart to the north, another poor, low-lying neighborhood known as Hell's Half Acre, transformed into public parks, ringing the downtown.[49] In 1893, Nashville condemned the Black Bottom block at the northeast corner of South Cherry and Demonbreun Streets, demolished tenements housing African Americans, and established the Hay Market, a designated area for produce and livestock sales.[50] That same year the *Daily American* likewise hailed the completion of the Wilson Spring sewer as an opportunity to reclaim Black Bottom, expecting that newly available land would facilitate new building construction, business, and wealth generation.[51]

Between 1870 and 1890, the city population nearly tripled, from 25,865 to 76,168 people. During these two decades, the city was nearly 40 percent African American.[52] "By the turn of the century, some 1,800 black people lived in the quarter mile area of Black Bottom," and the neighborhood's population increased by 21 percent.[53] The continued postbellum urban migration by African Americans was met with Jim Crow legal restrictions, threatened and real violence, and spatial segregation. For many African Americans, the new era of Reconstruction meant shared accommodations in a shack, a small, crowded rental house, or a single room in a purpose-built tenement located in a flood-prone district on the near edge of the city.

In the last decades of the nineteenth century, Nashville became a center of African American education and politics in the South, as demonstrated by a major protest against streetcar segregation that began in 1905. The streetcar conflict and the Black Bottom neighborhood became linked when whites refused to ride streetcars through the area, claiming that they were at risk of contracting disease from black passengers. They demanded segregated seating so that any physical contact between the races would be minimized. Newspaper editorialists argued that the whole neighborhood must be razed, proposing it be replaced by a park.

African Americans responded to these hostilities with a highly organized two-year campaign. They advocated for changes in state law, boycotted transit, developed an independent transportation company known as the Union Transportation Company, and founded a new weekly newspaper called the *Globe* to present a black perspective on civic issues and public conflicts.[54] Lawyer, former city council member, property investor, and bank founder James C. Napier provided crucial support for the effort, while Richard Henry Boyd, Henry A. Boyd (his son), Dock A. Hart, Charles A. Burrell, and Evans Tyree established the Globe Publishing Company.[55] Though the streetcar protest failed to prevent the segregation of the streetcars, it "showed that African Americans in Nashville, at a time of extreme racial violence, could freely meet, organize, and establish economic and rhetorical positions of resistance without the kind of reprisals likely to occur elsewhere in the South."[56] The protest served as inspiration for future organizing as Nashville's African American activists continued to fight for justice.

At the turn of the century, Black Bottom was only one of several Nashville neighborhoods where African Americans lived. Black physicians, professors, business owners, and ministers tended to live on the northwest side of the city. And although the neighborhood included a relatively diverse set of residents and mix of land uses and activities, its negative reputation persisted.

A Park to Eliminate Vice

Following the streetcar fight, Black Bottom became the subject of intense newspaper interest and public scrutiny. Reformers denounced immoral behavior and decried "vice" as a major urban problem, drawing the public's attention to whiskey drinking in barrelhouses, dancing in jook joints, and prostitution in brothels. They condemned gambling and noted the accumulation of garbage and the activities of ragpickers in Black Bottom. They railed against the property owners who would rent to the "lowest classes" of blacks and whites. They observed dilapidated buildings and junk shops and the presence of goats in the neighborhood's streets.[57] Nashville historian James Summerville writes that the "very mention of the name 'Black Bottom' conjured up visions of rambling tenement houses that overlooked dark and sinuous alleys, the sound of music blaring from the doorways of dimly lit dance halls, the scent of unbathed bodies huddled over a crap game in a basement den."[58]

The sights and sounds of the neighborhood attracted great interest from journalists, especially at night when, in the words of one reporter, "fun rules, and innocence goes to wreck, and pathos stares at you out of pallid faces, and crime slips in and out, dodging here and hiding yonder."[59] But most of all, they expressed repulsion at the neighborhood's foul odors. In 1905, the *Nashville American* editorialized: "No city in America or Europe can present a more disgraceful or sickening aspect of modern civilization than that part of Fourth Avenue that runs through the hideous heart of Black Bottom. If a conglomeration of dives, brothels, pawnshops, second-hand clothing stores, filthy habitations and the like—accompanied by the daily display of lewdness and drunkenness on the sidewalks and redolent with the stench of every vile odor—can make a 'hell-hole' then Black Bottom is that place."[60] The paper painted the neighborhood as a citywide threat and cause for civic embarrassment.

Between 1905 and 1910, the *Nashville Banner* and the *Nashville Daily American* campaigned for municipal action, either to clean up the neighborhood or eliminate it entirely. The journalists encouraged readers to associate what they read about the sights, sounds, and scents of Black Bottom with the purported immoral behavior of the poor. Stigma and blame were applied in racist terms, describing neighborhood environmental and social conditions as evidence of the state of development of the "Negro race." Paternalist progressives and other reformers often tried to refute the view that African Americans belonged in the bottoms by describing the "progress" of the race and by positive examples of successful individuals or attentive school children within the perceived context of social disintegration and disorderly conditions of the "slum."[61]

Many newspaper journalists stigmatized all lowland dwellers as immoral or less socially developed types of human beings, sometimes associating them with animals. They blamed African Americans for the poor housing and unhealthy living conditions that were in fact created by segregation and maintained by discrimination and violence. However, a few journalists pointed to class differences among blacks in an attempt to differentiate between good and bad people, middle-class and lower-class folks. In the *Nashville Banner*, for example, one journalist explained that "the best element of the colored people of the city does not dwell in Black Bottom ... they shun it, frown down upon it, and despise it with as much disgust and terror as the people of the white race. They do not associate with Black Bottom negroes, nor endorse their mode of life."[62] The neighborhood conditions, this reporter argued, could be explained by "the matter of finance, and the desire of the rougher element for a congregating place—the people who own and receive revenue from the shacks of the Bottom, and the people who find life in these hovels more to their taste than cleaner and more healthful surroundings."[63] Such descriptions were commonplace, portraying lowland residents as primitive, countrified, dirty, and undeserving. In the reform view, the "people who own and receive revenue" were also complicit.[64]

Nashville reformers' efforts to eliminate Black Bottom peaked with their attempt to pair slum clearance with a proposal to create a new park. *Banner* journalist Will Allen Dromgoole called Black Bottom "a menace to the beautiful city which sits serenely among her hills."[65] On August 4, 1905, the *Banner* ran a front-page editorial cartoon dramatizing the reform campaign (see figure 3.5). The neighborhood is represented by a black cat with the words "Black Bottom" written over its body. The city appears as a white woman marked with the words "Greater Nashville" looking down over a fence toward the cat, wielding an implement labeled "public sentiment." The cat, a symbol of bad luck or evil, stands atop a whiskey barrel, surrounded by bottles, including one labeled crime, and appears fearful. The black cat further serves to symbolize blackness, black people, and the black presence in Nashville. The scene depicted, with a white woman fighting back against the cat, also carries sexual connotations, alluding to the vicious stereotype that black men were sexually dangerous and a threat to white women, an accusation that frequently became the pretext for lynching in the South.

In December 1906, Nashville Mayor Thomas Morris announced a campaign to round up prostitutes and loiterers, and "redeem" Black Bottom.[66]

FIGURE 3.5. Black Bottom as black cat, *Nashville Banner*, August 4, 1905. Collection of Nashville Public Library.

The interest in breaking up commercial sex, gambling, and drinking activity in Black Bottom presented a problem for reformers, however, and it invited opposition in unexpected quarters. White homeowners in surrounding districts worried that the class of people who frequented the area's dance halls and whiskey joints, and the "downfallen population" who lived in the Bottom, might take up residence in their neighborhoods.[67] The *Nashville Banner* editorialized in support of the mayor, arguing that police action would make "vice" unprofitable there, setting the stage for a neighborhood transformation, remaking Black Bottom into "an entirely respectable residence or business section or a public park or market place, with respectable and inviting surroundings," noting that "the Banner's suggestion of a public park secured by condemnation proceedings appears the most feasible."[68] Proponents were well aware that landowners in the area could mount political opposition and legal challenges based on property rights arguments. They contended that the need to eliminate the neighborhood outweighed any concerns over eminent domain.[69] Furthermore, the Hay Market clearance project a decade earlier had provided an important, legally defensible, and purportedly successful precedent in achieving resident removal.

While the police conducted raids, clearance advocates sought state funding. In 1907, the Tennessee State Legislature, with the support of the House Committee on Municipal Affairs, authorized Nashville to issue $500,000 in bonds for the park project.[70] However, not until 1910 was the bill passed by the state legislature and taken up by the city council. Approved by the council 16–5 in September 1910, the proposed slum clearance and park plan was placed on the ballot for a vote: a $300,000 bond issue to be held November 8, 1910.[71]

One prominent opponent was Charles A. Martin, the councilman for South Nashville. Martin believed that the lowland was best suited to industrial purposes and that a public park should be on higher ground located to the south. He also argued that removing slums was not part of the park commission's purpose.[72] Proponents countered that Black Bottom was a "disgrace to the city," "menace to public health," obstruction to travel, and that it created "a bad impression" in the minds of visitors to Nashville, among many other justifications and claims.[73] They characterized their opposition to the area as being more concerned about money than morals, explaining that "the landlord is the king of the Bottom . . . the city's pest hole" and noting that "some of the property owners fight the project of elimination of the district for the reason that they make money out of it [while] the negroes and low whites hug their hovels for the reason that they have fallen to that depth, most of them, that they prefer Black Bottom to a saner and cleaner existence."[74] The wording here is worthy of note, as "whites" was modified by "low," with the phrase "fallen to that depth" suggesting a fall from God's grace due to immoral behavior, thus white city leaders racialized poor whites by throwing them into the same category as African Americans.[75]

Proponents argued that slum clearance justified the entire plan, that "the wiping out of the Bottom would alone be sufficient to commend this proposition to the entire city." They suggested that their proposal would eliminate ugliness: "Like a beautiful lily growing from the ooze of a stagnant pool the new Central Park will spring up out of the slime of Black Bottom." And, invoking a medical analogy, they described the neighborhood as "a malignant tumor poisoning the municipal blood current, which the civic body cannot overcome except by the prompt and radical surgery of complete elimination."[76]

Proponents also suggested that property values surrounding the neighborhood would increase to such an extent that the increased tax revenue from that part of the city would offset the expense of the bonds. They minimized the estimates of the number of people to be dispersed by the project and rejected Nashvillians' fears that Black Bottom's current residents might move into their neighborhood, stating that "there are infinitely better and cheaper homes out in the exclusive colored quarters of the city where the hard-working population of Black Bottom would be welcome and happy."[77]

Some prominent African Americans supported the clearance proposal. One Nashville paper published an "appeal from colored people," urging support for the measure as being in keeping with "the moral uplift of the race." It emphasized that project was justified because it would reduce crime and get rid of criminals.[78] The black-owned *Globe*, which reached thousands of subscribers in the city, approximately 20 percent of the city's total population at the time, editorialized: "Black Bottom! The very name has a horrifying affect. For years and years this section of our fair city has been a menace to the peace and happiness of our homes." The *Globe*'s editorial suggested that if the neighborhood's residents could "change their way of living," they would find plenty of places to live and, in any case, "these people could not be forced in a worse condition than they now live under."[79] Successful African Americans, many of them business and property owners, thus allied with white park proponents to favor slum clearance in one of the city's black neighborhoods. In doing so, they registered a political belief in capitalism, entrepreneurism, property ownership, and individual efforts to achieve improved economic status and better housing conditions.

None of these arguments persuaded voters, and in November 1910, the ballot measure failed. Black Bottom was not "eliminated," and the proposed Central Park was never constructed. Despite the shared faith of the proponents in increased property values and improved business opportunity, they were ultimately unsuccessful.[80] "Fears that slum dwellers would migrate to middle-class neighborhoods" prevailed at the ballot box.[81] Containment trumped clearance and dispersal. Racist attitudes perpetuated the notion of the bottoms as a neglected and despised urban district, designated for unwanted land uses and the poor.

Black Bottom's Decline

As slum clearance and park proponents considered their options in the wake of their loss on the bond issue, Nashville's population continued growing, drawing more migrants, both black and white, from its Middle Tennessee hinterland. In what historian Louis M. Kyriakoudes has explained as a response to "a sustained period of crisis" in agriculture driven by "Malthusian pressures" of population growth, rural residents fled the countryside.[82] Meanwhile, the Black Bottom neighborhood's population shrank by 27 percent between 1910 and 1920. Residential displacement by commercial and industrial development, changes in the demographics and residential location of the black community, and institutional decision making all influenced the decline.

Job discrimination by unions, limited economic opportunity, and Jim Crow segregation made Nashville a difficult place for black migrants to live; nonetheless, the city continued to draw black rural newcomers before and during the Great Migration to the North.[83] Nashville's overall population grew from 110,364 to 153,866 between 1910 and 1930, but while the total black population increased from 36,523 to 42,836, as a percentage of the population it decreased from 33 percent to 28 percent. The city began to draw larger numbers of rural white migrants, the poorest of whom settled in places like Mud Flats and Kalb Hollow, which was "named for the preponderance of migrants from DeKalb County."[84] The new lowland neighborhood names associated with rural whites proved to be short-lived. Nevertheless, these "white" bottoms, hollows, and flats demonstrate how the stigma attached to poor people living in low places could manifest itself in many different linguistic forms.

The built environment of Black Bottom changed in significant ways after the park bond referendum. Floods, poor sanitation, and dilapidated housing continued to be problems. Major floods in 1912, 1929, and 1937 hit Black Bottom, endangering lives, destroying belongings, and displacing residents.[85] The 1929 Cumberland River flood, for example, made homes uninhabitable and swamped "factories and other commercial institutions [that] had no relief from the water, which . . . covered valuable machinery and stocks of goods, and . . . deposited heavy layers of mud throughout the city's river section."[86] The bottoms were the place where the dirt and debris settled or landed. It didn't take much imagination for city dwellers to connect this "dirt" with the city's lower classes, settling into the low spots.

Key social, educational, and religious institutions left the neighborhood in the early part of the twentieth century. Many relocated to northwest Nashville and the area around Fisk University. Equally important, other institutions decided against locating in the neighborhood, including a new Negro Branch of the Carnegie Library, which opened at Hynes and Twelfth Avenue North in 1916.[87] In 1917, the city's only segregated black public high school relocated from Fifth Avenue South near Demonbreun to Sixteenth Avenue North and Grant Street.[88] In 1931, the prestigious Meharry Medical College moved from First Avenue South and Chestnut to Eighteenth Avenue North.[89]

At the same time, Nashville's civic and business elite urged real estate brokers and manufacturers to locate within the neighborhood for the purpose of displacing low-cost housing, a decision that would be institutionalized and intensified in the light industrial designation of the heart of the neighborhood for uses in the city's first zoning ordinance.[90] In 1888, city health officer Dr. Mitchell stated that "he was making an earnest effort to have Black Bottom well drained," but "he believed that if capitalists would buy the property, which could be had no doubt at very low figures, redeem it, build warehouses and manufactories upon it, they would make money . . . and relieve that part of the city of the small shanties that exist there."[91] The approach of favoring private action to address public problems would be reiterated after the defeat of the bond measure in the 1910. The *Nashville American* editorialized "do not be discouraged. The plucky fight just ended will enable you to carry on the battle even more forcefully at the next opportunity."[92] "Business Men Favor Plan" announced another news item, under the headline "Black Bottom as Warehouse Dist."[93] Mayor Robert Ewing explained that he wanted "those lots in Black Bottom to be utilized for small manufacturing institutions so that with electric power furnished to them and having our raw materials here on hand they will furnish the means of giving profitable employment to all our people."[94] The *Tennessean*, in turn, featured photographs of newly constructed commercial buildings that replaced residences as improvements in the neighborhood, including photographs of "modern stores" and factories.[95] One former saloon became a factory called the Kerrigan Plant.[96]

City infrastructure projects and other improvements had also targeted Black Bottom's buildings for demolition through the creation of the Hay Market and the construction of new public building there, the replatting and widening of streets, and a major new bridge across the Cumberland River at Sparkman Street.[97] City leaders renamed all the north-south streets using a numerical scheme intended to modernize and unify the street pattern. A map published in the *American* during the park bonds debate shows how city leaders also envisioned east-west street extensions through the Black Bottom neighborhood as integral to creating a new neighborhood identity.[98] Street modifications, less expensive and less publicized, were politically easier to implement than clearance, and they also led to targeted demolition of tenement buildings where poor African Americans lived.[99] Just prior to the vote, former councilman Martin, an outspoken opponent of the park proposal, had claimed that African Americans were making an "exodus" from Black Bottom due to the opening of the Sparkman Street Bridge.[100] After the bond measure was defeated, he argued that the "foul spot" was being corrected as the result of the road widening and bridge projects, making property "suitable for business purposes."[101]

In the midst of these demographic and land use changes, the neighborhood still provided a significant number of rental housing units in courts, flats, and tenements (see figure 3.6). Along Fourth Avenue South, barrelhouses and dance halls expanded their business. Alcohol shaped the neighborhood and its reputation for decades, but the rise of the temperance movement and federal Prohibition (1919–33) shifted the city's focus back to Black Bottom. In the rhetoric of one advocate of Prohibition, alcohol metaphorically flowed through the city much the way earlier observers had seen cholera's path or the movement of rural migrants to the city, like a "stream [that] came in fresh from the country, meandered through the immoral shoals and eddies, and disappeared in oblivion and early death."[102] At the center of several conflicts over alcohol in the city were Nashville's legendary pro-saloon Mayor Hillary Howse and an infamous saloon-keeper named Sol Cohn. Born in Nashville, Cohn opened his first saloon in the neighborhood in 1891.[103] It would become known as the "Bucket of Blood," and reportedly included a grocery store, barbershop, dance hall, gambling room, and a billiard parlor.[104] African Americans were his primary customers, and the saloon was frequently raided by the police.

In 1907, before national Prohibition, Nashville adopted a city ordinance restricting the location of saloons, and Tennessee adopted Prohibition statewide in 1909. The state law was enacted "following a notorious duel in downtown Nashville that ended in the death of newspaper editor Edward Ward Carmack, a martyr to the temperance cause."[105] During the trial a stenographic report published in the pages of the *Nashville American* included defendant Duncan Cooper's description of Cohn, his "dive" of a saloon, and the "notoriously disreputable" Black Bottom. The dialogue includes reference to the neighborhood as "the blackest spot" and the "lowest down" and Cohn's place as a location where "lewd" people of different races met and mingled.[106] Rhetorically, Nashvillians combined alcohol consumption, sexual activity, blackness, and lowness to reproduce the image of Black Bottom.[107]

"Boss" Howse was first elected in 1909 on an anti-Prohibition platform. He would serve until 1915, when he was removed from office. He was elected mayor again in 1923 and served until 1938. Characterized a "political champion"

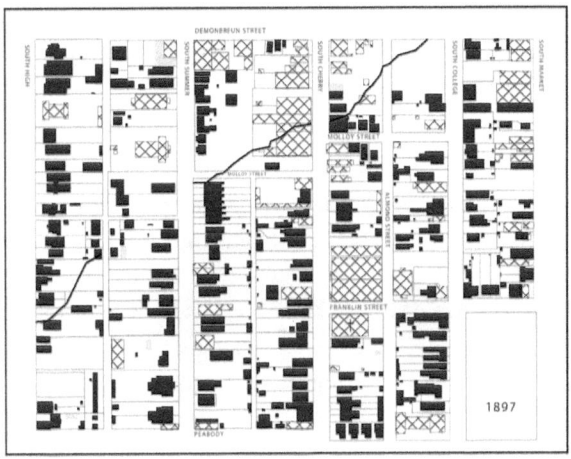
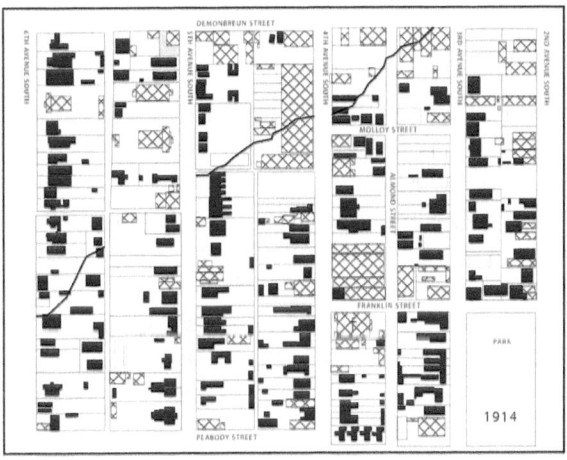
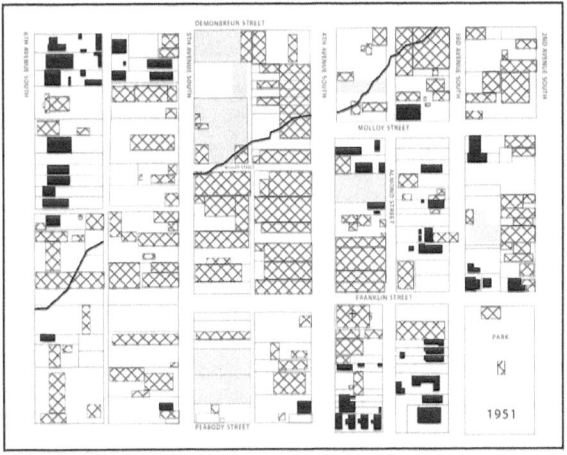

FIGURE 3.6. Land use change in Black Bottom, 1897, 1914, and 1951. Black indicates residential buildings. Map by Clelie Fielding.

of "the rural migrants, blacks, and poor people" who assembled a machine based on a coalition of "city employees, policemen, ward-level politicos, saloonkeepers, and bootleggers," Howse allowed the alcohol to keep flowing in Black Bottom. Cohn and other saloon-keepers continued in operation then embraced bootlegging after the enactment of a "'bone-dry' [state] law banning all out-of-state liquor shipments and making it illegal to possess or receive intoxicants." Prohibition would persist in Nashville until 1939.[108]

Illegal alcohol and nightlife also led to the widespread popularity of the phrase "black bottom" and a dance of the same name, based in part on the Nashville neighborhood's reputation. In the 1920s, the jook joints and bootleg stands of Fourth Avenue South gained great notoriety. As novelist Zora Neale Hurston, who lived in the neighborhood as a young woman, later observed, the neighborhood's name was connected to a dance craze that swept the country in the mid-to late 1920s.[109] White performers appropriated the dance and modified it for mainstream consumption.[110] The Black Bottom dance became one of many popular cultural expressions that were linked implicitly or explicitly to Nashville's Black Bottom neighborhood and others like it.[111] Ragtime and jazz legend Jelly Roll Morton composed "Black Bottom Stomp" in 1925. Blues musicians from Ma Rainey to Joe Evans used the phrase "black bottom" with its multiple, overlapping connotations of space, race, and the body. In Evans's version of "Down in Black Bottom" from 1931, it's a place where "they'll take your money and they'll take your clothes." As blues historian William Barlow has noted in *Looking Up at Down*, the blues themselves drew upon metaphor and lived experience in low places as source material; as a genre, he wrote, the blues were "bulwarks of cultural resistance, providing a composite view of American society from the bottom."[112] Historian Richard M. Mizelle Jr. observes, in *Backwater Blues*, the music could bear witness and provide a means for coping with tragedy.[113]

Between 1930 and 1940, the population of Black Bottom again declined, dropping from 1,125 to only 811 residents. A 1937 study of housing conditions titled *Low Standard Housing in Nashville Tennessee* mapped Nashville's population according to race and other variables.[114] Blacks and whites were roughly equal percentage-wise in the neighborhood, with African American residents clustered around the west side of Fourth Avenue. In 1938, the opening of two new Public Works Administration public housing complexes, one black and one white, led to further shifts in Nashville's poor population, away from Black Bottom and toward other neighborhoods. The black-only complex, like many other segregated institutions of this period, opened near Fisk University. Mary Elizabeth Rogers, who was born in Black Bottom and living in nearby Trimble Bottom, recalled how few houses in the area had electricity or plumbing, leading many residents to seek out better housing in other parts of the city.[115]

Nashville's civic elite and elected officials used race-restrictive covenants, zoning, redlining, public housing, highway construction, and urban renewal to displace and segregate the city's African American residents on a scale that far exceeded previous attempts to "clean up" Black Bottom. While Black Bottom declined, Nashville became more segregated by race than ever before. Legal contracts, municipal law, and government action, rather than topography, created new boundaries and racially marked spaces in the postwar urban landscape.

"Black Bottom Is Now Only a Name"

Between March and April 1946, the same small advertisement appeared four times in the pages of the *Nashville Tennessean*. "Black Bottom Is Now Only a Name," it read, explaining to readers that "that part of Nashville . . . is now one of the best sections of the city for business locations, and property there is in demand." In the ad, Eric Tatom of the Madison Real Estate Company announced that he had "several properties south of Demonbreun Street, including some warehouses and some sites for wholesale and distributing businesses."[116] The advertisement attests to how quickly the neighborhood had declined, after decades of attempts to remove its residents. Unlike the north side of downtown Nashville, where a massive urban renewal project unfolded in the 1940s and 1950s, Black Bottom's decline did not have a single cause. A combination of factors had drained the area of most of its population: small-scale housing demolition, zoning and land use changes, the availability of housing in other parts of the city, and Nashville's changing downtown.

From the 1960s through the early 1990s, cheap bars on Broad Street, Black Bottom's northern edge, fostered the burgeoning music scene and famous country musicians playing the nearby Ryman Auditorium, located a half block north of Broadway on Fifth Avenue, frequented them before and after shows.[117] While the name Black Bottom fell out of use by the 1990s, it had not been forgotten either.[118] Several newspaper articles from the 1990s recounted Black Bottom's history, featuring former residents such as William Daniel who lived there from 1930 to 1948 and described it as "a poor neighborhood" but also "a wonderful place to grow up" where people looked out for one another and shared a sense of community, and where backwater floods sometimes led to school to be canceled.[119] By the early 1990s, however, few houses or apartments remained in the old neighborhood as decades of small-scale industrial displacement were followed by a rise in the number of surface parking lots serving downtown office buildings and awaiting speculative development.

In the 1990s, a massive wave of public-private redevelopment transformed the area and the city rebranded it SoBro. A proposed seven-lane high-speed connector through the old neighborhood sparked a major battle among landowners, planners, and design advocates such as the Nashville Civic Design Center, and transportation engineers beginning in 1995.[120] Then in 1998, a tornado damaged several buildings on the south side of Lower Broad.[121] Alternative proposals suggested the "SoBro" name and urged a mixed-use development approach. The proposed highway was defeated.

Planners, downtown business owners, tourism promoters, and real estate developers partnered together to shepherd a set of multimillion dollar investments through to completion, including a major new sports arena on the south side of Broadway between Fifth and Sixth Avenues, home of the Nashville Predators professional hockey team, opened in 1996; the Country Music Hall of Fame on the south side of Demonbreun Street between Fourth and Fifth Avenues South, opened in 2001; and the Schermerhorn Symphony Center, on the north side of Demonbreun between Third and Fourth Avenues South, opened in 2003.[122] Looking back, singer-songwriter Lucinda Williams described how the live music and bar scene on Lower Broad from the 1960s to the early 1990s was replaced by tourist-oriented development and themed restaurants like Planet Hollywood and Hard Rock Café. Corporate interests, she complained, removed "all the sweet, original landmarks that spoke of the romance and creativity of an earlier time."[123]

Located in the block bounded by Demonbreun, Almond, Molloy, and Third Avenue South, one of the lowest topographical points in neighborhood, a 333-unit building dubbed Encore opened in March 2008.[124] The twenty-story building offered office tenants and condo residents sweeping views of the changing metropolis, or as the twenty-story luxury condominium tower advertises: "So you can see where you've been and where you're going."[125] Adjacent to the Schermerhorn performing arts hall where the symphony plays, it offers proximity to downtown restaurants and entertainment, the development's name signifying social acclaim, the opportunity to live life as a performance, and a place to enjoy one's later years in life.

After 2008, high-rise development continued with the Pinnacle at Symphony Place, a twenty-nine-story office tower at Third Avenue South and Demonbreun, opened in February 2010.[126] In May 2010, a major flood temporarily delayed construction of the new Music City Convention Center, a 2.1-million-square-foot complex located on the south side of Demonbreun Street between Fifth and Eighth Avenues South. For that project construction crews excavated more than two hundred thousand cubic yards of rock and soil across the sixteen-acre site over twenty-four weeks.[127] The center opened to the public in 2013. Hockey fans, concertgoers, country music enthusiasts, conventioneers, and out-of-town visitors frequent the reconstructed area, rarely encountering any mention of Black Bottom. The scale and intensity of development in the buried floodplain of Wilson's Spring Branch and the associated rise of a major tourism-entertainment district removed nearly all traces of the neighborhood's history. One building from the neighborhood's early history remains: the former Saint Paul's AME Church, which was converted to warehouse space, then an architect's office, before becoming an event space for wedding receptions and parties.

Topography, Class, and Race

The Black Bottom story reveals how topography, class, and race have influenced Nashville's city form: the significance of Broad Street as an urban boundary, the trajectory of land uses in lowlands, the neighborhood location of institutions, and the timing and availability of land for urban redevelopment. Nineteenth-century miasmatic disease theory, based on the belief that low places harbored dangerous air that threatened the public through odorous emanations, and a related cultural bias against flood-prone environments made urban lowland neighborhoods suspect. Geological structures, political economic systems, and legal frameworks made urban lowland neighborhood conditions possible, but the social meaning and political significance of topography was based on class and race.

The deadly cholera epidemics of the nineteenth century came to an end and the science of germ theory eventually triumphed in public opinion, but urban lowland neighborhoods like Black Bottom retained their negative reputations well into the twentieth century. Repeated contests over urban land, particularly attempts to foster commercial and industrial development to displace residents, played out within a political atmosphere where whites relentlessly identified African Americans and "low whites" with the spaces where they lived and then denigrated those spaces as dangerous, immoral, and threatening to the city as a whole.

The Nashville case is not unique. In many southern cities, African Americans moved into tenements or constructed their own housing in bottomlands at the city's edge after emancipation. They also established small independent towns in lowlands, places like Princeville, North Carolina. Discrimination and violence meant that the only available land for most African Americans was low value due to inadequate drainage, proximity to a city dump or cemetery, steeply sloped, or otherwise unwanted, a pattern evident in cities like Lexington, Atlanta, Durham, and Richmond.[128] Urban lowland neighborhoods were important places in African American community formation and institution building following the Civil War, including religious and educational institutions such as Saint Paul's AME Church, Pearl School, and the nearby Meharry Medical College in Nashville. During Jim Crow, these neighborhoods became part of a "world-within-a-world," where poor people lived, but also where black business owners operated stores and black physicians attended to patients.

The history of urban lowland neighborhoods, especially in southern cities like Nashville, serves as a reminder of the challenges faced by free people of color after slavery and emancipation. The sickness, suffering, and death encountered by African Americans during the Civil War would continue in lowland neighborhoods into the 1870s. Neighborhoods like Black Bottom, where cholera struck dozens dead within a two-month period in 1873, suffered from poor sanitation and municipal neglect for decades: in fact, they were literally the dumping grounds for the rest of the city's waste. When free people of color sought and obtained land title after the war, new communities faced discrimination, marginalization, and violent attacks by whites. In the early twentieth century, restrictive covenants, deed restrictions that prevented the sale or rental of property to nonwhites, became a common tool used by whites to attempt to keep blacks out of white neighborhoods.

Racial hatred and violence was intertwined with urban planning; it influenced local elites' and elected officials' decisions about urban land use, real estate, infrastructure, housing, and redevelopment.[129] Community marginalization through association with disease, immoral behavior, and crime perpetuated the structures of an unjust urban order, where the social hierarchy was easily read in the physical landscape of the city. Jim Crow laws erected legal and societal barriers that reinforced the physical phenomenon of topographical separation established in the nineteenth century. Segregation in the bottoms made racist spatial practices seem normal, inevitable, and natural.

4

Swede Hollow
Saint Paul, Minnesota

Milkman Bengt Jakobson walked home through city streets past freight yards and railroad lines before descending into a deep ravine. He lived in a small wooden house alongside a creek with his wife, Anna, and their three sons, Svante, Alfred, and Carl, and two boarders in a place called Swede Hollow. Almost all of the Jakobsons' neighbors were born in Sweden, with twice as many men as women, and several dozen children in a community of more than 170 residents. The men made a living as tailors, a clerk, a bricklayer, a plumber, and carpenters, but most, like the Jakobsons' two boarders, worked as laborers. Among the children, about a third had been born in Minnesota, usually the youngest ones. With no formal street names, the residents listed their addresses by their proximity to the named streets nearby: Phalen's Creek near Seventh, Phalen's Creek near Eighth, or Phalen's Creek near Hopkins. In 1879, there were thirty-nine houses in total. The small village rested on the valley floor and nestled among its lower slopes, sheltering families with surnames such as Ahlgren, Anderson, Esklund, Hammerquist, Jacobson, Johnson, Larson, Nelson, Norquist, Olson, Pearson, and Winquist.[1]

The Swedes shared space in the eighteen-acre valley with the Saint Paul Water Company, a private company that developed the city's first water system; the main line of the Saint Paul and Duluth Railroad, which traversed higher ground on the ravine's terraced western slope; the Saint Paul Mills flour-making operation; and Theodore Hamm's Excelsior Brewery, located at the top of the hollow (see figures 4.1 and 4.2).[2] It was a busy, active place where freight and passengers on railcars whisked past men walking to their jobs, children played beside the tracks and in the creek, and women tended to gardens and cleaned houses and yards. The brewery bustled with workers who

FIGURE 4.1. Railroads transformed the Trout Brook Valley into a major rail corridor (*left*), while a single set of tracks ran through Swede Hollow (*right*). Saint Paul, circa 1885. Map by Julie Kim.

delivered supplies, operated and maintained equipment, and brewed, stored, and transported beer. A ravine is perhaps an unlikely place for an urban community, but Swede Hollow, or *Svenska Dalen* as it was known in Swedish, was just one of many such urban lowland neighborhoods in American cities.[3]

The first Swedes settled in the valley in the late 1850s; they were likely a few lumbermen and other seasonal workers.[4] During the 1870s this urban lowland neighborhood developed into a small village. Recently arrived Swedish immigrants built dozens more houses in the hollow during the 1880s and 1890s. The "Swede" in the "Swede Hollow" name evoked foreignness and "old country" ways to the native born and recently assimilated within a city striving to become a new American metropolis, the capital city of the new state of Minnesota, which joined the union on May 11, 1858. Saint Paul's population, building stock, railroad connections, and economy grew tremendously fast during the 1870s and 1880s. This rapid growth required an influx of new residents, people relocating from the East, but also tens of thousands of foreign immigrants. The name Swede Hollow tied together people and place. The toponym ascribed an ethnic and national identity to a recognizable geographic feature of the land, and it suggested the presence of an unassimilated group, isolated from others and concentrated in a particular location at the margins of the urban landscape. But just as the label became a commonly accepted place name, one that appeared in newspaper articles and city reports, the hollow and city itself were changing. Within a few decades, the Hollow's residents were no longer mostly Swedish. By the 1910s, the majority of residents were Italians.

FIGURE 4.2. Saint Paul Mills, mill pond, and upper Swede Hollow, circa 1885. Note the tunnel below the railroad tracks at center left. Collection of Minnesota Historical Society.

Swede Hollow was both denigrated and romanticized as a community. The urban lowland was seen by outsiders as both culturally and physically separate from the city, what in the language of the time was called a "foreign colony." Some observers described this urban lowland neighborhood as scenic and picturesque, exotic and quaint, while others labeled it disordered, dirty, shabby, and ugly. The shape and character of the built environment, from the architectural styles of the cottages and building materials used for houses to their spatial arrangement in a neighborhood without streets, evoked curiosity and comment. Community descriptions, both positive and negative, repeatedly suggested that the neighborhood was rural, close to nature, and primitive. Analyses by health inspectors and housing surveyors and statements by public officials blended together descriptions of the physical environment with observations on the moral behavior of the residents, the prevalence of drunkenness, housekeeping standards, and the potential for Americanization and assimilation.

Geology, Railroads, and the "Swede" in "Swede Hollow"

Phalen Creek descends more than 150 feet in elevation from Lake Phalen to the Mississippi River, a length of about four miles.[5] It cut through terrain formed of Trenton limestone and Saint Peter sandstone, creating a steeply sloped ravine. Downstream it joined Trout Brook, flowing through a cleft in the high bluffs at the river bend before reaching the Mississippi. Situated only a few miles downriver from the Falls of Saint Anthony, at the uppermost reaches of the navigable section of the Mississippi, Saint Paul developed at a bend in the river—on its north bank, but more significantly, its eastern side. Located in the Northwest Territory, which was established by the United States in 1787, it bordered the lands acquired by the United States in the 1803 Louisiana Purchase.[6]

The creek that ran through Swede Hollow took its name from Irish-born soldier Edward Phelan (sometimes spelled Felyn or Phalen). After immigrating to New York City, he enlisted in the army, serving three years in Fort Snelling in the Minnesota Territory before his discharge from the Fifth Regiment.[7] After leaving the military, he stayed in Minnesota, traveling a short distance downstream on the Mississippi River.[8] He built a cottage near the top of the stream valley in 1839 that has been called the first house built in the city of Saint Paul.[9] Phelan later sold his claims to land, then fled to California after being accused of murder.[10] Other white settlers followed Phelan into the valley, as Saint Paul quickly developed into a commercial river port oriented around the fur trade and steamboat traffic.[11]

When Minnesota was admitted to the union, Saint Paul became the state capital. By the 1870s, Saint Paul was a major rail hub, located at the nexus of thirteen separate rail lines.[12] Magnate James J. Hill headquartered both the Great Northern and Northern Pacific Railways in the city, connecting Saint Paul to the West; the Lake Superior and Mississippi linked the Twin Cities to Duluth in the north; and the Chicago, Milwaukee, and Saint Paul Railroad, among other lines, connected the city to the East. The city's population jumped from 20,030 in 1870 to 41,473 in 1880 then exploded in the decade that followed, reaching 133,156 by 1890. Along with the "smoke and clang of factory and mill, and the scream of engine and steamer" would come thousands of immigrants seeking a new home.[13]

The completion of the Lake Superior and Mississippi Railroad line in 1870 marked a key moment in the Hollow's early history. The laying of track on the west side of Phalen Creek brought railroad workers and materials and created the terraced contour on the hollow's western slope. The relative narrowness of the passage and the steepness of the ravine's edges meant that it would become the only line to use this route, as other railroads laid track through Trout Brook. The route of the Lake Superior and Mississippi Railroad (reorganized and renamed the Saint Paul and Duluth in 1877) followed the topography and snaked through the valley before entering downtown Saint Paul on the east side at the site of Lower Landing, the city's main steamboat docking point. A substantial district of masonry warehouses, commercial spaces, and merchant and railroad offices developed as "Lowertown" beginning in the 1870s and 1880s. The city's first Union Depot was constructed there on Sibley Street in 1879. Tens of thousands of immigrants and visitors arrived at the station, which went through several building iterations, during the late nineteenth century. From the depot, Swede Hollow could be reached on foot, walking along the tracks to the east and then north through the valley of Phalen Creek.

The rapid growth of Saint Paul's population corresponds with the increase in Swedish immigration to the United States and the city's emergence as a rail and manufacturing nexus of the Upper Midwest. Swedish immigration began in the 1840s, but increased dramatically after 1865 with a first peak in 1868–69, precipitated by crop failures in Sweden, then a second larger peak year in 1887 when a recorded forty-six thousand "registered emigrants" departed their homeland. Immigration continued unabated, and during the decade of the 1880s, more than 330,000 people left Sweden for the US, bringing the total number of Swedish born in the country to approximately 478,000.[14]

By 1875, when the Swedish immigrant settlement in Swede Hollow began to grow in size, a total of 36,333 people lived in Saint Paul: 20,122 were native born, 14,364 were foreign born, and 1,847 were of unknown origin.[15] At that point, Swedes were the city's fourth largest immigrant group behind Germans, Irish, and Prussians, and just ahead of Canadians.[16] The increase in the number of Swedish-born residents in Saint Paul during the early 1880s coincides with the newspaper coverage of the growing "hamlet" of Swede Hollow.

Between 1863 and 1884, three major construction projects defined the urban boundaries of the Hollow: railroad tracks on the western edge, a brewery complex at the upper end, and a massive viaduct at the lower end. Already physically isolated by virtue of the ravine's geomorphology, these projects served to physically enclose one stretch of the winding stream valley. On city maps, the irregular S-like shape of Swede Hollow appears in the gap between city streets (see figure 4.3). Bounded by the new viaduct at Seventh Street on the south and Minnehaha Avenue on the north, streets on the east and west sides of the Hollow dead-ended on either side of the ravine.

The Upper End: Theodore Hamm's Brewery and Mansion

German-born saloon-keeper and boardinghouse operator Theodore Hamm immigrated to the United States in 1854, settling in Saint Paul two years later.[17] He turned Phalen Creek water into beer and transformed the valley in the process. Where mills and other businesses failed, Hamm succeeded. In 1874, together with a partner named Phillip Thoen, Hamm purchased Brainard Flouring Mills for $21,000; it had been erected on Phalen Creek at a cost of $3,000 in 1856. They invested in machinery, including a new engine and engine house, employed three men, and produced a reported "sixty and seventy barrels" of Queen of the West brand flour daily.[18] The mill yielded a relatively small quantity of high quality flour for the local market, but this "temporary investment" that brought Hamm to Phalen Creek would eventually make him famous.

The mills on Phalen Creek were unsuccessful, despite the "fine waterpower." The location attracted a succession of sawmills, gristmills, and breweries under different owners and business names.[19] Mill explosions and fires doomed several. Saint Paul Mills, for example was built in 1867, then sold in 1869 and again in 1872. The new owner, a Mr. Schaber who "erected an engine house 20x30, and put in a twenty-five horsepower engine," was killed in 1879 in a railway accident. On New Year's Day 1880, the mill burned to the ground in a fire. Rebuilt in August of that year, it was destroyed a second time, by a September 1880 boiler explosion that killed the engineer. Rebuilt again, by 1881 the new flouring mill included a thirty-five horsepower engine and a twenty-eight-inch Leffel wheel.[20] The Phalen Creek flour mills faced intense

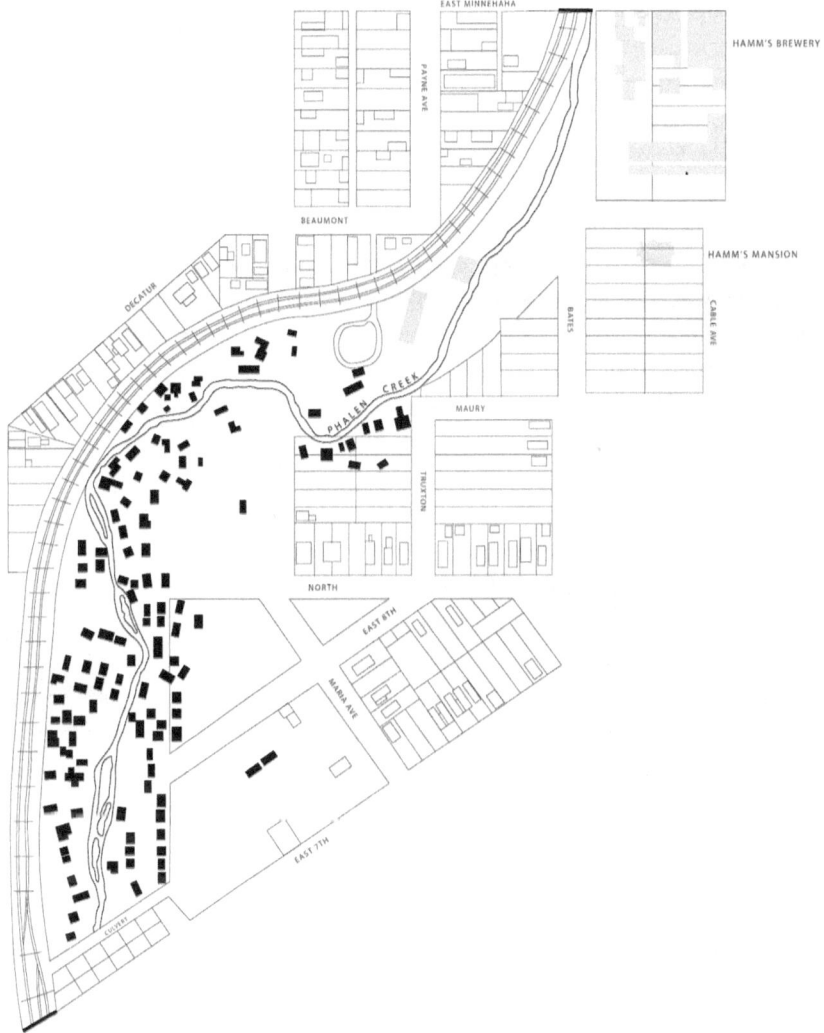

FIGURE 4.3. Swede Hollow cottages, circa 1890. Hamm expanded operations at an existing brewery during the 1870s (*upper right*), the city completed the viaduct at Seventh Street in 1884 (*lower left*), and the builders finished construction of Hamm's Mansion in 1886. Map by Clelie Fielding.

competition from larger industrial operations, as Minneapolis became an international center for the fast-growing industry. To make matters worse, their water supply and its rate of flow diminished.

Upstream Phalen Creek water was piped away as freshwater supply. Lake Phalen supplied the growing city's first waterworks, with construction completed in 1869. The Saint Paul Water Company constructed "17 miles of pipe" and "three miles of canals" to supply 1,100 buildings with water.[21] The company agreed to a deal whereby the mill and brewery owners would maintain rights to use Phalen Creek water for power generation, while in exchange the water company guaranteed "the maintenance of the water level" and a reliable flow of water.[22] But the mills would not last much longer. In 1881 state geologist N. H. Winchell noted that "since the railroads have encroached on the natural course of Phalen's creek and the city water works have diminished its volume, some [mills] have been abandoned."[23]

Into this contested landscape came Hamm, who made significant investments in Swede Hollow. In addition to the Brainard flour mill deal, he loaned money to the proprietor-owner of another company: Andrew F. Keller's Excelsior Brewery. When Keller was unable to repay the loan, Hamm "took possession of the brewery" as an "unpaid mortgagee." By 1870, Hamm owned $40,000 worth of business property and an additional $6,000 of personal property.[24]

In 1877, a reporter from the German-language Saint Paul newspaper *Volkszeitung* visited Hamm's Brewery finding that "the flow of water was ample for all immediate purposes and that it was not only adequate for the production of beer but that it could be used to keep the equipment clean and was even available in the event of a fire." Hamm's operation included a "copper boiler large enough to hold three hundred kegs of beer at one time," "mash vats," a "cement floor on which germination took place," "kilns used for drying," and "an area where kegs were cleaned and refilled." The brewery planned to expand from a four-day-a-week brewing schedule to daily operation. By 1879, the brewery boasted a capacity of eight thousand barrels, increasing to twenty-six thousand barrels three years later. Hamm reportedly also kept livestock on the property: "as many as forty steers in the fattening stalls in the vicinity of the brewery" and pigs raised for meat for sausages. Horses pulled the brewery's wagons. Theodore and his wife, Louise Hamm, opened a popular beer garden on the property.[25]

Theodore Hamm's successful investment in, and operation of, Excelsior Brewery made him a wealthy man. His personal fortune soon gained architectural expression in a new mansion overlooking Swede Hollow with views of downtown Saint Paul. In 1886, Hamm's son William contracted with "a young German-born architect named Augustus F. Gauger" to build an opulent new family home while Theodore traveled in Germany. When the father returned in early 1887, he discovered a new Queen Anne style, red-brick, three-story castle with eight fireplaces, five chimneys, and twenty rooms.[26] Located on Greenbrier Street, the mansion overlooked the hollow and Hamm's expanding brewery complex from the east. Visually prominent and architecturally

FIGURE 4.4. Hamm's Brewery and Mansion, circa 1890. Collection of Minnesota Historical Society.

ornate, the castle-like building claimed dominion over its site, projecting an image of symbolic permanence in stark contrast to the wooden cottages of Swede Hollow below (see figure 4.4).

The Dayton's Bluff neighborhood grew quickly after the first Seventh Street Bridge connected it to downtown in the early 1870s. By the time Hamm's Mansion was constructed, it had become a center for the German American community and a mix of "moderately-priced housing for working class families, including apartments, rowhouses, and double houses, mixed with the older, more high-style homes of wealthy businessmen."[27]

By the mid-1880s, Hamm's Brewery employed seventy-five workers, and brewed between twenty-five thousand and forty thousand barrels per year. The physical plant expanded to four acres.[28] The company continued to rely upon Phalen Creek for brewery operations, but not without conflict. In 1890, Hamm brought suit against the city for interfering with his business by "the diverting of Phalen Creek into the public sewer."[29] The city relented, canceled part of the proposed sewer project, and paid $3,000 in damages to Hamm. Phalen Creek continued to flow above ground through Swede Hollow, after passing around or through the brewery.

Hamm initiated a major expansion in 1894 "to include a bottling works and that was followed by artificial refrigeration in 1895."[30] The new architect-designed factory attracted an estimated ten thousand people for the grand reopening in September of that year. In 1896, the company incorporated with a capitalization of $3 million.[31] Production jumped from around forty thousand barrels per year in the 1880s to five hundred thousand annually in 1901, then a million a year in 1903, the year Theodore Hamm died. One early twentieth century observer called Hamm's Brewery an "immense plant," an industry that had been "inaugurated on a small scale" then "grown to . . . massive proportions."[32]

The Lower End: The Seventh Street Improvement Arches

As the highland neighborhoods of the East Side expanded, city leaders sought a new bridge to traverse the Swede Hollow gap. Growing by accretions of new tracts, additions, and subdivision developments, the city's street network took shape independent of Swede Hollow. At the north end near Hamm's Brewery, Minnehaha Avenue crossed over an embankment, where the ravine was relatively narrow. But to the south, at Seventh Street and below, the ravine was much deeper, and the distance between bluffs greater. Extending northeast in a straight line from the downtown street grid, Seventh Street served as an important link in the evolving street network.

By 1880, city officials had deemed the existing wooden bridge inadequate and unsafe. The bridge's state of disrepair was a cause of serious concern, and real estate interests and civic elites pushed for a new, improved structure to link the highlands. The city condemned the bridge in 1883, and shortly thereafter allotted funds for a massive landfill and bridge construction project known initially as the "Seventh Street Fill" and, later, as the "Seventh Street Improvement Arches."

The city hired William Albert Truesdell, a thirty-eight-year-old engineer working for the Saint Paul, Minneapolis, and Manitoba Railway, to design and implement the project. He responded to the complex challenges presented by the "Seventh Street Fill" site with an innovative helicoidal or spiral design. On the upper level, the new structure improved transportation access between downtown and Dayton's Bluff by allowing streetcars, carriages, and pedestrians to pass over the ravine and lowlands. On the lower level, it created a tunnel with arched openings on both ends for the Duluth and Saint Paul Railroad, and redirected Phalen Creek into a 320-foot-long culvert under the embankment.[33] Construction of the Seventh Street Arches began in September 1883; on December 18, 1884, the roadway over the arches opened to traffic.³⁴ Steep staircases descended from street level down into the valley. Below, the arched passageways created a portal that became a symbol of the entrance to and exit from Swede Hollow: a short, dark tunnel where freight trains rumbled.

The Seventh Street Arches marked the lower end of the immigrant village with a monumental engineering work designed facilitate rail traffic below and foot, horse, and streetcar traffic above. On the downstream side, the city recorded plans for a new road above the filled ground, aptly named Culvert Street. A man named Jacob Wagener, who owned the low-lying land on either side of the Improvement Arches, laid out a second new street south of the bridge, naming it after himself.³⁵

The Seventh Street Bridge project also coincided with an effort to shelter new immigrants from Ireland. Several Irish immigrant families moved into small houses downstream from the massive infrastructure project, on the east side of the creek between Fifth and Seventh Streets, after receiving initial assistance to immigrate to Minnesota from Saint Paul's Roman Catholic Bishop John Ireland around 1881.³⁶ The small village would become known as Connemara Patch, a derogatory reference. Local observers used many metaphors like patch to describe immigrant shantytowns and neighborhoods, including nest, warren, or roost, which frequently associated the human residents with patterns of animal habitation.³⁷ Swede Hollow and Connemara Patch developed on either side of what became a towering masonry wall, with arched passageways over rail lines, separating the stream valley into areas north or south of Seventh Street.

Debating Disease and Resident Removal

In the mid-1880s, Saint Paul newspaper journalists, as well as members of the board of health, were fretting about the possibility of a cholera outbreak. They identified Swede Hollow, and the increasingly polluted waters of Phalen Creek, as the most likely point of origin were an epidemic to strike the city. The Swedish immigrants living in the hollow in the late 1870s had occupied land controlled by the privately owned Saint Paul Water Company, which had negotiated water rights with the mill and brewery owners and purchased large sections of the valley floor.³⁸ But in 1882, the City of Saint Paul took over the waterworks system, and many of Swede Hollow's residents became tenants of the city.³⁹

In 1884, a letter from the health department noted that "built down in the valley of Phalen creek, are shanties for one hundred families."⁴⁰ A newspaper headline announced that the area was a "plague spot."⁴¹ City officials seriously explored the possibility of evicting residents and demolishing homes in Swede Hollow in the early 1880s. The Saint Paul Board of Health undertook a special survey effort to inspect sanitary conditions around the city. Henry F. Hoyt, MD, president of the board of health, who was also the city's chief health inspector, completed his report on sanitary conditions in November 1884, identifying Swede Hollow as one of the sections of utmost concern within the city. He concluded, "after careful investigation and thorough study of the matter from all its bearings, the only solution of this difficulty—in the opinion of the Health Department—is the removal of these people to some other portion of the city where the natural drainage and the water supply will not be so prejudicial to their own and the public health as their present site."[42] Saint Paulites read Hoyt's report with great interest, organizing subsequent tours of the Hollow and reports by newspaper journalists. Many citizens agreed that its residents must be removed.

Removal, however, presented its own problems. Members of the council objected to "compulsory removal," in part due to the potential cost of relocating residents. As the debate moved along, it was suggested that "a committee should be appointed to secure another location, estimate cost, etc., and report as soon as possible when action can be taken."[43] The Ramsey County Medical Society weighed in as well, bringing forward another potentially costly aspect of the removal plan: the need to reimburse property owners for the taking of their land. Special legislation was needed, but the medical society's sanitary committee pledged its "cordial co-operation and support.[44]

The call to confront the problem of Swede Hollow was sounded again two months later, this time by members of the chamber of commerce. They expanded upon the doctors' diagnosis of cholera risk, adding that the ravine emitted bad air causing typhoid and malaria. They exhorted, "something should be done toward cleaning out this hot-bed of disease," worrying that "should the cholera make its appearance here this summer it would find a splendid base of operations in Swede Hollow." The immigrant lowland, they argued, was "inimical to public safety from a hygienic point of view."[45]

The Swedish-language press covered the story, too. By the 1880s, several Swedish-language newspapers were in operation in the Twin Cities and around the country. A strong emphasis on reading within the state-sanctioned Lutheran church and mandatory schooling had produced a highly literate population.[46] In the August 6, 1884, edition of *Skaffaren och Minnesota Stats Tidning*, for example, the paper reported on the board of health's study of the cholera problem, identification of *Svenska Dalen* as the most likely location of an outbreak, and discussion over whether or not to relocate residents.

They advised "our friends" in the hollow to take careful notice of the city's deliberations.[47]

A consensus between the interested parties could not be reached, however, and three weeks later, the chamber of commerce, noting the impracticality of some of the proposed solutions, emphasized the need to enforce municipal ordinances regarding privies and sanitation. Members stated their concern that dispersal of the residents would only result in them reassembling in another location. One member noted, "communities like these have existed for the last twelve years in the city, first at the corner of Sibley and Third streets, later at Fourth and Rosabel; later at Fifth and Kittson, and now in Swede hollow, and as long as the owner of the land will permit this it appears as good a place as any. Drive them away and they will cluster in unoccupied streets and vacant lots."[48] The Hollow, according to some Saint Paulites, was an appropriate location for the containment of poor, foreign immigrants.

The board of health report suggested better enforcement of city ordinances. Then chamber of commerce members recommended another "method": city officials should go to Swede Hollow, together with an interpreter, to inform the residents in no uncertain terms that they were required to clean their houses. Those residents that did not comply with the order should be arrested, one chamber member argued. Inspections would take place once a week during the cholera "season." A "thorough spring cleaning of our city" was necessary "to maintain the same in healthy condition" and particular attention must be devoted to "Swede hollow."[49]

The *Globe* reported "considerable opposition." General Bishop argued that enforcement of the city ordinances in question would force "a good portion of the people to move somewhere else to live." Another member, "Dr. Day," "argued generally against the report, and declared that in his opinion Swede hollow was to-day a more healthy locality than St. Anthony hill." Meanwhile, "Mr. Murray asserted that Swede hollow was more healthy than any other part of the city, only two deaths having occurred there during the year and three not from sickness." The result was that "no action was taken on the matter and the report [went] over as unfinished business."[50] In the end, the city ignored Dr. Hoyt's recommendations. The chamber of commerce backed away, refraining from passing any resolution on the subject. Faced with the disease threat, the city opted to let Swede Hollow's residents stay.

The opposition had raised four main concerns about the forced removal of residents and the enforcement of city ordinances: first, that relocation and reimbursement to property owners might be costly; second, that residents might end up somewhere else potentially more problematic; third, that alternative measures such as mandatory inspections and housecleanings might be effective; and, finally, that the Hollow was actually a healthy place to live, not a source of disease as Dr. Hoyt had claimed or a "plague spot" as the newspaper headline proclaimed.

Hoyt filed his cholera report in the same month that the city officially opened the Seventh Street Arches over the lower end of Swede Hollow. The two efforts point to the dramatic, costly, and occasionally highly innovative civil engineering and municipal public works funded by late nineteenth-century cities. Voters and elected officials supported these infrastructure projects while at the same time expressing reluctance, and at times political opposition, to urban redevelopment initiatives that may have altered the city's sociospatial arrangement, specifically the location of the city's poor and immigrant classes. This failed attempt at removing residents to remake the Hollow into a healthier environment points to how lowland neighborhoods were stigmatized, but also defended, and by two quite different groups: containment proponents who wished to keep residents where they were and community advocates who argued for the community's right to be left alone.

Saint Paul's head medical officer feared that, should cholera "visit" the city, a widespread epidemic might kill hundreds, or even thousands, of residents. Saint Paul avoided a major cholera outbreak in 1885, and Swede Hollow avoided destruction. The community was presented as a potential threat to the whole city, but Swede Hollow's problems were interconnected with citywide ones. Phalen Creek had developed as both a source of water supply and waste disposal.[51] Residents continued to draw their drinking water directly from the creek and from wells. In 1887, the board of health raised the alarm again about this potential hazard in a brief note in its annual report. The city's health officer, Talbot Jones, MD, reported that a large section of the Fifth Ward emptied its sewage into Phalen Creek, recommending construction of a new sewer that was "very much needed, as a sanitary measure" to safely deliver waste from the city to the Mississippi River below Dayton's Bluff where it could be washed away.[52]

The Lowly of Life

Situated between downtown and the growing Swedish enclave on the East Side highlands, Swede Hollow came to be associated with a particular type of Swede and class of foreigner in a city with growing Swedish and Scandinavian populations. It could be understood both as a stepping-stone on one's path to a better future or as a place of last resort, where one fell in hard times, or struggled to escape. The word "low" pejoratively characterized both landform and people, a stereotype that coexisted with a romantic image of rural life and colorful folk traditions.

Between 1879 and 1892, approximately seventy-six new houses were constructed in the ravine.[53] Within the Hollow, the placement and orientation of small cottages and houses did not obey the typical geometric patterns of urban house lots and city blocks. There were no streets. The orientation of houses tended to respond to the twists and turns of the streambed, and people walked from house to house or through the hollow following a series of dirt paths. On either side, staircases, ladders, tunnels, and steep winding trails allowed residents to reach the residential neighborhoods above. All the houses were constructed of wood and were one story or one and a half stories in height, and they could be found on both sides of Phalen Creek.[54]

As reporters and other visitors ventured into the hollow, they frequently commented upon the arrangement of the houses, some seeing it as evidence of disorder and urban problems, others celebrating the little hamlet's pastoral beauty and charm. One newspaper story from September 1888 focused on poverty and dependency, and the headline offered the reader a view of the "Sights and Scenes as Observed among the Lowly of Life."[55] "The dwellings are uniform in but one particular," the reporter wrote, "their general air of ruin and desolation. They are placed at all angles . . . [and] the whole resembles an irregular mass of toy houses which a child has indiscriminately set down in accordance with the particular whim of the moment."[56] The writer continues, commenting that the "inhabitants of Swede Hollow . . . [are] of the lowest order of mental and moral intelligence," adding that "[a] stroll about the quarter shows an enormous amount of hidden and concentrated vice."[57]

But other journalists of this period described Swede Hollow as "a Paradise in Its Way" and a "Swedish Hamlet" of "Contentment and Thrift."[58] Ten years later, another observer praised the arrangement of the houses, sympathized with the hollow's residents, and imagined the small community as a metaphorical shelter from the harsh economic and social climate of the city.

> One house may turn its back on the water and face the bluff, thereby having its back door not six feet away from the next house, that looks toward the stream. Then there are others whose directions would puzzle the skilled eye of a surveyor, and yet there is an economy of space and originality of design which irresistibly fastens one's attention upon the necessity of this ingenuity. Herein lies the legend of Swede Hollow. These people years ago left the old country and came to this land, where they had heard of broad plains and fertile valleys, and where they had hoped there would be more room for them than there was in their native land. Those that came out here found room, but many of them were not welcome, for the highlands were pre-empted, and they found

no resting place till they found this deserted, but cozy little hollow made by the kindly hand of nature, refreshed by the airy stream that loiters through the ravine on its way to the Mississippi, and sheltered by the bluffs from the inclement winds.[59]

In the romantic account, Swede Hollow was already a place of "legend." By the turn of the century, Swedes and Swedish Americans had assumed a larger percentage of the total population of Saint Paul, Ramsey County, and Minnesota, eventually attaining positions of political and economic power and acting as one of the dominant white ethnic groups in the region. As Swedes joined the majority population, assimilating to American ways of life, the Hollow could be celebrated as a point of origin, not for disease, but for strivers and hardworking immigrants.

Swede Hollow residents built fences, tended gardens, organized cleanup days, celebrated holidays, and played games. One resident, a man named Paul Petterson, took out an ad in a Swedish-language newspaper offering English lessons in the afternoon.[60] Representatives from the free kindergarten movement established a mission in the neighborhood to conduct outreach and provide charitable services to local residents.[61]

Nels Hokanson, who lived in the Hollow as a young boy with his family in 1889 and the early 1890s, relocated there after first living in another part of town. His "father and mother . . . moved the family to St. Paul from Sweden in 1887" and their first "home was a cottage on Cook Avenue, which [his] father rented or purchased on the advice of his brother." But after only a little more than a year, they landed in the Hollow when his father "lost money in a land deal and could not continue payments on the house [moving into] one of a row of smoke-encrusted houses along the railroad tracks."[62] Hokanson recalled that in the 1890s, residents paid rent of five dollars per month directly to the city.[63] As it turned out, his family would only stay a few years, moving up and out as soon as they got the chance.

The dam and mill pond continued to be prominent features of the neighborhood, located at the upper end of the hollow near the brewery. Of Hamm's, Hokanson recalls: "A large pipe protruded from the brewery or at one side. Water from this pipe tumbled noisily into a pool several feet below, where men fished and big and little boys, naked as birches in winter, swam unrestrained by rules or regulations. Overflow from the pool formed the part of the creek which coursed through the Hollow and disappeared into a tunnel which I sometimes explored to a distance of five or six feet."[64]

The railroad tracks and shunting yards south of the Seventh Street Fill also attracted the attention of the children in the Hollow, with boys "dodging brakemen and hitching rides on the slow-moving cars." Hokanson writes: "The brakemen were popular with Swedish women who had a habit of calling to them 'Skalle ha litte kaffe?' (Would you like a little coffee?)," which led the railroad men to nickname the Saint Paul and Duluth the "Skalle Line."[65]

Swede Hollow's late nineteenth-century residents found and adapted living space next to the railroad tracks, and between the expanding brewery operations at Hamm's and the wall created by the Seventh Street Fill. Their homes clustered together around a seminatural creek that drained an upland watershed and provided habitat for fish and other animals, a meandering waterway periodically inundated with brewery wastes expelled from Hamm's. Yet Swede Hollow continued to grow. Located on both sides of the creek, more than ninety small houses could be found across the length of the valley floor, from the brewery to the Seventh Street Arches.[66]

Underlying the cholera and resident removal debates of the 1880s were societal questions about the city's responsibilities for securing the public health, providing services and infrastructure, and managing city-owned property. While faith in private solutions continued to reign as the dominant intellectual approach to municipal problems, the physical city was being transformed by engineers and architects, builders, and designers. Municipal-led engineering projects like the Seventh Street Improvement Arches and public health investigations redefined the scope and purpose of government in Saint Paul, and across the US. As new systems of water supply and waste disposal expanded, infrastructural questions bumped up against private claims and rights, such as Hamm's objection to the public sewer, and public health and housing concerns, such as where poor immigrant families *should* live. Social segregation by topography continued as new engineering techniques, medical discoveries, and political philosophies brought shifts in urban governance. In the new century, a focus on housing conditions and city planning reframed public debates over urban lowland neighborhoods.

Italian Swede Hollow and Aronovici's Survey

In the 1910s, Swede Hollow's residents worked in many of the same types of professions as they had three decades earlier. The 1914 city directory listed many laborers living along Phalen Creek, but also a machine operator, a charwoman, a washer, a carpenter, a clerk, a presser, a mangler, many apprentices, and dozens of laborers. And residents continued to list their addresses as "Phalen Creek": eighty-four separate addresses and 209 adults are listed in the city directory. Many of the addresses included fractions, such as 54 ½ North Phalen Creek, likely an indication of residences added after the house-numbering system began. Addresses were also listed as either north or south, reflecting further spatial organization and formalization of locations in the Hollow. "Phalen Creek North" was defined as "from Seventh [north] to Payne av between [Northern Pacific Railway] and Maria av" while "Phalen Creek South" was dedicated to addresses on the other side of the Seventh Street Bridge "from Seventh [south] to Third between [Northern Pacific Railway] and Hoffman av."[67] By this time, though, Italian immigrants had become the majority ethnic group in the Hollow with families with surnames such as Bonnello, Cicalo, Dipancrazio, Fragazzi, Gionda, Natalino, Oleito, Perillo, Ronoletti, and Sanchelli. While some residents thought of the community as a new "Little Italy," many continued to refer to it as Swede Hollow.

The experiences of Italian immigrant families were quite similar to Swedish immigrant families like the Hokansons. One former resident, Gentille Yarusso, recalled his family's long history in the Hollow: "thousands of Italian immigrants got off the train at the depot in St. Paul. . . . They all had tags on their lapels, and on each tag was written Joseph Yarusso, No. 2 Swede Hollow, St. Paul, Minnesota." Gentille's father, Joseph, would help new Italian immigrants with "a place to stay and a place to settle for awhile," and "by pinching and scrimping, in a year or two, when they had saved enough money, they, too, would move to better living quarters—Up on the Street."[68] Many families stayed in the Hollow for years, and children grew up there. Yarusso, who was born in 1912, explored many of the same features of the neighborhood landscape that Hokanson had traversed years earlier.

But the Italians also experienced the Hollow differently. Although more than two million Italians immigrated to the US between 1899 and 1910, relatively few came to Minnesota. In 1910, the Italian-born population of Minnesota was listed at 9,668.[69] In contrast, nearly fifty thousand Scandinavians lived in Ramsey County alone at the time.[70] Swedish businesses, churches, and cultural organizations thrived. In Minneapolis, publisher Swan Turnblad accumulated a fortune selling Swedish-language newspapers.

Most Italians who immigrated to Minnesota settled in one of three cities—Minneapolis, Saint Paul, or Duluth—or in the Iron Range, in the northern part of the state. In 1910, 1,994 persons born in Italy lived in Saint Paul; however, during the winter months, when seasonal railroad work was not available, the population was said to double.[71] The Great Northern and Northern Pacific Railways recruited an increased number of Italians as track workers after 1880, constituting one major "pull" factor in Italian migration to the Upper Midwest.[72] After arrival, railroad laborers received low pay, faced harsh working conditions, and worked long hours at great risk of injury or death.[73] Italian immigrants living in Swede Hollow came from "several regions: the Abruzzi (especially the mountain villages), Puglia (especially the province of Foggia), Campania, and Calabria."[74] Italian immigrants also settled in another urban lowland neighborhood called Upper Levee and located on the flats of the Mississippi. Established in the 1880s, upstream from downtown Saint Paul and below the High Bridge, this area became known as "Little Italy" or "the Flats."[75]

Urban lowland neighborhoods like the Upper Levee and Swede Hollow became the focus of housing studies and municipal plans in the early part of the twentieth century. Housing reformers and urban planners pushed for action to address dilapidated housing, lack of sanitation, and population congestion. By 1910, Saint Paul's population had grown to 214,744, and housing conditions had deteriorated across the city. Seeking to improve living conditions and remove "housing evils," Progressive era urban reformers organized to document the slums.

Sponsored by the Amherst H. Wilder Charity and directed by Carol Aronovici, PhD, *Housing Conditions in the City of St. Paul* reported on an extensive three-month-long field survey, documenting issues such as "condition of repair" of housing; "toilets and baths"; "sewers and water supply"; "garbage, ashes and rubbish"; and the "lodger problem."[76] Aronovici, himself an immigrant to the US from Romania, later became a nationally known housing expert. He received his PhD from Brown University in 1912, after completing bachelor's and master's degrees in architecture at Cornell University. Surveyors focused on eighteen city districts that they considered to be the most problematic. Districts included West Side Lower Levee, West Side Lower Flats, West Side Upper Levee, West Side Upper Flats, Upper Levee (under High Bridge), and Phalen Creek (Swede Hollow). The surveyors found that living conditions in "the homes of over 21,000 people ... demand attention."[77]

Aronovici and the Wilder Charity aimed to spur government action through a comprehensive presentation of the evidence of the problem. They sought to improve city life through city planning and made their case by emphasizing the need for standards and efficiency. The authors described how the survey was undertaken for "the purpose of revealing to the public sanitary conditions that may be a menace to the health of the residents of the poorer sections of the city with a view to stimulating more efficient service on the part of the municipality."

Aronovici discussed Swede Hollow and other lowlands as municipal-level concerns. "The sections generally known as 'Swede Hollow' and the 'Flats,'" he wrote, "which constitute the lowest types of residential districts not only in St. Paul, but of many cities that it has been the writer's privilege to examine, offer remarkable opportunities for replanning."[78] He recommended total clearance and replacement with a park, noting that the health benefits to the residents and the city as a whole.

The report, which included maps, tables, and photographs, featured an image of Phalen Creek that shows a young boy standing near the stream with outhouses behind him. Aronovici drew attention to nationality, collecting and reporting data on ethnicity and national origin and comparing housing conditions by ethnic group. Thirty percent of Saint Paul's Italian households, he noted, took in boarders—an "economic necessity" that was understood by social workers and reformers at the time as "dangerous" and "shameful." The authors offered fourteen conclusions, including the need for legislation, enforcement of existing laws by the health department, greater attention to the problem of structural defects and low construction standards, regulation of the arrangement of lots and placement of buildings, and the need for zoning.[79] Saint Paul's citizens found the results "shocking," and the report led to the adoption of the city's first housing ordinance in 1918.[80]

Connections between topography and good city planning continued to be a municipal issue when the city adopted its first comprehensive plan and zoning ordinance in 1922. The plan, prepared by consultants Edward H. Bennett and William E. Parsons with city planning engineer George H. Herrold, prominently features a map of city topography with the city's "lower levels" indicated in dark shades. The plan begins with a description of survey work, and the first item it addresses is topography, referring readers to the map. "The higher levels" of the city, the authors wrote, "are not adequately connected with the lower levels and ravines form barriers which must be bridged over in order that the city may be in good position to compare with other cities with flat topography."[81] The city's first zoning map designated Swede Hollow as a "heavy industry district" while the preliminary city plan indicated future use as a park.

Swede Hollow, meanwhile, continued to decline. By 1926, when the Sanborn Company updated its fire insurance map of the area, the cartographer documented only thirty-nine dwellings in Swede Hollow plus another twenty-one detached outbuildings (see figure 4.5). One building is marked old and vacant. The area is labeled as "Phalen Creek, Formerly Known as Swede Hollow," and the mapmaker included a note: "Italian settlement in ravine about 60 feet below East Seventh Street grade."

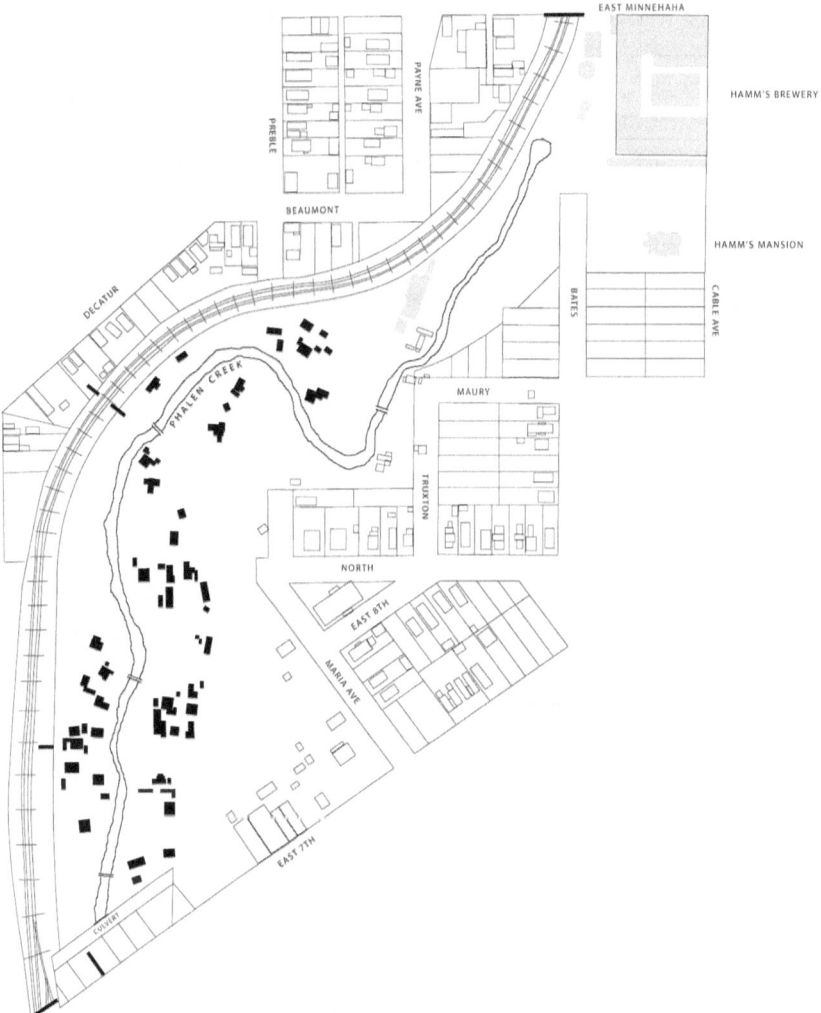

FIGURE 4.5. Swede Hollow cottages in the 1920s. Map by Clelie Fielding.

Painting Swede Hollow

One of the most remarkable and unusual aspects of Swede Hollow's history is the attraction it held for artists. Artistic depictions of the neighborhood suggest how the "legend" of Swede Hollow continued well into the twentieth century and how it was reinterpreted for new purposes and new audiences. Painter Dewey Albinson first visited Swede Hollow in 1918, and after his "first glimpse" he would "make the excursion to spend the day" whenever he had the opportunity.⁸² For the Minneapolis-born Albinson, the son of Swedish immigrants, Swede Hollow in Saint Paul and Bohemian Flats in Minneapolis were a striking visual departure from the rest of the city.⁸³ "After passing through monotonous streets," he wrote, "it was like entering a fairyland to descend into these settlements."⁸⁴ He was particularly attracted to Swede Hollow, and his 1925 lithograph *Shacks and Snow* would become one of his most well-known artworks. It was exhibited in museums around the US and the world, and inspired other artworks about Swede Hollow.

Shacks and Snow depicts Swede Hollow in winter, a geometric composition that emphasizes angles and planes through a depiction of snow-covered staircases, fences, trees, rooflines, and gables. Several houses are shown, with a two-story structure as focal point at the center left, to represent human presence in the landscape, although no human figures are visible. The human-built elements of wooden houses, staircases, and fences occupy about two-thirds of the composition and extend to the edges of the frame. The hillside forms the backdrop and encloses the scene; there is little sense of open sky or life outside the hollow. Snow blankets the rooftops and hillsides, linking people and nature, suggesting a harmonious, albeit crowded and densely inhabited, relationship. The people of Swede Hollow, Albinson indicates, are living in close relationship to the contours of the land.⁸⁵

In 1926, Albinson painted the same *Shacks and Snow* scene in color at a larger scale, thirty by thirty-four inches, and painted other scenes of Swede Hollow including the paintings *Hamm's Brewery and Swede Hollow* and *Winter Scene, Swede Hollow*.⁸⁶ The *Shacks and Snow* lithograph toured "Scandinavian museum sites in 1930 as part of the Exhibition of American Art, under the auspices of the American-Scandinavian Foundation and the American Federation of the Arts."⁸⁷ Albinson created several prints of *Shacks and Snow* during the 1930s.

Decades later Albinson related his own view of Swede Hollow. He wrote: "This settlement was started by a group of Swedish immigrants who, by the time they arrived at St. Paul, were out of funds. Some, I heard, had been clipped. However, as soon as they prospered they bought a piece of property set on the Hill.... By 1925, there was only one of the originals left, a Mrs. Lindquist, a widow with two sons—one of them had 'gone bad'—so she never made the Hill."⁸⁸ For Albinson and other artists, Swede Hollow became a subject of social realism.

Swede Hollow attracted at least six other regionally known modern artists. Artworks that take Swede Hollow as its subject include *Swede Hollow* (1933) a lithograph by Vera Andrus; *The Other Side of the Tracks* (circa 1940) and *Swede Hollow* (circa 1945), two paintings by Robert (Bob) Brown; *Landscape* [Swede Hollow] (1934), a lithograph by Wilby Hausener; *Swede Hollow* (circa 1920), an etching by George Resler (see figure 4.6); *Swede Hollow* (circa 1928),

FIGURE 4.6. *Swede Hollow*, etching by George Earl Resler, circa 1920. Collection of Minnesota Historical Society.

an etching, and *Swede Hollow* (circa 1935), a painting, by Theodore Sohner; and *Winter* (circa 1939), a painting by Bennet Albert Swanson.[89] Many artists, some of whom were involved in Depression-era New Deal federal arts programs, painted similar scenes of Bohemian Flats or the Levee.

The concept of landscape itself is closely tied to landscape painting.[90] The landscape of Swede Hollow offered twentieth-century Minnesota artists a subject for interpretation with social resonance during the rise of the modern city and the suffering of the Great Depression. As art historian Thomas O'Sullivan wrote, "The interplay of human actions with the natural environment is an enduring theme in American landscape art."[91] Public health officers, journalists, and housing reformers characterized Swede Hollow as a slum or a countrified village, but for artists like Albinson, Swede Hollow could evoke nature and culture, pathos, independence or separateness from mainstream society, or the beauty to be found in the everyday. The Swede Hollow landscape juxtaposed symbols of city and country, a tableau of built and natural forms: dramatic and often barren hillside slopes, the curving lines of railroad and creek, trees and water, brick factories and wooden houses, simple fences and kitchen gardens.

Swede Hollow Park

Swede Hollow continued to draw curiosity seekers, artists, visitors, and new residents through the 1930s and 1940s. Calls for resident removal and redevelopment also continued, echoing the recommendations of medical and housing experts in earlier decades. In 1932, landscape architect George Nasen advocated for a new Hamm Park at Swede Hollow to memorialize William Hamm, Theodore Hamm's son who died in 1931, and his advocacy on behalf of parks in Saint Paul.[92] Like Aronovici's recommendation from 1917, Nasen's proposal for a park at Swede Hollow was not realized.

In 1936, however, the Saint Paul Department of Public Works embarked on an engineering project that buried Phalen Creek in a massive new sewer through the valley bottom. Measuring eleven feet tall and ten feet eleven inches wide at its widest point, the concrete sewer pipe employed an elliptical design to convey storm water and wastewater underground through the valley toward the Mississippi River.[93] Despite the disruption of heavy equipment, earthmoving, and work crews, several dozen families continued to live in the valley through the end of the Depression and World War II. Swede Hollow's lack of services, such as no electric lighting or indoor plumbing, became more stark over the decades, in an era where modern appliances and new modern ways of living received strong emphasis in both consumer culture and government housing and urban development policy.

The park proposal resurfaced again toward the end of the war. On January 13, 1945, the *Saint Paul Dispatch* reported that the "property along the Phalen Creek from E. Seventh st. to the Hamm Brewing Co. plant" belonged to the state, "which holds the property under tax forfeiture."[94] The land was previously owned by the Hamm's Brewery and the estate of former Ramsey county sheriff John Wagener. The City of Saint Paul requested that the state deed the property to the city for use as a park, and city planning engineer George Herrold proclaimed that the families in the thirty-three remaining houses would be evicted, derisively and incorrectly referring to the residents as "squatters." The tract reportedly totaled twenty-three and a half acres, and it was considered a key piece of the proposed park. Tennis courts and picnic grounds were envisioned, to be inserted on a newly level flat ground atop the "lump" in the valley created by the Phalen Creek sewer, and "a municipal forest" on the "heavily wooded slopes" of the ravine. This proposal, too, would fail. Swede Hollow's residents, many of them Mexican immigrants by the 1940s, continued to reside there for several more years. When the Sanborn Company's mapmakers returned to the hollow in 1951, they documented only seventeen dwellings and nine miscellaneous detached outbuildings.

In the end, the Hollow's last homes were destroyed by fire. Hamm's Mansion, which had become a nursing home, then was left vacant, burned down in April 1954, the fire set by "a 14-year-old arsonist . . . out of boredom, he said."[95] Down in the hollow, the city began evicting Swede Hollow's residents. On December 11, 1956, the Saint Paul Fire Department burned the last remaining houses to the ground. A news report explained that the remaining houses "were burned on order of the city health department which had been working with the St. Paul Housing and Redevelopment Authority for months on vacating the area as a health hazard," adding that "the homes had no sewer or water facilities and obtained water from a spring found contaminated. Outhouses lined the creek."[96] Families had reportedly been paying "token rent of $5 a month" to the city, the same figure that Hokanson recalled residents paying in 1890s. The city had finally removed the ravine's residents, but the neighborhood's future was uncertain. Some Saint Paulites imagined "modern manufacturing plants" and other industrial uses.[97] Other residents proposed filling in the entire ravine or building a new highway through it. None of these projects came to pass, and the old immigrant hamlet became a dumping ground for many years. In 1973, after a concerted campaign to clean up the ravine and recognize its history, the hollow became a city park.

After 1973, park design efforts were directed at improving public access and developing bike and walking trails. The railway tracks, a defining feature of the ravine since 1870, were abandoned and then removed, replaced with an asphalt path. In 1994, local community members formed a group known as Friends of Swede Hollow, an organization that advocates for the park's maintenance and organizes programs. Hamm's Brewery (later Stroh's) at the top of the hollow closed down, and was fenced off for many years. One interpretive sign may be found at "Swede Hollow Overlook," a grassy park with shade trees on the former site of Hamm's Mansion. According to geographer David Lanegran, Swede Hollow's unofficial historian, interpretive signs installed in the 1970s were defaced and then removed. Several landscape artworks were installed, including a miniature Stonehenge-like arrangement of boulders and a stone pylon on a raised berm and, a few hundred feet to the south, a designed landscape of paving stones, a bench, and overgrown decorative plantings where a section of the old stream emerges above ground into a constructed open channel lined with paving stones. Walking tours frequently bring visitors to learn about Swede Hollow's hidden histories.

Poverty and Geography

Artists, engineers, and journalists assessed Swede Hollow. So did housing reformers and physicians. They all studied the place and its people, offering their own evaluations to the public. Romantics like painter Dewey Albinson celebrated the folk traditions, distinctiveness, and beauty of an immigrant community in a rustic landscape while professional experts and officials tended to emphasize unsanitary conditions and the risk of disease contamination. The same details in the built environment, such as the spatial arrangement of homes, were used to support both positions.

Since the 1990s, local newspaper accounts, museum exhibits, and magazine articles tend to portray Swede Hollow in heroic terms, celebrating it as a distinctive place where immigrants struggled before finding success. Stefanie Kowalczyk's 2015 article in the online journal *Open Rivers*, for example, is titled "An Enchanted Landscape: Remembering Historic Swede Hollow." In contrast, Swedish journalist Ola Larsmo's historical novel *Swede Hollow*, a best seller in Sweden, focuses on the injustices that working-poor immigrants faced in the nineteenth-century American city and the fight for a better life.

Swede Hollow was a highly imageable urban landscape, but its meanings were contested. The question of what to do about Swede Hollow was a persistent, public issue that challenged city officials, manifesting as several different problems: cholera in the 1880s, poor housing conditions in the 1910s, sewer infrastructure in the 1930s, and condemnation proceedings in the 1950s.

Although Swede Hollow was sometimes imagined as a rural or natural environment, it was a highly constructed and engineered landscape: embankments and ballast for railway operations, dams and races for mill operations, culverts and drains and pipes for directing the flow of creek water and wastewater, fill projects, and bridges. The urban lowland was subject to repeated conflicts over the use of resources and rights in the valley, leading to the water company and the mill owners' agreement of 1869, and Hamm's successful 1891 complaint against the city. But throughout, the residents were public tenants of a city agency—the water company. Although the Hollow was neglected and poorly served by city services, it became de facto housing for an overflow population. Swede Hollow was a paradoxical urban landscape: a permanent-temporary settlement. Like the housing shelters or homeless services of today, residents were shunted out of sight, near industrial areas, away from residential neighborhoods of single-family homes.

Swede Hollow's steep hillsides both sheltered and isolated its residential community and, due to limited access, inhibited clearance and redevelopment. The Hollow's physical and social isolation did not, however, prevent city engineers from submerging Phalen Creek in an underground sewer in the 1930s, or evicting the last residents in the 1950s, burning the wooden houses to the ground. Over the more than seven decades of its existence as a residential community, the physical and social changes in the hollow, and public debates over how to define the community and what to do about it, demonstrate how attitudes about immigration and ethnicity combined with beliefs about nature, disease, and lowlands as lived environments.

Historically Swede Hollow was understood two ways: to outsiders it was viewed as the place where immigrants belonged because they were foreign and poor, but for immigrants themselves it was seen as the place where the poorest of the Swedes or Italians lived, often only temporarily. The latter perspective emphasized the class differences within immigrant groups and the potential for assimilation and upward mobility. In the narrative arc of the American Dream story, where opportunity and success is available to all, immigrants arrived under harsh conditions, encountered many difficulties, suffered at times, but ultimately built a new life for themselves in their new country, achieving success and, perhaps, a small amount of material comfort or wealth. This narrative of "up and out" is one that is frequently told about Swede Hollow. As Lanegran has described, the Hollow was a "slum," but it was also a "funnel" and a "stepping stone"—"a temporary home where immigrants stayed only until they could afford to move up the hill. It was a place where impoverished newcomers could find cheap housing while they got started. It also served as a refuge for people who had fallen on hard times and needed a place to stay while they pulled themselves together again."[98] But, as historian Rudolph Vecoli has argued, harsh living conditions made it difficult to leave. He warns that a narrative that focuses only on assimilation and upward social and topographical mobility misrepresents the facts. Many immigrants, he writes, were "defeated and crushed by the harsh conditions they encountered in America."[99]

Structural forces unleashed by railroad building, industrialization, and urbanization after the Civil War, created urban lowland neighborhoods. Elected officials, physicians, engineers, and planners reinforced them through local action and city policy. Lowland residents exercised agency, albeit limited, by fighting off eviction and displacement, physically modifying their surroundings, and supporting one another through social, ethnic, and religious networks and communities.

Throughout its history, municipal decisions defined Swede Hollow: the use of water, the lease of publicly owned land to residents, rights granted to develop railroad lines, and construction of public works. The Hollow was both a human-constructed environment and a natural one, its history echoes the rise and fall of the railroad era in cities and demonstrates how the meaning of topography within the urban landscape changed between the 1880s and 1950s. Swede Hollow shows how the physical environment of the American city including creeks and streams, ravines, and the arrangement of houses in a community, has been understood through the lens of social attitudes and disease fears. And it also shows how the city itself was transformed as a result.

5
The Flats
Los Angeles, California

Laborer Moisado Joaquino, peddlers Jacob and Moses Krom, and terra-cotta maker Ludwig Lundberg and his wife, Caroline, were five of the first residents on Anderson Street, a new block of homes located next to the Los Angeles River. During the late 1880s, the Los Angeles real estate market boomed as the Southern Pacific and Santa Fe Railroads brought thousands of newcomers to the city. Property owners near the river plowed under cornfields, orchards, and vineyards while millions of dollars were exchanged in land transactions. They demolished old adobe houses and subdivided land for resale. On the east side of the river, below the bluffs of Boyle Heights, a new neighborhood began to take shape: the Flats.[1]

The railroads built freight yards and passenger stations, warehouses and worker housing, river levees and embankments, transforming the agricultural landscape around the river. In 1888, the Southern Pacific constructed Arcade Station on the site of William Wolfskill's orange groves.[2] An agronomist, rancher, and prominent public figure, Wolfskill was highly influential in the development of California agriculture. Nearby, vintner Jean Louis Vignes's home, El Aliso, another local landmark of early Los Angeles with its extensive grape arbor and a massive sycamore tree, was razed.[3] The real estate boom came to a crashing end in 1888, but was followed by another speculative fever just a few years later.

The floodplain of the Los Angeles River was a risky place to build. The river was not navigable, and often ran very low, trickling across a mostly dry alluvial fan. But during periods of high rainfall, it raged as a torrent. Floods were a serious threat from the unpredictable river.[4] Spanish settlers had established the pueblo of Los Angeles on the site of a Yangna village, below the

Elysian Hills on the river's west bank, in 1781. The pueblo was located close enough to access freshwater but distant enough from floods. To make the best use of limited water supplies in an arid climate, they also developed an extensive irrigation and water-supply system using ditches known as *zanjas*.[5] During the 1880s, as industrial and residential development edged into the riverbed, farmers and residents continued to rely upon the river and the zanjas as a source of freshwater (see figures 5.1 and 5.2). As population and development pressures intensified, water quality and supply rapidly deteriorated while floods remained a danger.

Over the next three decades, engineers and builders constructed the Flats. City workers and private contractors removed the zanjas, installed a sewer and drainage system, reinforced levees along the Los Angeles River, platted streets, built houses and factories, expanded railroad facilities, and piped in freshwater supplies. Thousands of new residents moved in, as more houses, apartment buildings, stores, and factories spread out across the lowlands, from the riverside around Anderson Street to the bluffs. But despite the "improvements" and "progress" cited by city boosters, journalists and housing

FIGURE 5.1. Aerial view looking east toward the Los Angeles River, June 27, 1887. The Macy, Aliso, and First Street Bridges link the city to its east side. The Flats is visible on the opposite side of the river (*top*) including newly platted streets. Security Pacific Collection, Los Angeles Public Library.

THE FLATS   115

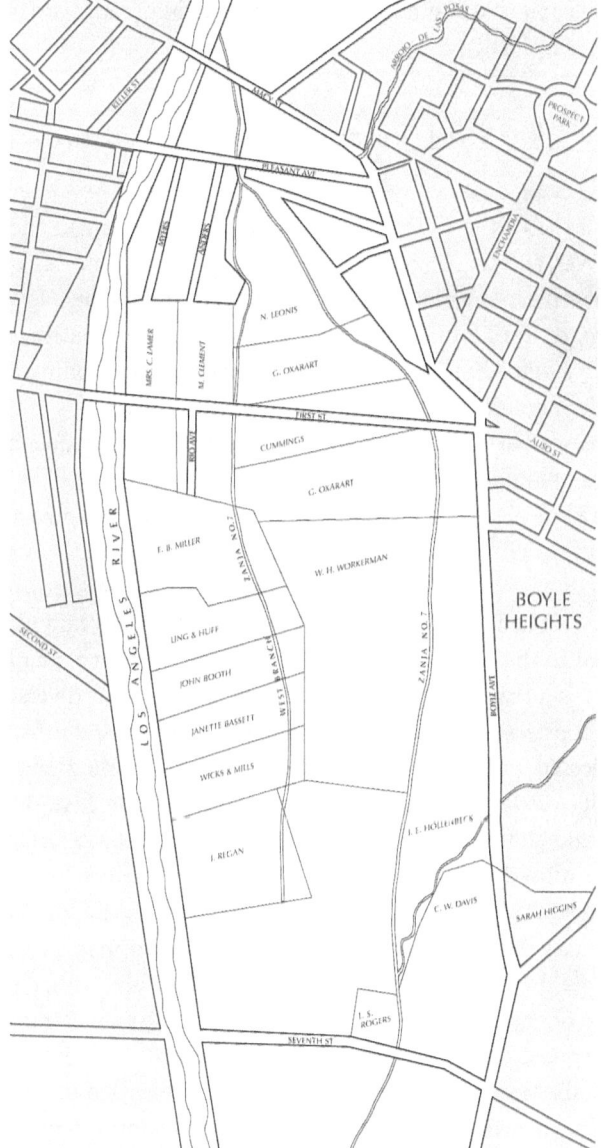

FIGURE 5.2. East and west branches of zanja #7 and property lines in the Flats, circa 1890. Map by Clelie Fielding.

reformers almost immediately labeled the neighborhood a "slum" and a "disgrace."[6] After 1905, the Flats was repeatedly identified as a place beset with disease, overcrowded housing, and sanitary problems. The story of the Flats reveals how the perceived qualities of the lowland environment, social prejudice and xenophobic anger, and attitudes about urban poverty led Angelenos to the conclusion that the neighborhood was a failure and a danger to the health of the city.

The Social Geography of Los Angeles in the 1880s and 1890s

Four decades after the Treaty of Guadalupe Hidalgo ended the Mexican-American War, and the US had claimed California, Los Angeles was a city of multiple identities. The oldest part of the city around the pueblo was known as *la placita*, or the Plaza. The Anglo downtown to the southwest included new masonry office buildings housing financial service companies, as well as wholesale markets, churches, hotels, and stores. Railroads and streetcars linked disparate parts of the region, and new cities sprung up across a geographic area of hundreds of square miles.

The old Plaza area became one of the most densely populated and densely built parts of the city. It included sections known as Sonoratown and Chinatown. In a city that had once been part of Mexico, the Sonoratown label suggested that the Mexican presence in the city was physically bounded and historically tied to the old city and, perhaps, to the Mexican state of Sonora, a characterization that did not reflect the actual origins of its diverse residents. Anglo city boosters marketed Los Angeles as a healthful and prosperous destination, blessed with a perfect climate, and they embarked on a campaign to remake its Mexican past. In literature, public spectacle, historical societies and clubs, and cultural exhibitions, boosters developed a myth of Southern California suffused with "romantic nostalgia."[7] Journalists, promoters, and land developers celebrated what historian Carey McWilliams has called a Spanish Fantasy Past. They devoted special attention to Spanish colonial missions and the preservation of architectural and cultural artifacts, and they downplayed or obscured connections to Mexico.[8] The publication and subsequent widespread popularity of Helen Hunt Jackson's novel *Ramona* and the founding of the Historical Society of Southern California and the Landmarks Club by magazine editor Charles Fletcher Lummis contributed to the movement in the 1880s and 1890s. Throughout, prominent Anglo business and cultural leaders like Lummis and real estate developer and Venice founder Abbot Kinney voiced their belief in white supremacy.[9]

These actions relied upon "invented tradition" to obscure the complex demographic and spatial reality of Los Angeles's multicultural, multiethnic, and international population.[10] While Anglos became the dominant group during in the 1880s, many other ethnic and racial groups chose Los Angeles, including African Americans and European-born immigrants from other parts of the US, Chinese, Japanese, Native Americans, California-born people of mixed ancestry, Mexican immigrants, and Mexican Americans.

Using data from the 1880 census, historian Richard Griswold del Castillo calculates that most Mexicans lived in the historic core and the southern, agricultural portion of the city, or wards 1, 2, and 4.[11] By the late 1880s, however, some families with Spanish surnames had moved across the river into predominantly Anglo subdivisions, including Brooklyn Heights, Boyle Heights, and along Mission Street in the lowlands. Many Mexican Americans lived east of Main Street and north of First Street on the west side of the river. Adobe houses remained a prominent feature of the urban landscape in this part of the city, whereas new houses of brick and wood dominated elsewhere. Between 1880 and 1900, the population of Angelenos who were either of Mexican origin or born in Mexico doubled.[12] During the same period, the Anglo population increased by a factor of nine.[13] By 1900, less than 15 percent of Angelenos were Mexican or Mexican American.[14] The city was also home to more than 2,100 African Americans, 2,100 Chinese, and 2,500 Jews. These numbers were relatively small, but were significant influences on future demographic trends, in a city with a total population of 102,479.[15]

Around 1900, Mexican emigrants began what historian Ricardo Romo terms the "peaceful 'reconquest' of the Southwest."[16] Unemployment stemming from mechanization and population pressures combined with inflation and rising food prices to push Mexicans northward. They departed from many home states within Mexico, especially the agricultural and mining region of Durango. While many Mexicans living in Los Angeles in the late nineteenth century called Sonora their home, by the early 1900s they would be joined by people from the northern and central states of Chihuahua, Zacatecas, Jalisco, Michoacan, and Guanajuato. Two important rail connections developed by the Southern Pacific facilitated this migration, both completed in 1885: the Mexican International Railroad, which reached nine hundred miles into the country, and the Sunset route, linking New Orleans and Los Angeles over a 1,200-mile stretch that ran close to the US-Mexico border.[17]

The workforce needed to support railroad expansion, track operations and maintenance, and freight handling found housing in the lowlands. By the 1890s, the railroads' recruitment efforts and promises of steady work focused almost exclusively on Mexico.[18] Railroad companies housed some Mexican workers in discarded boxcars, located near work sites.[19] Others found cheap rental housing or constructed their own simple dwellings. Railroad construction transformed the physical and the social environment of the flat lands in the topographically varied landscape of fast-growing Los Angeles. Laying track, building houses, packing citrus, producing bottled wine and distilling brandy, and extracting, processing, and transporting oil required workers. Labor demands quickly outpaced local availability, leading railroad companies and other businesses to recruit laborers.

Anglo white supremacists touted a vision of the future city that was rooted in a hierarchy of the races, but the definition of race in Los Angeles differed from that of East Coast, midwestern, and southern cities in several dimensions. Whereas many Americans understood race in "dichotomous terms" of black and white, sometimes referring to Slavs, Jews, and southern Europeans as members of other races, Angelenos saw various forms of "nonwhite" in between, a category that included the Chinese, Japanese, and Mexican populations of the city.[20] Using a racial hierarchy that defined whites as superior, they ranked the position of immigrants according to perceived potential for assimilation.[21] Compared to other American cities, Los Angeles continued to have lower percentages of European immigrants and African Americans.

One domain of public discourse in particular came to be defined by racial categorizations and racialized fears. In late nineteenth- and early twentieth-century Los Angeles, public health officials focused their attention on the diseases found in Chinese, Japanese, and Mexican communities.[22] Lowland geography and the patterns of low-cost housing development reinforced these cultural assumptions about disease and race. Sociologist Diego Vigil notes that early Mexican emigrants "settled in neglected and inferior locations, areas usually initially bypassed in the development of urban Los Angeles—the 'flats' or lowlands; the areas beneath bridges; and the undesirable gulches, ravines, and hollows."[23] These locations were not chosen by accident; the proximity to railroad work sites and lands owned by railroad companies were the determining factor in the housing of the area. Historian Mark Wild writes: "Along the floodplain below the bluffs railroad companies soon established Boxcarvilles for Mexican and other workers in Dogtown and the Flats. East of the bluffs, a series of gullies riddled a landscape that undulated by property value as well as elevation. Into low-lying areas like Fickett Hollow and Bernal Gully, where the constant threat of flooding depressed property values, moved settlers of modest means and various ethnicities."[24]

Massive in-migration, mostly from other places within the United States, produced an enormous new city within the span of three decades. Native-born whites, variously referred to as Yankees and Anglos, created the dominant culture, establishing a rigidly segregated city. Anti-Chinese prejudice was widespread, and Chinese immigrants were the victims of brutal violence. Many Anglos held racist views, believing that "foreigners" belonged in the industrial areas around the Los Angeles River. In an 1889 editorial in the *Los Angeles Times*, for example, one writer's hateful screed suggested that "steps were being taken" to drive the Chinese to the east side of Alameda, down toward the river flats.[25]

The river areas became associated with foreigners, tramps, hobos, scofflaws, and outsiders.[26] A 1901 *Los Angeles Times* article with the headline "They Build Nests in the River Bed" describes in a bemused and mocking tone the story of "unrequited love" and an old pioneer, a white man who once had riches, who has landed in the river area, built himself a shack, and become known as "King of the Bottom." "Among the quaint residents of Los Angeles are the ever shifting class that inhabits the river bed," the article begins. "While preferring a solitary existence, they nevertheless establish themselves within sight and hearing of the busy world."[27] The Los Angeles River lowlands became a railroad and industrial district where one could find people living in small houses and shanties among factories, warehouses, junk piles, and freight yards. Journalists, health officers, and visitors who went "slumming" in the river district portrayed the river as "a place of bad smells and bad people, a place where, Anglos expected and insisted, crooks, Mexicans, Indians, and Chinese congregated."[28] They framed the Los Angeles River according to race and ethnicity as an urban swampland and a refuge for the marginal, criminal, diseased, and foreign.

Heights and Flats

By 1888, construction of a third transcontinental line into Los Angeles was underway. Founded by a Utah syndicate, the Los Angeles and Salt Lake Railroad proposed to connect the two cities with a route through Nevada. Of the three major rail lines, the Los Angeles and Salt Lake would have the greatest impact on the Flats. The city granted a sixty-foot right-of-way along the east bank of the Los Angeles River from Hoff Street in Lincoln Heights to the city's southern boundary, requiring the company to construct a levee along the eastern edge of the official bed of the river, to commence work within a year, and complete the work within three years.[29] These railroad-built levees were among the first of many engineering efforts that ultimately defined the path and constrained the flow of the Los Angeles River.

Almost immediately, city leaders raised questions about whether or not the new company had the financial and organizational capacity to complete the project, speculating that its proposal was meant to secure the rights to a line that had little backing. The *Los Angeles Times* editorial board noted that the city's support was risky, but that the logistical advantages of an eastern route through the river flats and arroyos, along with the economic advantages of a potential supply connection to Utah's coalfields and other mineral deposits, outweighed the risks. The *Times* estimated that city-granted land was worth $250,000 and noted that the route was "the last inlet to the city for a big railroad," a troubling prospect given that mystery surrounded the project and its financing.[30]

Residents of East Los Angeles questioned whether or not the route was secured as a speculative move with plans to sell the right-of-way to another company. As it turned out, local citizens were right to be suspicious. The Salt Lake City line was delayed for twelve years before a conglomerate led by Montana copper king and former senator William Andrews Clark and backed by J. P. Morgan and Edward Harriman took over and completed the route in 1905.[31] In the interim, a local railway used the tracks to connect Pasadena, Glendale, downtown Los Angeles, and the port at San Pedro.

Taking a name that signaled its connection to the terminus at the ocean port, the Terminal Railway invested in facilities located in the Flats.[32] The company constructed a major station with an office and associated storage and maintenance facilities at First Street and the river. In laying track through the Flats, the railway encountered environmental and legal obstacles, as well as political ones, including complaints from property holders. In 1890 the city council debated whether the railway would be allowed to run track within the stipulated three-hundred-foot width of the designated riverbed or blast out a rock outcropping in the riverbed near Macy Street. The Terminal Railway Company sought clarification, as specifics would be necessary to meet the city's requirement to construct the east side river levee. Meanwhile, forty-seven property owners, living on the river's east bank between First and Macy Streets, signed a petition urging the council not to artificially narrow the riverbed. The specific location in question was the very same area around Anderson, Myers, Rio, and Shenandoah Streets where the first houses had been built in the Flats, near the point of the earliest and most important river crossings.[33] Ultimately, the railway opted to divert the route slightly to the east side of the rock ledge.[34] The river's eastern edge was legally and physically redefined (see figure 5.3).

Improvements to bridges and transportation linked the two sides of the river and catalyzed new real estate development in the heights. On August 3, 1889, the *Los Angeles Times* trumpeted the arrival of a new bridge to span the river at First Street with "a magnificent double track" for a cable railway line. Replacing an earlier wooden structure, the bridge was one of three river crossings in the Flats, along with the Macy Street and Aliso Street Bridges. One problem with the river bridges was that heavy winter rains in the mountains sent torrents of water through the city, ripping apart structures and severing connections between east and west. The new bridge promised a stronger

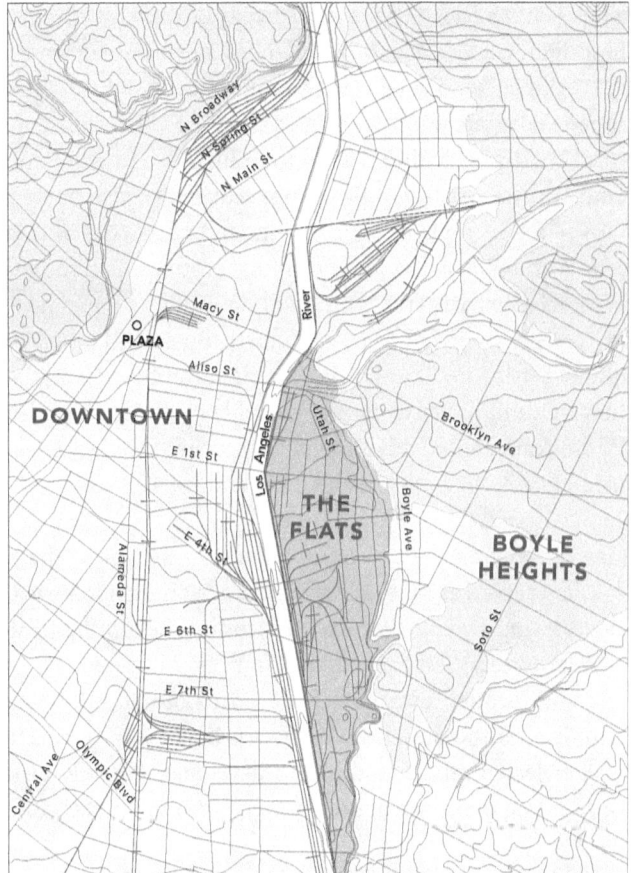

FIGURE 5.3. The Southern Pacific and Santa Fe Railroads took control of the west side of the Los Angeles River, while the Terminal (later Salt Lake and Los Angeles) Railway ran along the east side. Railroad company officials, city leaders, and engineers oversaw the straightening of the river's path, levee building, and the construction and replacement of river bridges and viaducts between 1880 and 1940 (compare to figure 5.2). Map by Julie Kim.

physical structure as well as a new symbolic link to the growing communities of the Eastside. Downtown and Boyle Heights were said to be "bound together by bands of steel that cannot be broken." The new bridge and transit line shortened travel times, lessened flood hazards and delays, and provided a more dependable route over the river.[35] Passing by the new Terminal Depot in the Flats, Angelenos riding the cable railway quickly and safely ascended the bluff. To the north they might catch a glimpse of Charles Stern's Model Winery and Distillery or the Southern California Packing Company, two companies in the Flats that processed locally grown grapes and oranges into products for export.

Prominent Los Angeles families had lived on the Eastside for decades. Among these families was the Missouri-born businessman and politician William H. Workman, who would later become mayor of Los Angeles. Workman developed real estate in Boyle Heights and the Flats, overseeing the transition from primarily agricultural uses to industrial and residential ones.[36] His own family history reflects this change. His uncle, also named William Workman, owned Rancho la Puente. Moving to Los Angeles with his family at age fifteen, Workman's father and one of his brothers died soon thereafter. Aided by his uncle, he partnered with his other brother to operate a saddlery business. In 1867, he married Maria Elizabeth Boyle and when his father-in-law, Andrew Boyle, died in 1871, he inherited the Boyle family's land, including vineyards and orchards on the east side of the river and a house on the bluffs.[37] Workman subdivided the land, procured the water supply, and named Boyle Heights in honor of his wife and his deceased father-in-law in 1876.

Workman became one of the most influential figures in the city.[38] His father-in-law had served as a city councilor, and Workman followed him into local politics, serving several terms on the council beginning in 1872. Over his long political career, Workman held the offices of city councilor, city treasurer, park commissioner, member of the board of education, and mayor. According to historian Rockwell D. Hunt, Workman was, in addition to his influence as an elected official and a land developer, "directly instrumental in securing or aiding the construction of every steam railroad which entered Los Angeles."[39]

From the old adobes and new Victorian homes on the river bluffs, Workman would have looked out over the river's floodplain toward downtown and Bunker Hill. After 1889, new bridges and transit services encouraged hundreds more residents to move to Boyle Heights, purchasing cottages and bungalows in the neighborhood. Below the bluffs, dozens of new homes went up in the Flats.

Celebrating the Flats

On Saturday, November 9, 1901, a crowd gathered near the Los Angeles River to celebrate with "free beer, claret, and sandwiches." The unlikely occasion was the opening of a new storm drain, but as former mayor Workman explained, the engineering work had significance for the future of East Los Angeles. The storm waters that flowed through the canyon known as the Arroyo de los Posas were diverted away from the Flats and sent directly into the Los Angeles River, making new land available for development. As he addressed the assembled citizens, he read aloud from a special resolution and thanked the city council. The project, he predicted, would lead to increased property values and increased tax revenues for the city. The *Los Angeles Times* explained that with the capacity to "carry a stream fifty feet wide by five feet deep," the project transformed a large area of "worthless" land into an area of opportunity.[40]

The Arroyo de los Posas carried a meandering stream through its narrow canyon, a small part of an immense natural hydrological system that drained the mountains above Los Angeles. Often dry, it could gush with mountain runoff and rainfall during storms. The creek bed formed a natural border at the northern edge of Brooklyn Heights (see figure 5.2). In the decade preceding Workman's proclamation, East Los Angeles residents had expressed alarm at the contents of the arroyo's flow. Upstream, the county hospital was discharging large amounts of sewage, passing it through "a straining box charged with quicklime" before dumping it into the ravine.[41] The treatment was not adequate, and the hospital's purification mechanism allowed large amounts of "filth" to be released. With a low, sporadic flow, the arroyo became polluted with stagnant water and medical refuse. Neighborhood residents demanded action from the county and the city when several typhoid cases were linked to the arroyo's polluted waters. The seven-hundred-foot-long concrete drain installed in 1901 channeled the stream's flow under Macy Street and toward the river.[42]

As Workman indicated in his speech, real estate development in the river's bottomlands required new pipes, storm drains, culverts, sewers, and levees. Los Angeles experienced repeated flooding in late nineteenth and early twentieth centuries, and floods inundated the Flats with water and washed over the zanjas.[43] Angelenos' collective decision to build on the floodplain was explained by culture as much as capitalism, as ignorance of the local environment combined with the seeming unpredictability of flooding and a fragmented governmental structure, creating a "hazardous metropolis."[44] Historian Norman Klein argues that tourist promotion and city boosterism served to "camouflage" environmental problems in the city, including the "filthy" state and insufficient volume of the city's freshwater supply in the 1890s and the frequency of winter floods and summer droughts.[45]

The zanjas supplied water for the pueblo of Los Angeles for decades, but the system could not meet the needs of the mid-nineteenth-century city, and they fell out of use. Their demise accompanied the city's increased demands for water supply, sewerage, and flood control. This phenomenon coincided with arrival of the railroads, the beginnings of industrial development around the river, and the development of Boyle Heights as a streetcar suburb. In 1876, for example, Los Angeles banned washing and bathing in the zanjas at the same time it required households to connect to a sewer and to install traps to prevent the escape of sewer gases.[46] Due to the city's infrequent but occasionally torrential winter rainfalls, city engineers oversaw the construction of a separate, rather than combined, sanitary sewer system.[47] The construction of the Los Angeles Aqueduct brought Owens Valley water to the city after 1913. Massive engineering works for storm water management and flood control followed, a process that unfolded over more than six decades.

But while the zanjas no longer served as essential city infrastructure, they continued to play a role in the evolution of lowland real estate. In the Flats, two branches of zanja #7 had provided water, diverted from the Los Angeles River upstream. As speculators subdivided their lands, the zanja's course became a legal property boundary. Just as Workman anticipated, builders and manufacturers quickly developed the reclaimed flats, first in the vicinity of the Terminal Depot and then spreading toward the bluffs on the east. But while the newly available land increased in value, providing income for city coffers, it also became deeply problematic for municipal boosters and urban reformers who sought to establish the modern image of the city of Los Angeles. The presence of poor people, especially Mexicans, and the possibility of immigrant districts, like those seen in big cities of the Northeast, alarmed them. The conflict pitted one group of business and civic interests against another. As labor recruiters pulled new workers into the city and region, property subdividers, land developers, and manufacturing interests profited. Meanwhile, Anglo elites kept promoting the city as a paradise that had no poverty, no disease, and no crowded tenement districts. Places like the Flats ran counter to that myth.

The Molokans

Beginning in 1904, Molokan refugees, pacifist orthodox Christians from the Caucasus fleeing religious persecution and conscription into Russia's war with Japan, began arriving in Los Angeles. Initially settling on the west side of the river, in the downtown area, they did not stay there long, instead purchasing homes across the river on Clarence and Utah Streets in the Flats.[48] Joining Mexicans, Armenians, African Americans, Japanese, Chinese, and Syrians on the rapidly growing Eastside, they attracted specific notice from Anglo newspaper reporters. The *Herald* described how the sight of women's colored headscarves and men's long beards and the sound of their language made the newcomers stand out on city streets, calling them "a source of curiosity" and labeling their presence as "a bit of medieval color" in modern Los Angeles.[49]

Religious practice and faithful adherence to the sect's beliefs defined community life. Many Molokan community members were related by blood or marriage, and intermarriage with other groups was prohibited.[50] The group called themselves Spiritual Christians, not Molokans, a label meaning "milk drinkers" that originated in the 1700s and was ascribed to them by the government of Tambov.[51] The Los Angeles press followed this old practice and referred to them as Molokans in the newspapers. Journalists treated them as a curiosity and focused on their foreignness as civic and charitable leaders debated their potential for assimilation into American society. The Molokans received assistance from several local groups, according to newspaper reports, including a Captain P. A. Demens, the president and general manager of an association of mill owners, who helped pay for their transportation to Los Angeles, and the Bethlehem Institute, which was located at Vignes Street. Captain Demens is likely the wealthy Russian American railroad magnate and founder of Saint Petersburg, Florida, born Pyotr Alexeyevich Dementyev, who had initiated a national campaign help religious refugees from Russia come to the US.[52]

Sometimes called the Lower East Side of Los Angeles, Boyle Heights and the Flats became a multiethnic, multicultural, and multireligious community in the early twentieth century.[53] According to historian Ricardo Romo, "The Molokans settled originally in the 'Flats' because they found low-cost homes and lots, an environment that readily accepted the foreign born, and easy access to the various industries and commercial shops immediately east of downtown."[54] The Molokans arrived in the Flats just as the Salt Lake Railroad line was completed; soon thereafter, landowners closer to the bluff subdivided their property into blocks and lots, the city opened new streets, and contractors built sewers to drain the lowland.

In February 1905, the *Los Angeles Times* announced the arrival of a "Fresh Batch of Molokans," reporting that "another company of the Russian peasants of the sect of 'Molokans' or Russian Quakers, arrived yesterday in Los Angeles. They were received with a warm welcome by the colony located east of the Los Angeles River, in 'the flats' of the Ninth Ward."[55] The reporter noted that more Molokans were on the way, forecasted that the "colony" in the Flats would soon reach four hundred people, and predicted that the newcomers would become "industrious, frugal, and desirable citizens." The *Times* expressed both amazement at the exotic newcomers, calling the community "one of America's strangest foreign colonies" and disapproval at the apparent unwillingness of the strangers to assimilate to American ways of living.[56] By 1907, only a few years after the Molokans' arrival, contestation over the representation of this urban lowland neighborhood was underway, a phenomenon that architectural historian Sophie Spalding has described as the "contradictory perceptions" of the Flats.[57] As in urban lowland communities in other cities in the US, newspaper reporters repeatedly connected foreignness, ethnicity, and neighborhood. "The Flats," a term which newspaper reporters used frequently after 1905, linked low social status and low-lying land.

The neighborhood's immigrant population grew as speculators and home owners built more small houses in the Flats. One *Los Angeles Times* writer commented in 1907 that the Molokans were in the middle of "a slum sandwich": "On one side of them are the Mexicans; on another are Armenians."[58] This awkward and disparaging metaphor suggested that the mere presence of people from any of the three "foreign" groups could be considered an indication of slum conditions and that neighborhood spatial organization neatly aligned with ethnicity/race or national origin. Both of these underlying assumptions caricatured the neighborhood and its people. The author continued, "It is a picturesque place—a place which is not of America. But it is picturesque only so far as people go. In itself it is a squalid region, a huddle of flat houses and tenements, of squat cottages and dilapidated huts."[59] The reality was more complex, as the neighborhood had a wide mix of housing sizes and types, from the earliest homes on Anderson Street to multifamily "housing courts" and brand-new bungalows.

In November 1906, the city council approved a comprehensive sewer plan for the neighborhood, catalyzing the construction of hundreds of homes plus stores, factories, and apartment houses in the Flats.[60] A wholesale bakery operated by the Pacific Coast Biscuit Company opened at the corner of First and Pecan, several blocks from the riverfront. The Utah Street Public School opened at North Utah Street and Kearney. Small single-family dwellings on narrow building lots filled many blocks, such as the one bounded by East First Street, South Utah, East Third Street, and South Clarence.[61] On that block alone, one could find forty-four one-story dwellings, one one-story duplex, and one two-story apartment building. However, on the similarly sized block immediately to the east, approximately of the same size and number of building lots, only seventeen dwellings stood, all of them one-story single-family houses. A greater number of apartment buildings could be found closer to the river and the former Terminal station, which was now called the Salt Lake Depot (see figure 1.5). Other uses in the neighborhood included greenhouses, on Clarence Street, closer to the bluffs, a feed and fuel lot on East First Street, a blacksmith's shop, and several small repair shops. Several Molokan families constructed small bathhouses and outdoor bread ovens in the yards behind their houses. They did not build a large church, instead choosing to meet for religious services in existing buildings adapted for the purpose or in community members' homes.

As the Flats community grew in size and population, journalists and city leaders expressed greater concern. In 1907, the *Times* estimated that five

THE FLATS 127

thousand Molokans lived east of the river and declared the foreigners were too detached and not American enough, and potentially a threat to the health of the city. The Molokans were reportedly suspicious of doctors, they performed marriages without obtaining city licenses, and they gave birth to babies without registering them with birth certificates. Their communal mode of living was considered to be out of step with American ways of life. The *Times* editorialized, "They had come here to avoid laws. They had come here to form colonies on a socialistic basis where statutes would not bother them."[62] While they were a "simple, harmless people, hardworking and thrifty," their religious practices, housekeeping, and living conditions were a "never-ceasing source of wonder" to health officials who visited them in their homes.[63]

The Progressives

Progressive urban reformers took a particular interest in the Flats in the first decade of the twentieth century. Two figures in particular became very involved in the community, interacting directly with residents and serving as public intermediaries by speaking about the neighborhood and its people to the press and public officials. Reverend Dr. Dana W. Bartlett was a preacher, settlement house worker, and reform advocate associated with the downtown charity the Bethlehem Institute. Johanna von Wagner was a housing inspector and civic leader who was recruited from New York to become the director of the city's housing commission.

Originally from Maine, Bartlett studied theology at Yale University and the University of Chicago and worked in settlement houses in Saint Louis and Salt Lake City before arriving in Los Angeles in 1896.[64] He lived at Bethlehem Institute, a Congregationalist settlement east of downtown and near the Los Angeles River at Ducommun and Vignes Streets, with his wife and five daughters. The institute ran a men's hotel with seventy rooms for permanent boarders, renting them for between one dollar and $1.25 per week, and received praise for its home-like atmosphere.[65] They served meals and coffee, provided clothing, ran a library, sponsored events, and offered bathing in a swimming pool. They provided medical services, English language classes, job placement, and counseling.[66]

In 1907, Bartlett authored an urban reform treatise called *The Better City* in which he blended City Beautiful ideals, an optimistic outlook, and faith in the Protestant work ethic with a settlement house worker's attention to poverty and social problems. Bartlett argued that the city had no slums due to its excellent streetcar system, which provided access to the countryside, and building pattern of cottages and yards. But Bartlett also described how the "coming

INSPECTOR DOING EDUCATIONAL WORK.
A Kindly Use of the "Arm of the Law" Far More Effective Than Force.

FIGURE 5.4. Johanna von Wagner in the Flats. Source: *Report of the Housing Commission*, 1908–10.

of Russians in large numbers to this city caused for a time much unhealthy crowding, with several families in houses intended for only one family."[67] He added that Angelenos should not worry too much, however, as the problem was temporary, and "these people are industrious and thrifty, and are now buying houses of their own."[68]

Bartlett began visiting and providing aid to the refugees as soon as they arrived. In a 1905 interview in the *Herald*, he explained that the Bethlehem Institute had the ability and the responsibility to assist these foreign newcomers. He added that the institute was committed to helping them and others like them as part of its mission.[69] He emphasized that the institution's work aimed to turn the newcomers into productive American citizens. He rejected the label missionary and added that "we are of these people, not sent 'down' to them at all."[70]

Nurse Johanna von Wagner began her career in Yonkers, New York, as part of an initiative organized by the Woman's Civic League (see figure 5.4). Within a few years, the board of health appointed her tenement house inspector.[71] She traveled the country speaking to city groups and inspired a movement to hire women in the roles of visiting nurses and social workers who met with families living in tenements. A few years before a group of Los Angeles reformers recruited von Wagner to move to the city, the *Times* profiled her in an admiring biographical sketch, noting that she was particularly adept at building trust with her clients, a trait that contributed to her "distinctive value... as distinguished from that of men inspectors."[72] Overcrowded living conditions and infant mortality placed high on the list of concerns articulated by these reformers, as did concerns about immoral behavior and the need to Americanize immigrants. Von Wagner believed that housekeeping lessons for girls and young women would improve society, and she argued that higher wages would also improve living standards. Von Wagner spoke four languages, including Russian, and she arrived in Los Angeles to begin work with the housing commission in December 1908.[73]

Bartlett and von Wagner each participated in housing reform under the auspices of the housing commission of Los Angeles. This effort rested upon years of political activism and campaigning by Los Angeles Progressives who sought to eradicate corruption in city government, rationalize and improve the delivery of municipal services, and build the future city. The Municipal League of Los Angeles, founded in 1902 by Charles Dwight Willard, served as a federation for the coordination of multiple groups' efforts.[74] One such group, the Los Angeles College Settlement Association (LACSA), led a movement to focus Progressives' attention on housing reform.[75] The group's first published report detailed their history and activities while also drawing attention to the old adobe houses of Sonoratown and the problems of overcrowding and disease.[76] Women's social and civic organizations, such as the Friday Morning Club and the Young Women's Christian Association, also hosted talks by outside experts, including Jacob Riis, on the problems of poverty and the need for municipal health and sanitation campaigns.

These groups initiated a comprehensive survey and inspection effort in poor immigrant districts in Los Angeles. They began with a publicity campaign that encouraged newspaper articles based on visits to poor immigrant districts of the city, arranging for a reporter to accompany a public health nurse from LACSA. The reformers affiliated with the LACSA and the Municipal League had a special focus on the built environment, especially types of dwellings that they believed fostered overcrowding, disease, and social problems. While they were interested in boardinghouses, tenements, shacks, and cottages, they zeroed in on house courts: groups of very small, one-story, and usually wooden houses arranged around a common courtyard or open space, often with a shared pump for accessing freshwater. These types of building arrangements, they argued, fostered disease by subjecting their uneducated and unaware occupants to dangerous environmental conditions.

In older sections of the city, landlords had subdivided interior spaces of adobe houses with new partition walls, creating small rooms for rent, and they constructed additional small wooden rooms in courtyards. As housing became more scarce and in higher demand with the increased arrival of newcomers to Los Angeles, people looked for living accommodations anywhere they could find them. In some cases, property owners converted horse stalls into living quarters. In other areas, property owners constructed, or allowed tenants to construct, new house courts by grouping small wooden structures together around a common courtyard.

The house courts soon became notorious. Housing conditions in Los Angeles and house courts in particular received national attention when, in a December 1905 essay titled "Courts of Sonoratown" published in *Charities and Commons*, LACSA founding member Bessie Stoddart referred to the courts as "nests of humanity" and "human hives."[77] While praising the gentle manners and friendliness of Mexican families, she also fretted that many young Italian and Russian men had recently moved into Sonoratown. Observing that many neighborhood homes had dirt floors, she highlighted the presence of dirt, mud, and dampness, and the possibility for disease. Photographs illustrated the article, including one captioned "The court yards of the old Adobes are honey-combed with narrow alleys and dilapidated shacks." She blamed landlords for the situation and argued for building codes to prevent overcrowding in house courts, proposing to require access to "enough air," provide "proper plumbing," and limit lot coverage.[78]

Reformers' efforts to publicize the problem and to pressure the city's mayor eventually succeeded, as charity-led reform efforts joined with municipal interventions in public health and housing policy. In February 1906, the Municipal League pushed Mayor Owen C. McAleer to establish a housing commission of five appointed members.[79] The new municipal body, they explained, would be charged with eliminating slums. In an open letter published by the *Los Angeles Times*, they presented their case, and claimed that disease from house courts represented a special threat to the city as a whole. Mayor McAleer agreed and, shortly thereafter, appointed the first commissioners: building superintendent J. J. Backus, physician Titan Coffey, attorney Elizabeth L. Kenney, LACSA member Mary Adair Veeder, and Reverend William Horace Day.[80] The league maintained a close relationship with commissioners and exerted a powerful influence. They provided staff, resources, and offices to the commission as well.[81]

Not all elected officials agreed with the commission's charge, however. Councilman Arthur D. Houghton from the Sixth Ward criticized it as an insult to poor people—a way for the rich to demean and make fun. He urged his constituents to refuse any inspector the right of entry, advising them to use a revolver if necessary.[82] His objection, however, did not persuade any of his fellow council members, and the commission commenced its work.

Whereas earlier efforts highlighted Sonoratown, the commission immediately began investigating the Flats. Reporting on the new commission in late February 1906, a *Times* journalist cited "the Flats" as the foremost example of the "ugly slums" under investigation. Commission members reportedly "made discoveries of conditions which they declare are a disgrace to a civilized community."[83] Later that year, the *Times* reported "War on the Slums Now to Be Pressed," featuring photographs of houses crowded together on Utah Street and in the vicinity of the Salt Lake Railroad at Aliso Street, a backyard cesspool, and a crowd of people.[84] The captions below the photographs explained that the commission's "crusade" focused on city neighborhoods beset with "filth, disease and immorality," directing particular attention to the disgraceful and menacing "Aliso-Utah street section." But, the article concluded, there was hope. The interventions of charity-affiliated reformers and social service professionals would make a difference. The Women's Civic Federation, it noted, encouraged Utah Street residents to plant beans, sunflowers, and other plants and awarded prizes for the best kept gardens, bringing beauty and improving health in the area. The Progressives' effort took hold, the new commission was at work, and the press was making the public aware of the problems of slums.

Dark Spots in the Land of Sunshine

Sunshine provided a powerful environmental metaphor for Los Angeles reformers: it represented health, agricultural productivity, light, visibility, clarity of purpose, and a bright optimism about the future.[85] Reformers dramatized urban problems by juxtaposing sunshine and darkness, especially when calling attention to slums and unsanitary housing conditions. Some reformers even rhetorically framed the region's healthy climate and good living as a possible impediment to reform. Stoddart, for example, wrote that "if it were not for the friendly Southern sun destroying disease germs the day long, frequent epidemics would draw attention to these places of incubation, and better sanitation and housing laws would be enacted."[86] The shadowy recesses of the city needed to be exposed, they contended.

House courts came to considered "dark spots" in the "land of sunshine."[87] Historian Natalia Molina has described how the statements, reports, and surveys produced by city health officers, beginning in 1879, shaped a related medical discourse about Chinese, Japanese, and Mexican communities in

Los Angeles.[88] The public health department explicitly linked unhealthiness to social and cultural behaviors considered to be un-American. Housing inspectors evaluated the quality of housekeeping during home visits. Public health and housing inspection reports often included an explicit sociospatial reference: low, wet, and dark spaces occupied by "foreign" people threatened the city as a whole.

Reformers faced a new challenge when Democrat Arthur C. Harper won a four-person race to succeed the retiring Mayor McAleer in December 1906. Reportedly surrounded by men of dubious character and a "rabble" who exerted powerful influence, Harper's candidacy had raised doubts at the *Times* about his suitability for office. He soon became known as one of the city's most corrupt elected officials.[89] Nevertheless, Harper played along with the Progressives. In late July or early August 1907, he visited the Eighth and Ninth Wards, including the Flats. "I have lived here a long time, and I thought I knew Los Angeles. But I found conditions last week that have given me the nightmare ever since." He added: "At one place I found a father, mother and ten children occupying a single room; there they eat, sleep and perform all family functions, living amidst conditions that would cause animals to sicken and die. There is too much land and too much sunshine here for us to tolerate such a state for human beings."[90] New surveys of housing conditions and field investigations of slum conditions were ordered.

Reformers planned to build upon an existing organizational structure for public health services in which the city employed and LACSA supervised a visiting nurse in the city's old town district. The city health officer already had the power to inspect private property and order landlords to clean up any unsanitary or unsafe conditions. The newly appointed housing commission exercised its power to conduct its own inspections and field surveys, tabulate data, research tenement reform in eastern cities, produce architectural drawings and plans, create maps, and publicize its findings. It was limited, however, in its ability to force changes: it did not have the ability to compel repairs, mandate upgrades, evict residents, or seize property.[91] As the commission went about its work, questions of its relationship to health authorities and its powers continued to surface.

The housing commission expanded to seven members, as the initial five members, who included "a minister, a physician, an attorney, an architect, and a settlement worker," were joined by a businessman and a plumber.[92] The commission became a city department in October 1908.[93] It employed two inspectors: one male, Nicholas Quierolo, and one female, von Wagner, who had sole responsibility for the house courts. A woman, many middle-class housing reformers believed, would be uniquely able to influence other women to improve domestic cleanliness.[94]

The commission was greatly impressed by reformer Jacob Riis's visits to Los Angeles, and their early reports twice quote Riis saying that he had seen larger slums in other cities, but none were worse than those in Los Angeles. Indeed, the commission's first report in 1906 opens as follows: "GENTLEMEN: A great surprise awaited the City Fathers and other residents of the Land of Sunshine, good air and abundant space in the discovery of congested slum conditions, as bad, according to Jacob Riis, if not as extensive, as anything to be found in New York City."[95]

The commission singled out Mexican residential districts as a specific area of concern, and they used a derogatory term for Mexican laborers, "cholo," to racialize their descriptions of the urban landscape. The 1908 commission report noted that "certain districts have become very much crowded by the increase in population among the Cholos, Russians, Italians, and Japanese."[96] Coffey, the commission's chairperson, showed a map of "Cholo and Mexican districts" within the city during a November 1906 presentation to the board of health.[97] The commission's reports refer to both "cholo courts" and "house courts," taking special care to locate the places where male Mexican workers lived. For example, the commission reported in 1908: "We found, also the peculiar growth of the Cholo court, which apparently was an outlet for the congested Mexican population, and enabled them to secure a site for a home at very small expense. The life in these courts is typical of the life among the peons of Mexico. Here we found filth and squalor on every hand. Miserably constructed houses, made of scrap sheet iron, old lagging and sections of dry goods boxes, were huddle together without any attempt at proper construction or order."[98]

The city adopted a legal definition of "house court" in the housing ordinance of 1907. A house court was "a parcel or area of land on which are grouped three or more habitations used or designed to be used for occupancy by families and upon which parcel or area the vacant or unoccupied portion thereof surrounding or abutting on said habitations is used or intended to be used in common by the inhabitants thereof."[99] The ordinance required owners to submit plans specifying materials, configuration, and details about sewerage and water supply; it mandated drainage and prohibited dirt floors; it required windows, regulated ceiling heights, and limited lot coverage to 70 percent. It set a standard for the number of toilets and water-supply hydrants per resident. The board of public works and board of health were charged with implementation, not the police or the housing commission itself. After receiving a notice of violation, property owners who did not comply could be subject to misdemeanor charges and fines or jail time. The ordinance applied to both existing and proposed courts, and the board closed hundreds of them, rendering several thousand residents homeless. Many of them built or moved into new shacks and other modest structures on vacant lots or in backyards.

The triangular block bounded by Anderson, Utah, and Kearney Streets provided a good example of the variety of housing conditions and the environmental characteristics of the house courts (see figure 5.5). Roughly bisected by the rear lot lines of houses facing Anderson or Utah Streets, the two sides developed quite differently. On the Anderson Street side, small single-family houses, one per lot, faced toward the depot, warehouses, and river. On the Utah Street side, multiple structures, smaller in size, crowded together on many of the lots. As noted above, the dividing line between these two areas follows the former path of zanja #7. Property owners and city engineers redeployed the old irrigation ditch as a drainage swale in the late nineteenth and early twentieth century, and builders erected these shacks and shanties on some of the most marginal and environmentally hazardous land within the Flats. In an era when land clearance and building construction, river levees, sewers, bridges, and road and railway grading projects were reshaping the terrain, housing for the poor and for immigrants filled in the cracks in the urban fabric.

In *The Better City* Bartlett made a distinction between the Molokan and Mexican communities in the Flats. He singled out Utah Street as the location of the worst crowding in Los Angeles, reporting that "those Mexicans ... were brought in from Mexico to work on the trolley lines. The land ... was divided into tiny lots which were rented for one or two dollars a month. On each of these lots was built a shack of hammered-out cans, old boxes, or burlap, with no yard space nor sanitary appliances of any sort. The toilets were of earth, and were used in common."[100] A report from the housing commission called out "Utah street court" in the Flats as an example of the worst conditions in the city. Inspectors counted between four hundred and five hundred men, women, and children living in sixty-eight small houses with seven water faucets and eight toilets in an area one-third the size of "a city square."[101] The board of health expressed concern that the house courts were places where "disease spawned in overcrowded rooms, including tuberculosis, cholera, typhus, and pneumonia."[102]

The Utah Street court was demolished, and the response from some landlords was immediate.[103] "In several instances," Bartlett wrote, "the landlords, rather than submit to the expense of renovating the houses and repairing the

FIGURE 5.5. Shanties on Utah Street, 1906. Note the contrast with surrounding housing types. The rear lot line in the block between Anderson and Utah Streets traces the same path as the former zanja #7. Map by Clelie Fielding.

courts, have evicted their tenants. This is especially true on Utah Street, where nearly all the courts were cleaned out."[104]

A few business and civic leaders proposed to build new model house courts, an effort endorsed by the *Times*.[105] The Pacific Electric, the Southern Pacific, and the Salt Lake railway companies built a few such projects. Immigrants, especially Mexicans, continued to draw particular attention, as evidenced by the commission's 1909 report: "Already difficult problems of overcrowding and unsanitary conditions have existed in Los Angeles, a city of homes and open spaces, too long to make their solution easy. With the coming of every carload of colonists, our task increases. The foreign population has grown incredibly in the last two or three years. Do uptown people know that we have about four thousand Russian peasants, two thousand Slavs, and a large number of Italians, Japanese, Chinese, Syrians, not to mention the original Mexicans, the rapidly increasing colored population and other elements of a cosmopolitan whole?"[106] From this perspective, which was commonly shared among elected officials and city leaders, the racial character of Los Angeles as a white American city was at risk. Housing officials echoed white supremacist concerns about the city's demographic composition, and used data gathering, field inspections, report writing, and testimony to precisely locate the presence of nonwhites in the environment and to associate their living environments and housing conditions with their race or foreignness.

This rhetoric drew upon decades of public health surveying and reporting. Reformers focused on cleanliness in domestic environments, connecting the interiors of homes with the urban landscape as a whole. For example, the commission's 1909 report notes: "Sanitation in daily life is the preventative medicine of the future. Dirt is the greatest enemy in private and municipal housekeeping and to rid the homes and streets of this deadly enemy is the problem of all Boards of Health and Housing Commissions."[107] The report identified home visits as the way to teach immigrant women about proper health and sanitation through instruction in American cultural practices. It related the "American" management of the home to the broader goals of urban planning and the making of a better city. In the 1909 report, a series of proposed measures, most of which the commission had no power to implement, included raising the standard of living for "the workingman," eliminating "wretched habitations," building new housing, and regular inspections.[108] The commission's 1910 report continued in a similar vein, warning of the threat of epidemic disease and fire posed by "the lowest form" of housing: "the dry goods box shack and the gunny-sack, tin-can tent house, often set on the bare ground, and so primitive in type that the original cave dwellers possessed at least a more water-tight roof and greater protection from heat and cold, winter floods and flies." Interspersed "with a better class of small houses in similar groups, in the heart of the city, as well as in the river bed and on the outskirts, [the] 'House Courts.' [were] so filled with humanity, dirt and disease, as to threaten epidemic; others were fairly clean, but fire traps."[109]

The housing commission's work continued through the early 1910s. The Flats became known as a slum and was stigmatized as a place for recent immigrants. But while the house courts elicited an immediate response, provoking eviction and dispersal, a great deal of other building was also going on, including the construction of dozens of small single-family houses, duplexes, apartment buildings, and stores. The housing commission and newspaper reporters had given the neighborhood a single, broad label, but the focus on the house courts, along with the fact that the city adopted an ordinance specifically about that housing type, dominated the reformers' and surveyors' attention.[110] New residents in the Flats came seeking work, with many laborers brought in to fill the needs of a rapidly expanding city. Many others sought and found religious freedom and new opportunities.

By 1910 the population of Los Angeles reached 310,198. After a major flood in February 1914, the city and county of Los Angeles began a massive infrastructure project that permanently transformed the bottomlands, bluffs, and gulches near the Los Angeles River. Flood control engineers channelized the river, confining it to a concrete channel that was ultimately more than fifty miles in length. While sewerage, drainage, infrastructure development, and housing construction gave the Flats a more developed urban landscape, other "instant communities" spawned by the railroads "in undeveloped areas" continued to spring up.[111] Modest single-family houses and tiny cottages appeared in the city's gulches and arroyos, and many Mexican families purchased these homes on installment plans. One such area near Fickett Street became known as Fickett Hollow.[112]

Russian Town

By the time of World War I, the Molokan community was well established in the Flats. Although the Flats continued to be multiethnic and multireligious, a home to many Catholics as well as Spiritual Christians, Angelenos often referred to the neighborhood as Russian Town. According to a study penned by a sociology student at the University of Southern California named Lillian Sokoloff, the Molokans frequently owned their own homes, furnished them sparsely, and rented out spare rooms to boarders.[113] Many men worked in lumberyards prior to the war, then became shipbuilders, while young women tended to work in laundries, a few girls worked in a candy factory on Utah Street, boys sold newspapers in the downtown, and older women tended to work in fruit canneries or do housework.[114] Sokoloff, herself a Russian immigrant who worked at the Utah Street School for the previous four years, noted that about four hundred of the one thousand elementary school students were Russian.[115]

Progressive reformers developed a special connection with the Utah Street School, using it as an organizing point for a variety of initiatives including a free day nursery, programs that taught housekeeping skills, provided public health services, and attempted to inculcate American values and standards of living.[116] Mrs. E. B. Mapel, chair of the Home Economics Department of the Los Angeles Federation of the California Congress of Mothers, reported that children from a few months old up to kindergarten attended the nursery, which saw an average of sixteen to twenty-five children per day.[117]

Other programs included Russian language and cultural instruction as part of a literacy program, and an after-school and evening program included a playground supervised by an attendant, and a YWCA-affiliated "International Institute" clubhouse on Utah Street.[118] The Catholic Church established an outreach ministry in the Flats in 1925, supported by Saint Mary's, the first parish church in Boyle Heights, constructed in 1897. The effort led to the founding of Dolores Mission Church in the neighborhood, which obtained its own building in 1945.

Despite the focus on Americanization in many of these programs, Sokoloff reported that of the fifty families she interviewed not a single community member had yet become an American citizen, citing the sect's opposition to war and militarism as a primary reason.[119] Younger people, in contrast, were "rapidly becoming Americanized."[120] Many community members, she noted, did not plan to stay in Los Angeles permanently, and fewer new arrivals were purchasing homes. Concluding her study, Sokoloff praised the courage and perseverance of the Molokans.

By 1920 the Flats community featured a main street for shopping and gathering (East First), transit connections to Boyle Heights and downtown, the Utah Street Public School, several Molokan places of worship, and a diverse community of several thousand people (see figure 5.6). Whereas many of the parents in the community had recently immigrated to the US, with each passing year the number of children born in the city continued to grow. A short stretch of North Gless Street provides a snapshot. The nine-member Castro family lived at 135: Jesus (age twenty-three), Maria (age twenty), three children, and two grandparents. While most family members were born in Mexico, the two younger children were both born in California. The Castros reported to census taker Charles Ewing that they had immigrated to the US in 1917. A few doors down at 129 North Gless lived the nine-member Hopraff family: Nick (age thirty-one), Mary (age twenty-six), five children, and two grandparents. The Russian-born older family members immigrated to the US in 1907, while all five children were born in California.[121]

The Flats neighborhood was also becoming more industrial, especially in the blocks closest to the railroad tracks and the river (see figure 5.7). A major reason was zoning. Los Angeles adopted land use zoning, the nation's first such ordinance, in 1908. Amended and modified many times, it developed into a "comprehensive" system that was in place citywide by 1925. The city's

FIGURE 5.6. A commercial street in the Flats, likely East First Street. Photograph by Mae Thilo, circa 1930. Source: Pauline V. Young, *The Pilgrims of Russian Town*.

FIGURE 5.7. North-facing aerial view showing the Los Angeles River through downtown, circa 1925. The Macy, Aliso, and First Street Bridges connected downtown and the Flats neighborhood (*center right*). Security Pacific Collection, Los Angeles Public Library.

maps designated the area of the Flats closest to the river as Zone E, for heavy industry "without restriction . . . provided [it] is not prohibited by law or ordinance," while the rest of the neighborhood was marked as Zone D for "light industry." The line separating them ran along lot line behind Utah Street, corresponding to old zanja #7.[122] Industrial development brought additional odors, smoke, noise, and danger. Bigger, bulkier buildings located closer together further separated neighborhood residents from the river.

In 1932, sociologist Pauline V. Young authored a major study of the Molokan community in the Flats of Los Angeles. Published by the University of Chicago Press, *The Pilgrims of Russian Town: The Community of Spiritual Christian Jumpers in America* included an introduction by Robert Park. Young focused on the religious and social practices of the community, particularly the questions of interest to sociologists: customs and practices in immigrant communities, social integration and disintegration, conflict, and assimilation. Young portrayed the community in positive terms, and the study is filled with detailed descriptions of the environmental character of the Flats in the early 1930s.[123] She vividly described land uses and sensory experiences, revealing the expansion of industrial activity throughout the neighborhood.

> The atmosphere of The Flats is heavy. Factories, warehouses, small industrial plants of all kinds and description, contribute their share of pungent smells. Feed, fuel, and livery stables, a wholesale drug company, a co-operative bakery, a firecracker factory, a granite-works establishment, a creamery, a garment-manufacturing concern, are some of the varied types of industrial establishments which hem in the district to the north, south, and east, while the railroads define the west boundaries. Noisy engines, clanking over a maze of tracks, puffing steam in spirals, and emitting volumes of black smoke, spread a pall over the region.[124]

The influence of the Chicago school was evident: the Flats, Young writes, is located in a zone of "transition," and the Molokans are just one of many groups that have "invaded the district" like new plants in an ecosystem while the "most prosperous and active of the early American residents have moved away."[125] To outsiders, the Flats had a distinct reputation as an immigrant neighborhood, where one might encounter people with "Old World" customs and styles of dress in an environment of factory smoke and railroad noise. To residents, the neighborhood was home.

By the 1930s, Mexicans were the largest immigrant group in Los Angeles. In the Flats and in Boyle Heights, people spoke Spanish, Russian, Armenian, Japanese, and many other languages. A 1934 story in the *Los Angeles Times* described how the International Institute in Boyle Heights had reached 26,460 people from fifty-nine nations in the previous year.[126] Boyle Heights had also become a center of the Jewish community. In 1920, twenty thousand Jews lived in Los Angeles, and although immigration restrictions meant fewer European Jews entered the US as immigrants, migration within the US led the area's Jewish population to grow to seventy thousand by 1930.[127] During the same period, the Mexican population of Los Angeles grew from five thousand in 1910 to thirty thousand in 1920 to "at least 90,000 by 1930."[128]

An ambitious program of bridge building strengthened connections between the downtown and the Eastside, but the massive scale of the new engineering works further isolated the neighborhood. Between 1909 and 1938, the city constructed fourteen new reinforced concrete arch bridges linking the two sides of the river, including four in the Flats. Two of them bypassed the lowland streets entirely, soaring high above the neighborhood to connect downtown Los Angeles directly to the bluffs at Boyle Heights.[129] The new Spanish baroque–influenced Macy Street Bridge, which was completed in 1924, spanned 1,240 feet. Replacing the 1889 structure, the city completed the 1,300-foot-long First Street Viaduct in 1929. Two years later the city replaced the last remaining wooden bridge in the downtown area, opening the Gothic revival style Fourth Street Viaduct. The structure stretched 1,890 feet. Finally, in 1932, the Sixth Street Viaduct opened, the last and the longest of the monumental bridges. Designed with streamline moderne architectural elements and steel arches, it reached 3,546 feet, at that time the longest viaduct of its kind in the world.

Two major Los Angeles River floods, in January 1934 and March 1938, lent a sense of urgency to flood control projects. Singer Woody Guthrie penned the song about the 1934 event called "Los Angeles New Year's Flood." Eighty-seven people died in the March 1938 flood. These disasters brought national attention to the city and its river, leading Congress to authorize immediate additional funds in the amount of $25 million.[130] By the end of the decade, a concrete channel directed the river's path through downtown, extending as far south as Olympic Boulevard, about a mile downstream from the Flats.[131]

The Flats was a busy, thriving urban neighborhood in the 1930s. The commercial district along First Street in the Flats, Young noted, was occupied by "grimy store buildings; a variety of small Mexican and Armenian cafes . . . [and] a row of confectionary shops, soft-drink parlors, [and] pool halls, where young men congregate and talk local politics."[132] Frances Camareno, who grew up in the Flats and attended Utah Street School during the 1930s, described how her family moved to the area because "most of the people my father knew from Zacatecas moved there, and from Durango, so they all knew each other."[133] When flood of 1933 hit, river water came "right up to the floorboards" of her house. For residents, life in the Flats offered connections between people based on personal relationships and a shared cultural and linguistic heritage, and, for all the neighborhood's challenges, it also fostered a sense of place.

Aliso Village and Pico Gardens

In 1934, during one of the worst years of the Great Depression, a group of architects proposed that Utah Street in the Flats become the site of one of the city's first public housing projects under a Public Works Administration (PWA) program. This group of prominent architects, which included Lloyd Wright, son of Frank Lloyd Wright, assembled "a group in 1934 to obtain—if not create—a commission for the Utah Street housing project under the PWA program."[134] They called themselves the Utah Street Architects Association. The project never materialized, but according to architect Dana Cuff, anticipation of the possible seizure of property using eminent domain led to further deterioration in the neighborhood, as property owners delayed investments and repairs.[135] Three Los Angeles sites were identified for possible PWA projects, but none were built.[136]

When Congress adopted the Housing Act of 1937, Los Angeles planners and architects were ready. Established the following year, the Housing Authority of the City of Los Angeles (HACLA) would oversee the program. Of the ten sites selected for slum clearance and public housing complexes in the city, three were in East Los Angeles and three were in South Central.[137] The *Los Angeles Times* reported that the total undertaking would cost $15 million and yield 3,748 "new dwelling units."[138] Nine of the original ten proposed sites gained quick approval, but in May 1941 a councilman from West Los Angeles opposed a site in the Sawtelle section of his district.[139] Fickett Hollow was briefly considered as an alternate, but then rejected in favor of a site in the Flats. The neighborhood became the only area in the city with two major public housing projects: Aliso Village, located north of First Street, and Pico Gardens, south of Fourth Street.[140] A combined land area of fifty-six acres would be cleared for the two projects.[141]

The demolition of the Flats under the "slum clearance" provisions of the federal housing legislation did not require voter approval through a referendum. Instead, with federal money and authority to implement the project, and a federal provision requiring "equivalent elimination," HACLA planners quickly identified "slums" rather than undeveloped land. For three decades, the newspapers and municipal reports had characterized the Flats as a dark spot and a menace to the city. For city officials it was a logical choice.

THE FLATS 143

Demolition was preceded by a site-specific appraisal process and intensive photographic survey between October and December of 1940. As Cuff shows in *The Provisional City*, these photographs and accompanying field notes provide visual evidence of existing conditions, but also reveal volumes about the surveyors' prejudices and working assumptions. Supervisor Charles Shattuck was president of the California Real Estate Association and the National Association of Real Estate Boards as well as an official at the Home Owners Loan Corporation (HOLC).[142] His team compiled page after page of negative appraisal records and disparaging comments about residents' homes.

Pico Gardens (241 units on fourteen acres) and Aliso Village (685 units on forty-two acres) opened on August 1 and December 1, 1942, respectively (see figure 5.8).[143] Designed as modernist superblocks, these new communities featured garden apartments: light-colored, two- and three-story concrete buildings arranged in a composition designed to maximize open space and provide a dramatic visual contrast with the projects' surroundings. When the

FIGURE 5.8. View south over the Flats from the air, 1949. Two public housing projects are visible between the 101 Freeway and the concrete channel of the Los Angeles River: Aliso Village in the foreground (*lower right*) and Pico Gardens in the distance (*middle left*). Spence Air Photos, Security Pacific Collection, Los Angeles Public Library.

projects were leased up, more than 1,500 people lived at Pico Gardens and nearly four thousand people at Aliso Village.[144] On the east side of the Flats, transportation engineers routed the Hollywood Freeway along the edge of bluffs, creating a new barrier between the neighborhood and Boyle Heights. After World War II, a new round of federal public housing funds became available with the US Housing Act of 1949.[145] In the Flats, HACLA expanded Aliso Village, adding another 336 units in two blocks south of First Street.[146]

HACLA redefined multiple blocks with varied housing conditions and a mixed residential-industrial-commercial character as two project sites: areas to demolish and rebuild. While earlier studies recommended rehabilitation and small-scale rebuilding, the new federal public housing program imagined a major architectural statement. Cuff argues that the New Deal housing program was based in utopian ideals, fueled by modernist architectural zeal, and implemented with "totalitarian" thoroughness.[147] She emphasizes the rhetorical significance of the slum label, derived from stereotypical notions and racist fears about concentrated areas of immigrant settlement. The marginalization and stigmatization of the neighborhood over several decades, and the cultural association between low status and low elevation in the name the Flats, made that designation seem natural. Viewed from a landscape perspective, the neighborhood site was already defined according to its geological structure. The social and cultural understanding of that urban place brought together topography, class, and foreign "race." The cultural prejudice of public health officials and housing inspectors was reflected in the actions of planners and architects, too.

From "Green Bottomlands" to "the Flats"

Urban renewal, public housing, and freeway construction projects displaced thousands of people, demolished hundreds of homes and businesses, and erected new barriers that separated the community. After 1940, the Molokans left Los Angeles and moved in smaller groups to other communities in Southern California and across the US. Many Jewish families relocated from Boyle Heights to the Fairfax district, the Westside, and other parts of Los Angeles, as did Armenians who resettled in Hollywood and Glendale after the 1950s. Many Mexicans and Mexican Americans stayed in Boyle Heights and the Eastside. Angelenos of Mexican heritage or born in Mexico became the single largest ethnic group in the city, living in every neighborhood across the city. By 2010, more than 3.5 million Mexicans and Mexican Americans lived in Los Angeles County.[148] In Boyle Heights, Latinos comprised approximately 94 percent of the nearly one hundred thousand residents in 2010. Although the newspapers and city reports rarely used the phrase the Flats, many neighborhood residents still called the neighborhood by its old name.

"The Flats" described landform and a pattern of topographical segregation that was rooted in class but closely tied to nationality and race. In an era when census takers as well as newspaper writers and public health officials understood racial categories and specifically whiteness to exclude foreign elements, Anglos in positions of power in the city interpreted the presence of Molokan Russians, Mexicans, Armenians, and other immigrant groups in the Flats as a cause for multiple concerns, including disease and fire risk, but also the possibility that nonwhites would dilute racial purity, damage American culture, and mar the city's image.

In early twentieth-century Los Angeles, the house court and stereotypes about Mexican laborers and immigrants dominated public discourse about poverty and the environment. Reformers positioned themselves as uniquely able to document and describe these conditions, while inspectors sought to teach poor lowland-living foreigners better housekeeping skills, sanitary practices, and American cultural ways. Practices that deviated from Anglo norms, such as bread baking in backyard ovens or gathering and socializing in outdoor spaces, suggested to some that neighborhood residents were not worthy of citizenship and did not belong in Los Angeles.

The stigma of lowlands, partially rooted in nineteenth-century disease theory, would be reframed around nationality: race as miasma. Combined with the public attention aroused by newspaper reporters about the unfamiliar customs and religious practices of the Spiritual Christians (Molokans), who also called the Flats home, the neighborhood developed a reputation for an exotic foreignness. Sometimes using the name Russian Town or Russian Flats, observers tried to differentiate it as a separate community. But as the 1920 census shows and oral histories recount, Mexicans and Russians and many other groups of people lived together, often on the same block, in the neighborhood.

The power of the stigma that was attached to the built environment would eventually shift away from topography and toward race and housing types and forms. By the 1970s, public housing itself became stigmatized and marginalized. In 1998, through the HOPE VI redevelopment program, HACLA received a federal grant to demolish Aliso Village's 685 apartment units. They were replaced by 377 rental units and ninety-three homes for sale at a cost of $76 million. The new "mixed-income" neighborhood development, its name Pueblo del Sol inadvertently alluding to the historical use of sunshine as an environmental metaphor in slum housing campaigns, opened in 2003.[149]

6

Landscapes of Poverty and Power

Urban Americans created bottoms, hollows, and flats during the 1870s. They took advantage of property law, engineering techniques, and house-building practices to produce them. Then, for seven decades, they re-created them, through physical interventions and cultural constructions. Engineers built sewer systems, physicians inspected environmental conditions, journalists reinforced reputations, and experts planned new cities. Urban lowland neighborhoods like Harlem Flats, Black Bottom, Swede Hollow, and the Flats were not static. Between the 1870s and 1940s, they were constantly in flux and actively contested.

Once established, urban lowland neighborhoods collected poor and working-class residents and concentrated them in "low" environments, provoking fear and concern in American urban society. That paradox of containment and contamination, pejoratively expressed in phrases like "black bottom" and "foreign colony," was multifaceted. For lowland residents, it meant that engineering, health, housing, and planning efforts in their neighborhoods typically were not for their benefit. Rather, these interventions, from railroad and bridge building in the 1870s and 1880s to zoning and redlining in the 1920s and 1930s, were designed to control the urban landscape to the benefit of the middle and upper classes, landowners, and wealthy private interests.

Water problems, city building challenges, and "slum" reputations defined urban lowland neighborhoods of the late nineteenth and early twentieth centuries. Residents of Harlem Flats, Black Bottom, Swede Hollow, and the Flats confronted social and environmental challenges exacerbated by disease fears, racism, and xenophobia. Cultural bias informed the purportedly objective analyses of urban problems and neighborhood spaces published in

Progressive Era government reports, charitable organization studies, and planning documents. In debates over what to do about urban lowland neighborhoods, waged in the pages of the newspapers and meetings of local government officials, advocates for containment and proponents of reform often shared negative views about people who lived in "low" environments. Simultaneously, city officials, landowners, and developers wrestled with varying ideas of nature in the city as they imagined the urban lowland and its ecological and economic purposes within the city framework. Bottoms, hollows, and flats were both intellectual constructs and real places.

The phenomenon of urban lowland neighborhoods was an important phase in the history of poverty and environment in the American city. Stark economic and social contrasts were visible in the landscape as poverty and wealth were proximate. In Saint Paul, for example, brewer Theodore Hamm looked down from his mansion on workers' houses below in Swede Hollow during the 1880s (see figures 1.6, 1.7, and 4.4). Landforms expressed economic and social difference. Bottoms, hollows, and flats showed power in the landscape.

That visual separation and "natural" view of poverty in the urban landscape would slowly be replaced by a systematic program for creating and enforcing new modes of separation. Beginning in the 1890s, landowners, realtors, and developers created race-restrictive covenants to segregate newly planned residential communities as white only. In the 1910s and 1920s, planners and lawyers invented ways to establish class-segregated enclaves of exclusively single-family homes with yards through zoning ordinances. During the 1930s, federal government officials, mortgage lenders, and insurers steered capital investments toward restricted communities. Then, the accelerated suburbanization of the American metropolis after 1940 produced a dispersed horizontal landscape where segregation by race and class was inscribed over larger territories and enforced by new legal mechanisms and planning approaches.

The story of bottoms, hollows, and flats puts the constructed nature of these metropolitan landscape changes in historical perspective. Not only did modes of transportation change, from streetcars to automobiles, and their associated residential forms, from streetcar suburbs to automobile-dependent suburbs, but the overlay of the city on landform shifted. A more horizontal, segregated, and dispersed metropolitan landscape made urban lowland neighborhoods unnecessary. The history of bottoms, hollows, and flats tells historians and city planners about the places where poor and working-class people lived, the way that environmental problems and poverty were connected by urban Americans, and how racism and xenophobia were deeply embedded in public debates and the purportedly scientific expertise that informed American city planning. Comparing the cases of Harlem Flats, Black Bottom, Swede Hollow, and the Flats shows important commonalities and differences in how it happened.

Comparing Cases: Disease

Following the Nashville cholera epidemic of 1873, Presbyterian minister and health officer John Berrien Lindsley of Nashville urged his colleagues to learn the lessons of New York City's failures in sanitary reform. He advised that Nashville "avoid the mistake formerly made in New York and other places of neglecting the indications of nature," particularly the problems of springs and "fissures" in the city's geology where groundwater reached the surface.[1] He sounded just like Egbert Viele, the well-known New York City civil engineer and sanitary reformer who repeatedly criticized the filling of Harlem Flats. Cholera was the most feared of the lowland-associated diseases, and it was understood as an environmental problem. Cholera outbreaks or the fear of them were common to Harlem Flats, Black Bottom, and Swede Hollow.

Deadly cholera outbreaks hit New York City in 1832, 1849, and 1866. The 1866 *Report of the Metropolitan Board of Health* referred to Harlem Flats as "the most insalubrious district in the Twelfth Ward," an area "almost wholly rural in character" that nonetheless suffered from "a high death-rate from preventable causes." The report noted that "nearly 2,500 of the poor people" who lived there dwelled "in shanties and other temporary huts" and residents were "every year vexed by malarial fevers and fatal diarrhoeas."[2] During the 1860s, 1870s, and 1880s, journalists sensationalized these reports, pejoratively labeling shantytowns on the west side, in Central Park, and around Harlem Flats as "cholera and fever nests" (see figure 2.2).[3] Through the chaotic and malodorous decade-long filling of Harlem Flats, newspaper journalists invoked the risks presented by a miasmatic environment to push for a solution to the problem. Ironically, the original justification for landfilling was to combat disease. The act passed by the New York State Legislature in 1871 specifically stipulated that "whenever it shall appear necessary for the protection of the public health," land that was certified by the city sanitary inspector was to be drained.

More than a thousand people died in the Nashville epidemic of 1873. In the aftermath, physicians identified Wilson's Spring and its creek as a specific problem area, mapping the geographic location of reported deaths using the method first developed by John Snow in London two decades earlier. It was during the 1870s that newspaper reports began to refer to the neighborhood as Black Bottom (previously known as the Sixth Ward) reinforcing and amplifying existing cultural associations between low and unsanitary living environments, the presence of poor African Americans, and disease risk. In contrast to sanitary surveys and medical reports in the other cases, such as New York City's Citizens' Association report of 1865, Nashville physicians consistently identified statistics on sickness and death by race. This tendency was not unique to morbidity studies. City directories, newspaper stories, and even fire insurance maps labeled black residents, "colored" churches and schools, and "Negro tenements." However, in a southern city permeated by racial divisions, where African American residents were constantly under threat of racialized violence, this tendency in official record keeping highlights how race and racism informed purportedly neutral medical-scientific analysis. Indeed, physicians and journalists often blamed African Americans for disease, attributing it to poor diet, immoral behavior, poor housekeeping, or a number of other factors.

Physicians and health officers like Lindsley communicated with colleagues across the country, read the newspapers and medical literature, and gathered together at meetings and conferences of sanitary reform and public health associations. In the public health debates in Saint Paul in the 1880s, even after germ theory had made significant advances scientifically, the perceived risk of low-lying settlements within cities and the presence of poor people and immigrants alarmed physicians and elected officials. Dr. Henry F. Hoyt's 1884 study of sanitary conditions recommended resident removal. Fortunately, Saint Paul avoided a cholera outbreak, and the city government did not raze Swede Hollow in the 1880s; however, the notion that the urban lowland neighborhoods could be a threat to the whole city continued for decades, well into the twentieth century.

Only in Los Angeles, where the Flats did not become a large residential neighborhood until after 1905, was cholera not a factor. Nevertheless, disease fears and disease associations played a major role there as well. Public health officers and housing inspectors focused on issues of overcrowding, housekeeping practices, and immigrant assimilation to the American way of life in a sustained campaign of identifying, labeling, and inspecting "foreign colonies" and "dark spots" within the city. In the first three decades of the twentieth century, health and housing officials linked these xenophobic fears to the built environment and urban landscape. They targeted immigrant communities of Chinese, Mexican, Italian, Armenian, and Japanese residents located around the Los Angeles River and the city industrial areas and in the railroad-adjacent settlements built in the city's arroyos, gulches, and flats.

An outbreak of bubonic plague in 1924, the last instance of its kind in any American city, seemed to confirm these fears. Originating on the west side

FIGURE 6.1. A member of a government-contracted wrecking crew poses with children on Utah Street. The men were hired to demolish buildings and spray chemicals to combat an outbreak of the bubonic plague. The crews unleashed a wave of destruction on the homes of Mexican American families living in river-adjacent communities of working-class housing. The Flats, Los Angeles, 1924. Collection of the Bancroft Library.

of the river near the Plaza, it killed thirty people over a two-week period. Homes in the Flats were inspected, photographed, and treated with chemicals (see figure 6.1). A rapid response to quarantine the sick and eradicate rats, the vector for the disease, successfully quelled its spread, but at a high cost for working-class Mexican residents. Public health authorities demolished shacks on Utah Street and other streets in districts around the Los Angeles River, "over a thousand shacks and old houses in total" without providing any monetary compensation or replacement housing.[4] Historian William Deverell characterized it as "widespread and ferocious" destruction and "urban renewal as urban clearcutting." The outbreak and its response had long-term consequences. Historian Stephanie Lewthwaite argues that the episode led to a shift away from "sanitizing and rehabilitating" toward a campaign to "eradicate Mexican spaces and remove Mexican tenants."[5] Disease fears rooted in class, ethnic, and racial bias were never far from the surface of public discourse about poverty and environment in urban lowland neighborhoods.

The public health response and the public debates over waterborne diseases like cholera, informed by miasmatic theory, perpetuated the intellectual construct of the "slum" as a low, wet, and diseased environment. Nineteenth-century sanitary engineers and physicians framed Harlem Flats,

Black Bottom, Swede Hollow, and the Flats as public health problems. The four cases share a common trajectory: creeks identified as urban problems were buried underground. Polluted springs and creeks, unsanitary and inadequate drinking water supply, odors, shoddy landfilling practices, and floods combined with the threat of disease outbreak. Removing water by sewering lowlands and providing public access to a clean water supply decreased morbidity, but it did not rid lowlands of cultural stigma or floods.

Miasmatic disease theory, along with the lag time before widespread public acceptance of germ theory, contributed to the persistent negative reputations of lowland areas, whether they were sites of disease outbreak or not. In the early twentieth century, ethnic and racial prejudice in the survey and analysis of housing conditions perpetuated an environmental-disease discourse and pushed policy makers toward demolition and slum clearance. Americans viewed urban nature through the lenses of class, race, and ethnicity; lowlands were framed as diseased and dangerous environments in multiple ways. Actions to address these supposed dangers repeatedly grappled with the question of containment versus dispersal of lowland residents.

Comparing Cases: Water Problems

Creeks and streams created unpredictability in the urban environment. In the reciprocal exchange between hydrology and geomorphology, the creeks influenced the landform, and the landform influenced the creeks. People living next to one of these creeks (prior to sewer projects) would have witnessed creeks that jumped their banks during a "freshet," backed up during river floods, carried and deposited debris, and fluctuated with tides. The creeks changed paths and reworked the margins where land and water came together.

Harlem Flats was a huge wetland complex where the relationship between land and water shifted daily and where creek, marsh, and river merged together. Black Bottom's urban creek originated in an upland spring in limestone hills. It descended through a small valley to the Cumberland River. In Saint Paul, Phalen Creek traveled a longer stretch, running from upland Lake Phalen down a four-mile path to the Mississippi. In Los Angeles, the now-forgotten urban stream called Arroyo de los Posas carried water down through mountainous terrain and across the Flats before joining the Los Angeles River. Hydrological dynamics varied: tidal changes in a salt marsh in New York; back floods in Nashville; surges in stream flow through a narrow ravine in Saint Paul; and mountain-fed flash floods through arroyos in Los Angeles. Despite the range of conditions, all these sites had serious water and sanitation problems.

The common problem of dumping is seen clearly in Swede Hollow and the Flats. Former Swede Hollow resident Michael Sanchelli recalled that when Hamm's Brewery was "operating at full blast the sewers would be full of sewage" and the minnows in the creek would float to the surface.[6] In Los Angeles, residents of the Flats fought with Los Angeles County Hospital, which expelled medical wastes into the often-dry Arroyo de los Posas in the early twentieth century. Residents demanded a stop to the practice and advocated for new sewer construction in the area. Urban lowland neighborhoods had water problems because they were built on wet, marshy land. The challenges of each physical site were exacerbated by landfilling using garbage; disposal or leakage of human wastes in waterways; dumping of factory wastes; and use of waterways and nearby springs as a freshwater supply for drinking, cooking, washing, and bathing. In both Los Angeles's arid warm climate and Saint Paul's frigid conditions, where spring snowmelt produced seasonal floods, lowland neighborhoods encountered downstream effects of dumping waste in streams.

Sewer construction ranged across a wide time period in these four lowland neighborhoods, from 1872 to 1936. As railroad engineers and road builders constructed embankments, culverts, and drains to facilitate transportation, sanitary engineers tackled the problem of polluted waterways, overflowing streams, and wet ground due to inadequate drainage. Sanitary engineers frequently buried the creeks and streams that ran through these urban neighborhoods. These waterways had attracted people who built houses but also mills and factories that used water, when possible, for power and waste disposal. But while sewer projects displaced residents in the immediate vicinity of the earthmoving and water-moving construction zones, they also created new land for building. Historic circumstances vary, but the development of bottoms, hollows, and flats was generally tied to the uses and abuses of small urban waterways and infrastructural systems for storm water and waste.

Of the four cases, Harlem Creek was first, buried in a sewer by 1872; and Saint Paul's Phalen Creek was last, with sewer construction completed in 1936. Both sewers were enormous: the elliptical concrete sewer pipe needed to contain Phalen Creek was eleven feet high and ten feet eleven inches wide at its widest point, while the 110th Street sewer in Harlem required pipes eight feet wide and twelve feet high to drain a seven-hundred-acre watershed.[7] Sewer projects both precipitated further development in New York and Los Angeles and lagged behind it in Nashville and Saint Paul. The sequence and timing of these events suggests that larger cities exerted a greater ability to summon the massive amounts of capital investment needed to organize such projects, while medium-sized cities, even when experiencing rapid growth and real estate development, weighed political decisions and technology choices within a more constrained fiscal environment. In Saint Paul, it was New Deal funds and job creation benefits during the Depression that changed the political calculus, finally putting Phalen Creek completely underground.

Sewer projects did not end floods. Floods occurred before, during, and after these projects. Nineteenth-century sewer projects were modest compared to the flood control works of the twentieth century, much larger in scale. These engineered systems increased the rate of outflow into rivers and harbors and the faster output tended to increase the height of peak flow during floods. Dikes and levees exacerbated downstream flooding by preventing storage in floodplains. Impervious surfaces in the urban landscape decreased soil infiltration and increased the volume of runoff. Putting urban creeks underground in sewers improved sanitary conditions and public health, but it also created "buried floodplains."[8]

Nashville's Black Bottom has flooded repeatedly.[9] An 1887 *Atlanta Constitution* report was typical in the way it linked poverty and environmental hazard: "hundreds of the wretched poor, who will be driven from their cheap homes in the lowlands, will suffer, if not helped by the citizens."[10] In 1926, displaced African American families took shelter in the Ryman Auditorium and in churches.[11]

In Los Angeles, federally funded and constructed flood control interventions created the infamous and iconic image of a concrete river: an instantly recognizable symbol of the city.[12] Depicted in thousands of movies, commercials, and televisions programs, this highway-for-water became the setting for car chases, murder mysteries, and police dramas. The City of Los Angeles and Los Angeles County began planning this system of engineering interventions on the Los Angeles River following the flood of February 1914, "the catalyst for the creation of the flood control program."[13] "Two disastrous floods," on New Year's Day 1934 and in March 1938, precipitated extensive federal government involvement. The 1938 flood inundated 108,000 acres of land, killed eighty-seven people, and damaged more than $78 million in property in Los Angeles County.[14] Engineers constructed dams and catch basins in mountains, straightened and redirected upland streams, and altered arroyos and washes, resulting in what geographer Blake Gumprecht has termed "51 miles of concrete." The system has prevented flooding in the neighborhood formerly known as the Flats, but at significant cost, eradicating any sense of the natural qualities of the river or its place in the city's pre-twentieth-century history.

Floods reinforced the stigma and marginality of lowland districts. Flood events and flood lands were trapped in a negative symbiosis, a mutually reinforcing bad relationship that was paradoxical and contradictory in its effects.

Floods reinforced negative ideas about place, but also stimulated the desire to rebuild there or remake the area. Floods served as catalysts for new opportunities or incentives to locate in lowlands with cheaper property values following the disaster, and lowlands became a place for newcomers with no other options.

Federally funded engineering projects within cities, implemented by the US Army Corps of Engineers, produced thousands of flood walls, levees, drains, culverts, underground conduits, and dikes. The Flood Control Act of 1936 catalyzed the construction of large-scale projects like dams, upstream reservoirs, retention basins, and spillways.[15] These modern engineering projects were ambitious and expensive efforts to reduce property damage and human injuries and deaths by flood. Geographers, engineers, and planners reframed lowlands as floodplains and proposed new controls and mechanisms for limiting floodplain development.

The modern use of the term "floodplain" dates to the 1930s, when the human impact of floods became an area of scientific research.[16] Floodplains can be defined as areas of land that flood—water in the wrong place—but in terms of natural processes, floodplains can be defined as "natural detention areas for storm water."[17] While the difference may seem subtle, the consequences of ignoring natural hydrological processes have been significant, leading to displacement, destruction, and death in many lowland communities.

Urban lowland neighborhoods manifested many puzzling contradictions: both nature-like and human-constructed, they became a regular and familiar aspect of the urban landscape. These neighborhoods were persistently maligned and neglected, yet subject to targeted actions when municipal leaders found it necessary. By the early twentieth century, the scale of these engineering and planning interventions increased, aided by new technologies of earthmoving, drainage, and flood control. When American engineers and city builders modified nature to mold the city, they reinforced and concentrated inequality to create what historian Matthew Klingle labels an "unnatural ecology of urban poverty." Their actions forged urban boundaries and neighborhood identities that most Americans accepted as normal—a remarkable demonstration of power in the landscape.[18] But they were "unnatural" only in the sense that they were constructed by humans who were intent on profit and control. Urban lowland neighborhoods were natural places because dynamic natural processes of hydrology and geomorphology never disappear from the city; they are continuously interacting with urban systems and built form. The former Black Bottom neighborhood was inundated during the May 2010 Nashville flood, and the former Harlem Flats neighborhood in New York City flooded during Hurricane Sandy in 2012. The fundamentals of lowland hydrology have challenged even the most advanced engineering systems.[19]

Comparing Cases: City Building

The question of how lowlands fit into the city was both a land use issue and a social one. Physical obstacles to urban "progress" included steep slopes and unsuitable soil conditions. When railroad builders encountered wet places or soggy ground, they constructed viaducts or raised beds of ballast for laying track, as seen at Harlem Flats. At Swede Hollow, engineers for the Duluth and Saint Paul Railroad established a passage through the ravine by carving and leveling out a flat section on the western edge, just below the bluff line. Street plans, bridge building, roadwork, culverts, and earthmoving were a few of the techniques employed for organizing, planning, and implementing the human conquest over nature. But while physical "improvements" like Saint Paul's Seventh Street Improvement Arches received significant capital allocations and became major construction projects, housing was considered a matter for the private market or individual initiative. In Saint Paul that led to the construction of private houses on land owned by the city water company. Often a short walk away, and sometimes immediately overlooking a lowland, one might find homes of the wealthy. Rich and poor were separated by topography.

During the late nineteenth century, railroads reinforced these boundaries and edges in several ways: first, seeking gradual grades or flat terrain, the location of track often paralleled waterways, creating corridors; second, railroad lines extended into urban centers and nodes of commercial activity where they linked together river-based transportation, warehouses, factories, stations, and other facilities; and third, freight yards and side tracks frequently located in these same areas. Railroad company decisions by surveyors, engineers, and construction crews from 1870 to 1910 had a lasting impact on the American urban landscape. Lowland neighborhoods were what Mumford called "railroad slums."[20] But, just as with the diversity in geomorphological forms, the spatial arrangement of built forms, including railroad tracks, yards, and buildings, varied from neighborhood to neighborhood and from city to city. Swede Hollow and the Flats were proximate to major rail yards while Harlem Flats and Black Bottom had significant areas of industrial development, but less track in the neighborhood.

During the early twentieth century, suburban builders began using new legal mechanisms to enforce the spatial organization of the city according to race, class, and ethnicity. New suburban developments invoked the healthfulness of elevated sites by including "heights" or "highlands" in subdivision names. After 1920, architectural styles, street layouts, house types, and even nature became strongly linked to socioeconomic homogeneity and racial or ethnic exclusion in the built environment. In particular prejudice against African Americans became institutionalized and systemic in housing markets through race-restrictive covenants, zoning, and redlining. Real estate brokers, planners, and elected officials centered city planning and zoning efforts around the creation and "protection" of neighborhoods of single-family homes with yards.[21] In contrast, the lowlands were typically zoned "unrestricted" or industrial (see figure 6.2).

New York, Nashville, Saint Paul, and Los Angeles enacted zoning ordinances between 1905 and 1933. Los Angeles was the first to adopt zoning, a partial measure oriented toward designation of industrial districts. New York City's 1916 law was the first comprehensive zoning ordinance in the country, Saint Paul adopted zoning in 1922, and Nashville, a relative latecomer compared to other American cities, adopted it in 1933. The process of creating the first zoning maps often involved reserving space for desirable residential areas and industrial zones first, then figuring out the rest.[22] Rental housing and apartment buildings were typically considered incompatible with single-family residential neighborhoods.

When Los Angeles completed a comprehensive zoning plan for the whole city in the 1920s, the residential areas of the Flats received a "light industry" designation, and the railroad-linked manufacturing district east of Anderson Street along the river was designated for "heavy industry."[23] In New York City's East Harlem, on the blocks that covered the former salt marsh and wetland complex, the bulk of the immigrant neighborhood of tenements, small stores, and churches was zoned as "business" while the blocks between First Avenue and the river, and south of Ninety-Ninth Street, between Second Avenue, were zoned "unrestricted." Saint Paul's first zoning ordinance designated all of Swede Hollow and the entire lowland between downtown and Dayton's Bluff as "heavy industry." Curiously the city plan, also adopted in 1922, shows Swede Hollow as future park space on a map of the city. In Nashville, the city zoned most of Black Bottom as "industrial A" for light industrial use.[24] These policies signified an official municipal stance that barely tolerated lowland residents. Planners and developers viewed lowlands as sites for manufacturing and warehousing purposes. Industrial designations promoted factory expansion and pushed out residents through "expulsive zoning": the new codes incentivized redevelopment of residential property.[25]

In the 1920s, zoning's proponents argued that it embodied a modern business approach that favored organizational efficiency and the wise use of

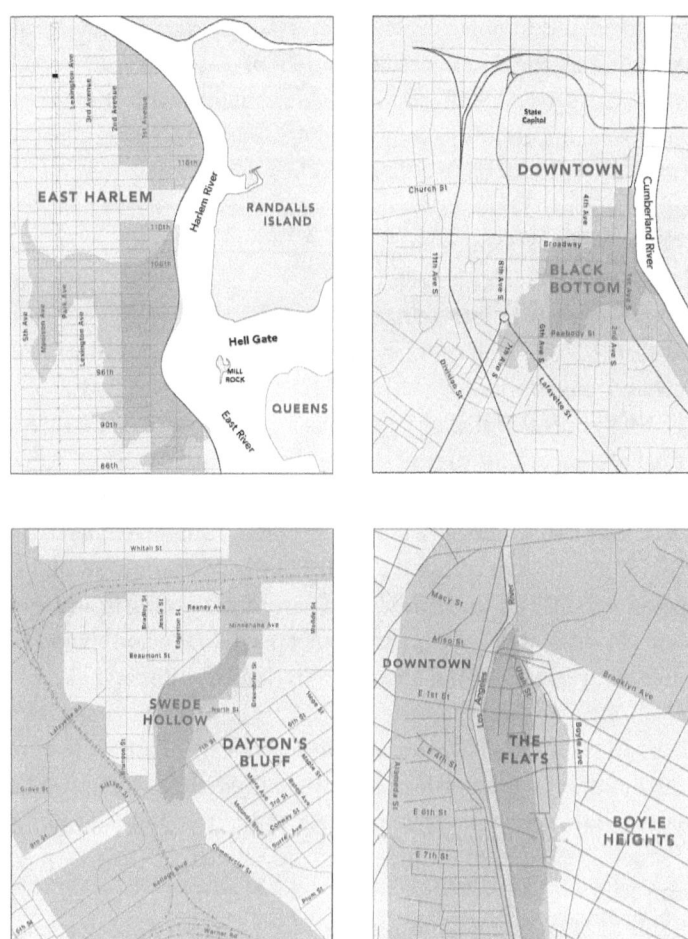

FIGURE 6.2. Areas zoned for industrial use in relation to urban lowland neighborhood boundaries in Harlem Flats (East Harlem), Black Bottom, Swede Hollow, and the Flats, 1920s and 1930s. Map by Julie Kim.

standards and procedures to improve city life.[26] This ostensibly rational and modern framework for regulating the built environment was explicitly biased and unjust: it aimed to solidify patterns of residential segregation by class and race.[27] These municipal policies and legal agreements drew political and cultural support from an emergent ideology of homeownership-as-citizenship along with the social and economic necessity of the automobile and a new type of consumer society.[28] By explicitly directing industrial development toward lowlands, zoning ordinances accelerated residential disinvestment. Mixed residential-industrial districts, common in lowland neighborhoods, were considered undesirable, suspicious, and dangerous. Simultaneously, "exclusionary zoning" codified the establishment of class-segregated residential neighborhoods as a policy objective. In combination with the use of race-restrictive covenants, trends in demography, suburban housing construction, and housing demolition, these policies led to a more segregated city.

During the 1930s, redlining by the federal Home Owners Loan Corporation (HOLC) made explicit use of race and ethnicity, among other variables, to guide investment and risk decisions. New Deal programs "systematically instituted segregation into housing policies," discriminating on the basis of class and race.[29] New Deal mortgage and housing programs identified most urban lowland neighborhoods as "slums." HOLC maps identified all four lowlands as either nonresidential or hazardous for investment (see figure 6.3).

On the Eastside in Los Angeles, where Mexicans and Mexican Americans and Molokan immigrants from Russia lived in the Flats, and Jews, African Americans, Japanese Americans, and many other groups lived in relative harmony, HOLC surveyors expressed alarm. They labeled the Flats and its surroundings area as "D" for undesirable and hazardous, noting in an area report that the neighborhood was a "'melting pot' area, literally honeycombed with diverse and subversive racial elements."[30] In Saint Paul, mapmakers labeled Swede Hollow as "D" and the once-prestigious but declining Dayton's Bluff neighborhood received a "C" rating. In New York City's East Harlem, surveyors marked all the blocks north of Ninety-Sixth Street as hazardous, except a one-block-wide stretch of riverfront area to the east that was not graded because it was industrial, and a one-block-wide stretch of Fifth Avenue to the west, from Ninety-Fifth to 103rd Streets along Central Park, marked "green" for desirable or "first grade." In Nashville, Black Bottom was not graded, and simply considered nonresidential. This omission was a telling reflection of how planners and real estate professionals felt about the nearly one thousand residents who lived there. On all sides of Nashville's downtown, surveyors marked the neighborhoods surrounding downtown as hazardous, including the Watkins Park neighborhood near Fisk University that many African American doctors and academics called home.[31] Statistics, field surveys, and interviews with bank executives and other business leaders contributed to these findings, as did underlying assumptions such as "the proposition that the natural tendency of any area was to decline" due to age and obsolescence.[32]

In some field reports, investigators made explicit reference to lowlands, reflecting commonly held beliefs about bottoms, hollows, and flats. In Chicopee, Massachusetts, for example, one HOLC surveyor described a "low and flat" neighborhood where Polish mill workers lived as "completely flooded in the Spring of 1936." But, the surveyor commented, floods were common

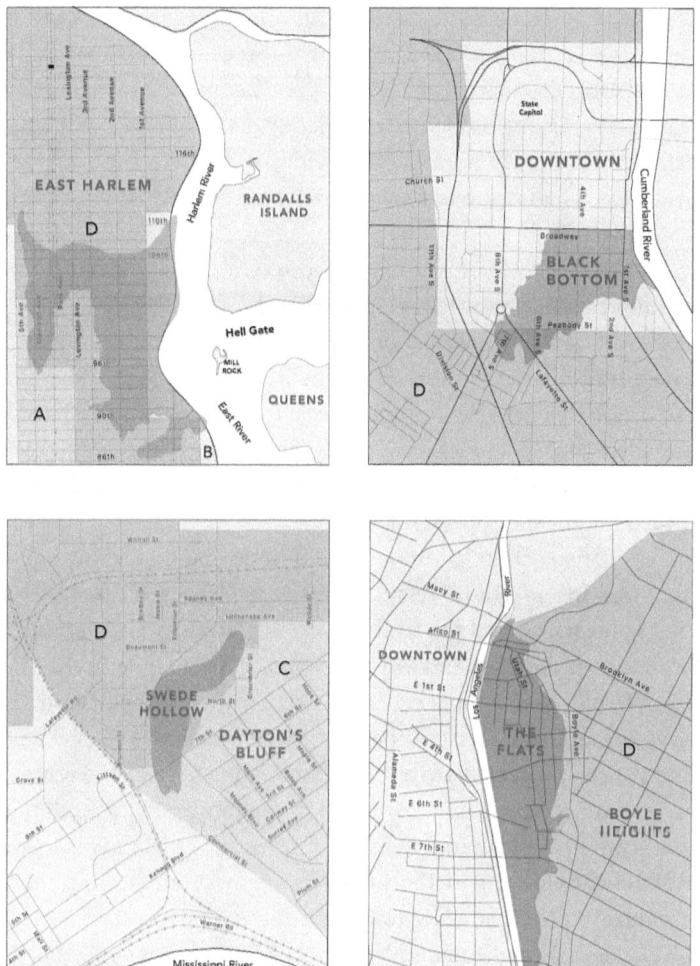

FIGURE 6.3. Redlined areas in relation to urban lowland neighborhood boundaries in Harlem Flats (East Harlem), Black Bottom, Swede Hollow, and the Flats, late 1930s. Map by Julie Kim.

and the "inhabitants . . . do not seem to mind these periodic floods. . . . They seem to prefer to exist under these circumstances and to be left alone in their colony than to move to higher ground at an increased cost to the family wage earners."[33]

By the 1930s, in the midst of a national economic crisis, a new coalition of reformers and business interests began to advocate for redevelopment of urban lowland neighborhoods. The physical condition of the American city deteriorated significantly during the Great Depression, and economic problems strained cities' abilities to fund public services, repair infrastructure, and maintain urban systems. As unemployment soared, Hoovervilles and shantytowns appeared in the cracks and at the margins of the city. Unemployment, hunger, and homelessness forced many poor people into low places in the urban landscape, taking desperately needed shelter anywhere they could find it. Encampments in river bottoms and below bridges symbolized how many more Americans had come to find themselves in low places, often desperate and demoralized.

Race-restrictive covenants, zoning, and redlining accelerated central city deterioration by starving urban neighborhoods of investment.[34] Urban lowland neighborhoods lost population due to restrictions on immigration and widespread housing demolition. In Nashville's Black Bottom, the main destructive factor was expulsive zoning, while in Los Angeles and New York it was slum clearance. The function of lowland districts also shifted with the decline of the railroads, the rise of the private automobile, and the shift to truck-based freight transportation.

Highway construction led to demolition in lowland neighborhoods, and it restructured urban spatial relationships (see figure 6.4). In Los Angeles, highway engineers located the Hollywood (101) Freeway right at the edge of the bluff between the Flats and Boyle Heights. In East Harlem, they inserted East River Drive, later renamed FDR Drive, on the neighborhood's eastern edge, separating residents from the East River waterfront. Nashville's highways and parkways created a circle around the downtown, and a major new roadway and bridge crossing were added in the former Black Bottom neighborhood. Saint Paul planners briefly considered running a highway through Swede Hollow, linking it to the interstate highway at the neighborhood's southern edge, a plan that never reached fruition.

Nationwide, railroad route mileage peaked at just over 250,000 miles in 1916.[35] A steady decline ensued as tracks were abandoned and dismantled in the decades that followed.[36] At the city level, Los Angeles and New York built motorized parkways and highways in the 1930s. Highway engineers identified housing demolition and slum clearance as ancillary benefits of these projects, an approach that historian Raymond Mohl labeled the "two birds" theory.[37] The nexus of railroad-river-lowland housing would be displaced by new nodes centered around truck-accessible and later cargo plane–accessible distribution points. This macroscale economic shift in the organization of commerce in relation to the built environment would lead to deterioration of infrastructure and abandonment of buildings in urban lowlands.

Highways dramatically altered the scale and character of the American metropolis, further facilitated trends of suburbanization and decentralization, and introduced new walls and barriers into the city fabric, separating

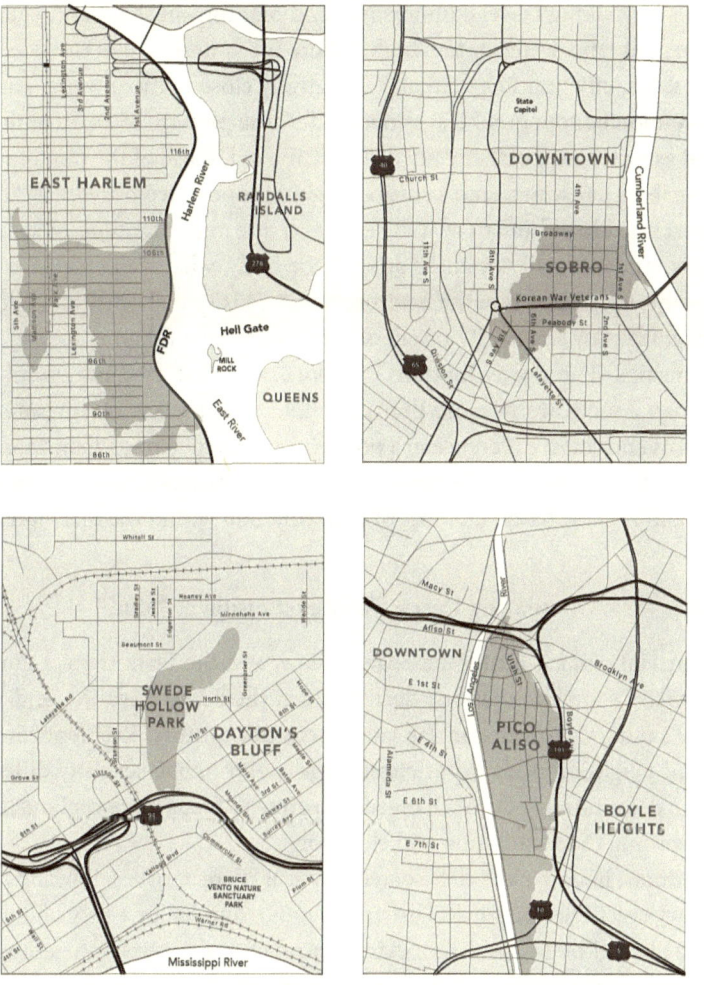

FIGURE 6.4. Highways in and around four former urban lowland neighborhoods, 2019. Map by Julie Kim.

neighborhoods from one another and blocking access to waterfronts. They also provided for new types of vehicle access and personal mobility, and they facilitated new paths and economic flows in the movement of goods to and from cities. Many architects and planners celebrated the new urban parkways and early highways of the 1930s and 1940s as symbols of speed, progress, and modernity.[38] As the automobile became ascendant, urban lowland neighborhoods faded from view.

Wide rivers, tall bluffs, and steep slopes had once informed a city dweller's cognitive map of the urban landscape, dividing one part of the city from another by making travel cumbersome and marking areas of landscape contrast such as land/water or low/high. Before the appearance of the skyscraper in the 1880s, city buildings remained relatively close to the ground, and built form reinforced topographical variation.[39] These physical features of the land served as reference points in city dwellers' mental image of the city, especially in describing late nineteenth-century neighborhoods. Geographer Yi-Fu Tuan has described how human spatial sense and our understanding of space and place is fundamentally oriented around the body, what we perceive as front, back, side, up, or down in the environment.[40] This spatial sense is reflected in the language American city dwellers used to describe urban places and their relationships. The words "bottom," "hollow," and "flat" became useful terms for urban Americans because they communicated a sense of environmental problems and social difference in a powerful spatial metaphor. Commonalities in city building and planning practices in the four cases show how they were made and remade based on ideas of their function within the metropolis.

Comparing Cases: The Redefinition of "Slum"

Harlem Flats, Black Bottom, Swede Hollow, and the Flats share a common trait: their "slum" reputations derived from their low elevation and water-related sanitary problems in the late nineteenth century. Residents of urban lowland neighborhoods experienced stigma and public scrutiny differently, and the definition of "slum" changed over time to focus more on housing and city planning than sanitation and elevation.

Bottoms, hollows, and flats shared physical characteristics: lowlands where tributary creeks flowed toward urban rivers surrounded by a mix of industrial and residential buildings. They shared social characteristics: a heterogeneous combination of poor and working-class residents. And they were unlike other urban neighborhoods, distinctive because of their low elevation and low position in the urban social hierarchy. Bottoms, hollows, and flats vividly illustrated the sanitary problems and economic polarization of urban society in the late nineteenth-century American city.

Yet each urban lowland neighborhood had its own distinct story. Key differences surfaced: when immigrants arrived and what countries they came from, when and why creeks were buried underground in sewers, and relative location within a city. The landscapes varied, too: a salt marsh and tidal inlet, a spring-fed stream valley, a ravine, and river flats below a bluff. Of the four cases, Harlem Flats occupied the largest site at 396 acres. Located in New York City, this lowland was home to farmers, squatters, and shanty dwellers before a massive filling project in the 1870s. It led to a dense grid of tenements housing more than one hundred thousand residents by 1900. At the other extreme, Saint Paul's Swede Hollow was smallest in size, less than one-tenth the area of Harlem Flats. It never developed a paved street system, and residents lived in small houses in a ravine. Swede Hollow's wooden houses, shacks, and cottages were oriented around the curves of Phalen Creek and the contours of the land. Black Bottom in Nashville and the Flats in Los Angeles were 154 acres and 251 acres, respectively.

Perceptions of race and ethnicity also varied. In Nashville, Black Bottom's population included African Americans, foreign-born immigrants, and native-born white migrants from the countryside. During Reconstruction, white southerners responded to emancipation by using the "black bottom" name to label places where African Americans lived as undesirable. In this racialized view of urban space, only so-called low whites lived in neighborhoods labeled as "black." In Los Angeles, the notion of race was constructed around Southern California's Spanish and Mexican past and its Pacific Coast connections to Asia, rather than being based on skin color alone. White "Yankee" newcomers and European immigrants to Los Angeles, who often arrived in Los Angeles only after living in other American cities first, brought racist attitudes with them from other parts of the country. Many African Americans who migrated to Los Angeles came from Texas, Louisiana, and other southern states. They often encountered virulent racism in a new setting. Anglos also combined class prejudice and racial bias toward Mexicans and Mexican Americans in regionally specific ways, such as the derogatory references to "cholo courts" by housing reformers in the early twentieth century.

The word "slum" originated in Britain in the early nineteenth century and entered American English around 1870. Sociologist Irving Allen explains that "*slum* originally meant a small, low, unclean, and possibly wet place of human resort and was later extended to an urban area of such buildings."[41] Historical geographer David Ward states that "the term referred to the most unsanitary and therefore the most poorly drained sections of the city."[42] Slums were also imagined places, a product of what historian Alan Mayne, quoting Charles Dickens, calls the "attraction of repulsion."[43]

The idea of the slum traveled. It traveled back and forth between Britain and the United States, and throughout the English-speaking world. It traveled with Jacob Riis, who presented his lantern-slide lectures on the problem of slums more than two hundred times between 1890 and 1914.[44] It traveled in newspaper reports that described local debates and municipal politics in cities across the US.

In the early twentieth century, Progressive Era reformers and journalists deliberately framed urban lowland neighborhoods as territories occupied by foreign people with foreign customs—strangers who were unfamiliar with American ways of life. Deviations from accepted norms, such as wearing traditional clothing or baking bread in backyard ovens, attracted curiosity, pity, and scorn. Outside observers remarked on the cadence or pitch of foreign languages and caricatured the sights, sounds, and smells of neighborhood places. In the newspapers and statements of public officials, an even harsher depiction of community life in "black bottoms" and other African American neighborhoods also focused on clothing, food, behavior, and speech. Racist language and white supremacist thinking dominated newspaper coverage of poor and working-class black neighborhoods. In all cases, the urban newspaper writers often drew upon stereotypical ideas of "country life" to highlight "uncivilized" or "folk" ways in the city.

The presence of animals in the urban landscape, and inside the home, became a common trope. Saint Paul housing reformer Carol Aronovici, who hoped to reframe public attention around policy and planning approaches to urban poverty, criticized newspaper stories that focused on peculiar anecdotes like the family with "potatoes in the bathtub" or "the goat in the parlor"—activities that were seen as an affront to civilized behavior, suggesting ignorance, ambivalence, or total disregard for the "proper" function of spaces within the home.[45] The goat was particularly common as a symbol, and it makes an appearance in newspaper accounts of Harlem Flats, Black Bottom, and Swede Hollow (see figures 2.2 and 2.3). An exposé featuring photographs of poor residents and goats amidst scenes of dilapidated buildings and urban poverty which ran in the *Nashville Banner* from 1905 noted that "few animals are to be seen in Black Bottom, but the billy goat seems to be something of a favorite."[46]

A romanticized perspective on life in Swede Hollow presents an interesting counterpoint to the associations between country ways of life and "slum" living in cities. The sinuous form of the meandering creek and deep ravine, the views of the cottages afforded from the edges, and the relatively small size and contained shape of the community were rendered as picturesque, even while public health and housing experts judged it to be a sanitary menace. Everything from the arrangement of the cottages to the cultural behaviors of the residents was used as evidence by outside observers to argue that Swede Hollow was (or wasn't) a slum. During the period when Swedish (not Italian) immigrants were the dominant ethnic group in the hollow, the perceived potential for the assimilation of Scandinavians into American society changed with the growing political and economic power of Swedish Americans in the Twin Cities.

The aesthetic fascination with Swede Hollow suggests how this urban landscape came to symbolize immigrant life in the Twin Cities. When artists like Dewey Albinson visited Swede Hollow, it was an Italian community. But visually, and in the continued use of the term Swede Hollow, these artists made an implicit link between the immigrant experience of Swedes and Italians. Swede Hollow became not only a picturesque landscape for painting and a visual opportunity for commentary on class and social reality, but also a symbolic landscape that represented ideas about assimilation and social mobility in American society. The creation of Swede Hollow Park in the early 1970s and the decision to give it that name point to the site's continuing relevance to immigration narratives and historical interpretation. Rather than being "other," poor and working-class Swedish immigrants (and the Italian and Mexican immigrants that lived in Swede Hollow in subsequent decades) became part of the history of the city.

Nevertheless, before it was a park, when poor and working-class people lived there, Swede Hollow was repeatedly labeled a "slum." Aronovici identified Swede Hollow and the Levee neighborhoods along the Mississippi River as examples of "the lowest types of residential districts," and he recommended demolition and comprehensive replanning by the city.[47] Saint Paul's Wilder Charity 1917 study focused on slums as areas of bad housing and proposed condemnation, model housing construction, adoption of building codes, and planning and zoning regulations. Swede Hollow's last dozen or so cottages were condemned and burned to the ground by the city in the mid-twentieth century.

In Los Angeles, racialized disease fears and xenophobic concerns about foreign threats shaped public discourse about urban neighborhoods. Many observers argued that containment remained the best strategy for addressing poverty and social difference in the city. Lowland neighborhoods attracted notice: all poor neighborhoods might have problems with drainage, flooded basements, or waste removal, but the downhill neighborhoods seemed to collect them, and poor foreigners, too. During the campaign against house courts, the *Los Angeles Times* referred to residents in the Flats as "peons" and Mexican children as "little brown specimens" and "brown-bodied babies." Drawing attention to drainage problems, cesspools, and standing stagnant water in the district, the *Times* announced, "the evils that come with a confirmed slum district have come upon us."[48]

Newspaper journalists weren't the only ones using the word "slum." During the 1920s, social scientists and planners took the term in a decidedly different direction. Sociologist Roderick McKenzie took a special interest in the topic of lowlands as slums. In his 1920 thesis, he examined social cohesion and community structure in the Bottoms of Columbus, Ohio, the culmination of his studies at the University of Chicago's Department of Sociology.[49]

It was published as a series of articles in the prestigious *American Journal of Sociology* and issued as a monograph, considered one of the foundational early studies in urban sociology. In 1924 McKenzie wrote in a study of Seattle that "the conservative, law-abiding, civic-minded population elements dwell" on the hilltops, while in the "downtown section and the valleys, which are usually industrial sites" live "a class of people who are not only more mobile but whose mores and attitudes . . . are more vagrant and radical."[50]

Sociologist Nels Anderson wrote in similar terms about Harlem Flats. His 1930 New York University dissertation examined social cohesion and the development of East Harlem. He contended that the slum "always remains the habitat of the socially and economically impotent folks; a retreat for the poverty-ridden and a last resort for the maladjusted." He continued, "Every city has its worst area; its unkempt houses along the tracks, its shanties on the river bottom, its row of houseboats, or, if it is a metropolitan city, its East Side, its West Side or some other area of mediocrity. It is not poverty alone that marks the slum, nor is it the antiquated building. It is in addition an area of social disorganization, low morale and high transiency."[51] Sociologists like McKenzie and Anderson continued the moral judgment and tone of disgust from the old lowland miasma discourse while reorienting it around scholarly investigations of social-behavioral patterns. They ignored environmental and social injustice as they intellectually constructed urban places as miniature social-behavioral "ecosystems." They located slums geographically in low-lying places while at the same time strenuously arguing for a cultural-behavioral definition. They ignored how urban lowland neighborhoods had been intentionally built.

Led by Robert Park, Chicago school sociologists theorized that slums and immigrant districts constituted discrete elements within a comprehensible urban spatial structure. They borrowed concepts of invasion and succession from plant ecology, and the approach would become known variously as "human ecology," "social ecology," or "urban ecology." Using words like "ecosystem" and "ecology" metaphorically, with little attention to nature or environment in the city, they established the modern field of urban sociology.[52] They explained residential segregation by class, race, and ethnic origin with the vague and actor-less notion of the "sifting and sorting" of urban populations. In this view, lowland residents fell to the bottom of the urban social-spatial hierarchy as a normal part of the process of urban differentiation. Their scholarship profoundly influenced ideas about poverty and the urban environment in the twentieth century. Planners, architects, and legislators took their ideas and modified them to create New Deal housing policies.

Housing expert and Harvard Professor James Ford virtually codified the definition of slum in a treatise called *Slums and Housing* in the 1930s. A slum, he wrote, was "a residential area in which the housing is so deteriorated, so substandard or so unwholesome as to be a menace to the health, safety, morality, or welfare of the occupants." This would be repeatedly cited as the authoritative definition of the slum for several decades.[53] Ford discussed the evolution of the term and its applicability to contemporary American urban conditions. Older definitions, he noted, included the sense that these urban areas were foul, low, squalid, and dirty; other observers focused on density, congestion, and overcrowding as key elements. Restricted air flow and darkness (in addition to filth) were key factors for tenement reformers, while isolated "back streets," poverty, and lack of cleanliness and order by residents could sometimes be highlighted. Ford argued that the most important part of a definition of "slum" was the sense that the physical environment was unfit, dangerous, injurious, and poorly arranged. He critiqued the Chicago school and its focus on processes of deterioration and transition in a concentric framework as an oversimplification of the urban pattern. And he rejected Zorbaugh's definition from *The Gold Coast and the Slum* (1929) with its focus on "submerged" and "detached" areas, urban decay, and processes of "disorganization and disintegration" before promulgating his own.

Housing became central to the political and legal definition of "slum." Earlier associations with wet ground and poor drainage faded from view. The housing-planning discourse about slums followed the successes of earlier municipal interventions and projects to improve public health, as Progressive reformers sought to expand the scope of intervention and rid the city of slums. Rather than attacking diseased environments they framed their work as a war on the problems of poor housing and degraded environments. Lowness, in its many textured metaphorical meanings of land, class, and morals, remained a potent rhetorical label and political descriptor. Whereas a nineteenth-century sanitary inspector like New York City's Dr. Farrington drew attention to Harlem Flats as lands submerged by water, and therefore a serious disease concern, social scientists of the early twentieth century began referring to poor neighborhoods as "submerged districts" where the social behavior was considered deviant and communities were lacking in social cohesion.

The US Housing Act of 1937 established a physically based definition of slum that departed from sociologists' focus on a place "beset by internal social dysfunctions."[54] It reflected Ford's emphasis on the potential danger to residents and the city as a whole while also referencing "dilapidation, overcrowding, faulty arrangement or design, lack of ventilation, light or sanitation facilities, or any combination of these factors."[55] It informed administrative procedures that allowed for the legal seizure of private property and the subsequent demolition of people's homes.[56] The 1937 housing act tied new construction to slum clearance through the so-called equivalent elimination clause. It was inserted to assure business interests that the new units would not compete with existing apartments or otherwise disrupt the housing market by mandating demolition while requiring no net increase in units.[57] The act's provisions strongly incentivized local housing authorities to construct new housing projects on the exact same footprint as the site of a demolished slum. It was more pragmatic in obtaining political approval, public support, and land, and it met allowable project construction costs. Paradoxically, this process of site selection often put housing in areas zoned for industry, with few residential amenities. Housing authorities argued that these new public neighborhoods would be bulwarks, protecting place by stabilizing property values in declining areas and preventing the further spread of blight.

Planners relied on maps as evidence: maps that showed zoning, housing conditions, demographic data, investment data, mortgage risks, transportation plans, and "blight" and "slums" became commonplace by 1940. Neighborhood boundaries and identities feature prominently in these visual representations of urban spatial structure. Urbanist Michel Cantal-Dupart critiques the modern tendency in planning to show "problem areas" or "redevelopment zones" on a map, arguing that the potato-like shapes visually communicate a desire to segregate people, analyze urban problems in geographic isolation only within small bounded territories, and ignore the potential for interconnectedness and city-scale urban thinking.[58] His point is an astute one. In the historical example of bottoms, hollows, and flats, the visual representation of urban lowland neighborhoods as industrial zones, as "natural areas" identified by urban sociologists, as "hazardous" districts for residential mortgage investments, as blocks of substandard "slum" housing, as public housing sites, and as redevelopment areas is common and persistent from the 1910s to the 1940s.

In an earlier era, the lowland neighborhood names bottom, hollow, and flat performed a similar function and a conceptualization of poverty and the environment. The cultural practice of marking urban space this way reflected a desire to establish boundaries of social status and to differentiate urban spaces by class, race, and ethnicity. But those boundaries were interpreted in many different ways: as temporary barriers to be surmounted, as impediments to social mobility, or as ghetto walls that imprisoned. Bottoms, hollows, and flats reveal the heterogeneous ways that Americans have imagined the physical spaces of the city in relation to social mobility and economic opportunity. To get up and out of the bottoms was the desire of most lowland residents. For some the lowlands were a temporary home, but others were not so fortunate. Still others moved out, only to return again at a later date.

Meanwhile the "black bottom" name continued to be used well into the twentieth century. Its origins, however, were often obscured. After the "black bottom" also became the name of a wildly popular dance in the 1920s, novelist Zora Neale Hurston, who lived in South Nashville as a young woman, explained that the dance did not get its name "from the black sticky mud on the bottom of the Mississippi river" but instead from "the Jook section of Nashville, Tennessee, around Fourth Avenue."[59] Musicians and dancers appropriated the name that had been used to label the city's Sixth Ward neighborhood as a dangerous and disease-ridden slum in the 1870s, using it for their own purposes. Hurston's analysis suggests how the notoriety of Nashville's Black Bottom in particular is related to the general phenomenon of using the term "black bottom" to mean the black part of town.

The replacement of "black bottom" and similarly derogatory place names by "ghetto" is the result of both changing conditions of urban life for African Americans and the changing meanings of "ghetto" as an intellectual construct. While the American use of "ghetto" is linked to the Chicago school of sociology in the 1920s, it was not in common parlance until the 1940s. Once used to refer to restricted urban spaces where Jews lived, urban sociologists and activists began to use "ghetto" to describe patterns of segregation, poverty, and exclusion experienced by African Americans.[60] In *Ghetto*, sociologist Mitchell Duneier describes how the Nazi ghetto served as a point of comparison when Americans started to use the term to apply to black neighborhoods in the 1940s.[61] The term, Duneier argues, carried a strong sense of political and social critique, now largely forgotten: associating Nazi theories of Aryan supremacy, religious-racial exclusion, and genocide with American society's racism, racial violence, and patterns of urban residential segregation. But just as "ghetto" replaced "black bottom" and similar place names, it too would be redefined over time, losing its political charge.

Bottoms, Hollows, and Flats in the History of the American City

Ideas of neighborhood and community animate the study of the American city. The history of bottoms, hollows, and flats shows why the connection between elevation and social status mattered to late nineteenth- and early twentieth-century Americans. In the social and cultural construction of the lowland neighborhood as a part of the larger whole of the American city, the significance of water-based sanitation problems and disease fears, race and ethnicity, and class are evident. These categories informed how Americans thought about the organization of the city: class was part of the structure of the physical landscape. But places like Black Bottom and Swede Hollow added two additional elements to this formulation. They were particular, even peculiar, types of places where relationships between landforms, water, and city building were visually apparent. They were places for "others" within the social framework of the city where customs, behaviors, spoken language, and community life were considered to be outside the American urban mainstream: countrified, exotic, morally suspect, and un-American.

The landscape element of the social construction of lowland neighborhood spaces is particularly striking. Like the spatial organization of first-, second-, or third-class spaces on a train or inside a railroad station, the nineteenth-century urban landscape was hierarchical. Not only was the American city class segregated, but builders, architects, and engineers molded city form in relation to existing sociospatial patterns. These measures included landfilling, railroad and bridge building, and drain, culvert, and sewer construction. These infrastructure and city building decisions involved both the implementation of new urban systems at the citywide scale, but also distinctly local impacts that resulted from site selection. The Black Bottom case shows that these decisions were often justified, indeed celebrated, as municipal actions that would destroy the homes of poor lowland residents without disrupting the overall spatial hierarchy through large-scale clearance. Municipal neglect in terms of police, fire, or sanitary services in these neighborhoods combined with carefully selected and targeted infrastructure projects to marginalize neighborhoods and the people who lived there.

A topography-and-poverty lens on American urban history in the Gilded Age and Progressive Era also highlights notions of morality, environment, and behavior. From the beginnings of American city planning, environmental determinism has provided the theoretical foundation for physically based urban interventions. Whether it was fueled by disease fears rooted in miasmatic theory or Progressive Era housing reform, the urge to modify the physical environment in order to improve the behavior of city dwellers and to address the problem of urban poverty was persistent. This foundational city planning concept led to some successes: it catalyzed the development of urban parks and modern sanitary systems, for example. But it also melded with racial and ethnic prejudice, white supremacist theories and nativism, and anxieties about class and space. The physical-environmental dimensions of poor neighborhoods are obvious in public debates over bottoms, hollows, and flats in a way that both complements and challenges the traditional focus on tenement districts.

Municipal debates and decisions about when, how, and where to intervene in bottoms, hollows, and flats influenced American culture, housing policy, and city planning for decades. Through zoning, redlining, highway building, and public housing, these neighborhoods were reconstructed within a new metropolitan framework. The social, political, and ecological ramifications continue to influence American city form. Urban lowland neighborhoods today contain the remnants of these past decisions. The echoes reverberate in the present.

EPILOGUE

Lowland Legacies

Bottoms, hollows, and flats virtually disappeared in the mid-twentieth century. By the 1940s, the population of Nashville's Black Bottom declined to fewer than nine hundred people. About 120 people lived in Saint Paul's Swede Hollow in 1940, and only a few dozen by the mid-1950s. In the Flats of Los Angeles and New York City's East Harlem, the wrecking ball and the bulldozer demolished thousands of homes, displacing thousands of families in "slum clearance" projects.

Just as many factors led railroad builders, landowners, and elected officials to create urban lowland neighborhoods, many factors caused their decline. Housing demolition for new highways and urban renewal projects, industrial zoning, demographic changes, and population movements broke up the old neighborhoods. Federal government policies catalyzed dramatic physical and social changes in the urban landscape. Federal immigration restrictions enacted in the 1920s cut off the flow of newcomers to the city.

Local elected officials in partnership with civic and commercial leaders used federal urban renewal and public housing funds to demolish older housing in many low-lying places. Public housing authorities planned and constructed new housing developments in mixed residential-industrial lowland neighborhoods across the US, including in Los Angeles and New York City. Planning and zoning commissioners enacted expulsive zoning measures to push out residents in favor of commercial and industrial development in lowlands. Highway planners used federal funds to restructure the modern American metropolis around suburban development, an automobile-dependent transportation system, and a dispersed low-density population linked by major arterial roads and interstates.

In many former lowland communities, city officials renamed lowlands. After

1949, the Flats in Los Angeles became known by the hyphenated Pico-Aliso, a combination of the names of two public housing projects. In 2003, the HOPE VI–redeveloped mixed-income project at the site of Aliso Village was rebranded Pueblo del Sol, but many people still call the neighborhood by the old name Pico-Aliso, or refer to it as a part of Boyle Heights. In the 1990s, redevelopment planners rebranded Nashville's Black Bottom as SoBro for South of Broadway. In Saint Paul, Swede Hollow became Swede Hollow Park. In East Harlem, the area of the former salt marsh and creek has been known as Italian Harlem, Spanish Harlem, or simply El Barrio. But Columbus, Ohio, residents still call the near west side "the Bottoms," even though no one wants to be referred to as the city's "rump" and "Bottoms" is not considered polite conversation or appropriate in certain social settings.[1] And Washington, DC, residents know Foggy Bottom as the location of the US Department of State, George Washington University, and the Watergate hotel complex instead of a working-class industrial neighborhood.

Nineteenth-century urban lowland neighborhood names relied upon a common understanding of the sociospatial structure of the urban landscape. The American city changed and so did the terms used to describe urban spaces. Since World War II, American city dwellers' perceptions of the urban landscape have changed due to bigger buildings on larger sites and "superblocks," high-rise architecture, and faster speeds of travel. Modern civil engineering and earthmoving practices modified landforms in new ways.[2] A revaluation of urban landscape features followed. Places names like the Heights or the Highlands no longer carried the same prestige. Newly developed riverfronts and coastlines with desirable amenities and high property values became known as "waterfront property."

Meanwhile, outside of the centers of big cities, and inland from ocean coastlines, Americans built new apartment complexes, mobile home parks, and public housing developments on floodplains. Not unlike the railroad-adjacent housing in the era of bottoms, hollows, and flats, new low-cost housing sprang up proximate to chemical factories and other heavy industries in low-lying places. A new spatial pattern, less visible and horizontally dispersed like much of the postwar American residential landscape, again links income, elevation, and environmental hazards.

In the twenty-first century, low-lying places, especially noncoastal, amenity-scarce urban lowlands, continue to be places where poor people, recent immigrants, and African Americans live. Geographers Jeffrey Ueland and Barney Warf found a strong statistical correlation between race and altitude in southern inland cities and the "inverse relationship near the coast, where whites dominate higher-valued coastal properties."[3] Areas adjacent to and reliant upon engineered urban systems of drainage, flood protection, or industrial development are strongly associated with lower socioeconomic status.[4] New Orleans's Lower Ninth Ward and New York City's public housing developments in East Harlem, the Lower East Side, and Rockaway are a few well-known examples. It is not that poor neighborhoods are the only places that flood, or that all poor people live in low-lying neighborhoods, but instead that poverty increases social vulnerability to environmental hazards like floods. The pattern reflects a legacy of decision making with deep roots in city planning and American society. One implication for urban planners and urban ecological designers is that environmental justice and sustainability require awareness of the historic processes that produce landscapes of poverty and power.

Lowland legacies continue in American language, too. In cities across the US, Americans still use the slang term "the Bottoms" to refer to a place that is derelict, down-and-out, depressed, or distressed. In the twenty-first century, the phrase is meant to signify the worst part of the city. In Jackson, Mississippi, for example, "the Bottom" is a place "where every fifth or sixth home is abandoned, with broken windows, doors hanging off hinges."[5] In Los Angeles, Skid Row's homeless residents refer to the blocks "where the missions and the street dwellers are concentrated" as "the Bottoms."[6] In Columbus, Ohio, journalists report stories of prostitution, addiction, and policing in "the Bottoms."[7] Twenty-first century "bottoms" are places associated with human desperation, physical decline, and urban death.

Historically, the question of what to do about poor neighborhoods in lowland environments involved debates about disease, water problems, and city building challenges. In the era of bottoms, hollows, and flats, decision makers favored containment, viewing urban lowland neighborhoods as threats to the whole city. Stigmatization was paired with municipal neglect. Many observers objected to the mere presence of poor and working-class residents in the lowlands, and they repeatedly spread racist and xenophobic fears. Lowland residents were imagined to be part of a diseased and dangerous urban landscape. By the 1930s, it was widely accepted that these "blights" and "cancers" on the urban body had to be excised. The mass demolition and dislocation of urban renewal, with long-lasting negative consequences for the American city, followed. The legacies of urban lowland neighborhoods are present in the urban landscape today. We should continue to recover their stories.

Acknowledgments

The urban landscape both celebrates and obscures the past. Historical patterns are sometimes only faintly visible as material traces of an earlier era, neglected or forgotten in the present. But places hold powerful clues, and a heightened awareness of the built environment is critical to making better cities. The story of urban lowland neighborhoods has been documented and interpreted over several decades by former residents, activists, preservationists, historians, museum curators, and librarians. My project to uncover the history of bottoms, hollows, and flats in the American city would not have been possible without the work of these many advocates for the power of place.

Colleagues, mentors, friends, and family have provided the support and guidance that shepherded this book into print. I am especially grateful to have been mentored by Lawrence Vale and Anne Whiston Spirn who have inspired me as a scholar and encouraged my interests in city planning history and the urban landscape. They have steadily guided me, sharing their wisdom and expertise over many years. Special thanks also to Leigh Graham, Marta Gutman, Dolores Hayden, Joseph Heathcott, Leo Marx, Robin Nagle, Megan Kate Nelson, Max Page, and Sam Bass Warner for their generous advice and many contributions to my thinking about this topic. Presentations and feedback at the Society for American City and Regional Planning History and the Urban History Association provided formative discussions, and I would like to especially thank Andrew Kahrl for his comments on an earlier version of this work. Thanks also to Melanie Kiechle and Kara Schlichting for conversation over many conferences about our shared interests in urban environmental history.

My colleagues at Smith College provided all types of instrumental support as well as a stimulating and thoughtful intellectual community that embraces cross-disciplinary scholarship. Elizabeth Pryor read an early draft of the Black Bottom chapter, and I greatly appreciate her insights, critiques, and suggestions. Thanks to Ann Leone, Reid Bertone-Johnson, and David Osepowicz in the Landscape Studies Program for the moral support, technical assistance, research funds, and dedicated time necessary to see this project through to completion. Ann Leone and Doug Patey read manuscript drafts, and I'm grateful for both their careful attention to detail in reading a text and mentorship on the various ins and outs of being a scholar at a liberal arts college. Students have shaped this project in many ways, and I would like to give a special thanks to research assistants Jessica Robinson, Manny Benard, Clelie Fielding, and Julie Kim for their contributions, including the creation of many of the book's maps. To my colleagues in the sciences who provided their expertise on geomorphology and hydrology, Andrew Guswa and Robert Newton, and to all the participants in the Kahn Colloquium "Destroy Then Restore," I would like to say thanks for all the great conversations. Thanks also to all the folks at the Spatial Analysis Lab, including Jon Caris, Tracy Tien, and Rachel Moskowitz; librarians Barbara Polowy, Shannon Supple, and Brendan O'Connell; and imaging specialists Nicholas Baker and Jonathan Cartledge. Financial and other support from Smith College, including a Picker fund award, a semester-long sabbatical, STRIDE project funding, and CFCD funds through the Provost's Office helped make this book possible.

This project has also benefited immeasurably from the opportunity to research and write, and to discuss my work at cultural institutions, museums, libraries, and archives, especially the New-York Historical Society through the support of a Mellon Foundation fellowship. Thanks to Nick Yablon and Gergely Baics for many conversations on the top floor of the N-YHS library. Likewise, an appointment as a faculty fellow in the interdisciplinary Draper Program at New York University facilitated many helpful discussions with colleagues and students about New York City history. The Environmental History Seminar at the Massachusetts Historical Society has provided another intellectual home over many years, and I am particularly thankful for the friends and colleagues I have met there. The American Swedish Institute and the Los Angeles Public Library have had a long-lasting influence on my sense of what cultural organizations, museums, and libraries can and should be.

Archivists and librarians from around the country aided in the research that went into this book. At Los Angeles Public Library, special thanks to Glen Creason and Christina Rice. Thank you also to the many librarians who provided assistance at Los Angeles City Archives, New York Public Library, New-York Historical Society, New York City's Municipal Archives, Minnesota

Historical Society, Saint Paul Public Library, Nashville Public Library, and Tennessee State Library and Archives.

Thanks to Bruce Karstadt, Gregg White, and everyone at the American Swedish Institute for my first introduction to Swede Hollow. John Hesse-Moline and his family generously hosted me on a research visit to Saint Paul. I can't recall now how many conversations I've had with Jeff Caltabiano about the bottoms in ragtime, jazz, and blues. Thanks also to LaDale Winling for redlining maps and to Michael Needham and Humanities First for editing assistance. At the University of Chicago Press, I am grateful to Tim Mennel for his steady support for the project; Tim Gilfoyle, series editor, for his careful editing and thoughtful recommendations; and the two anonymous readers on behalf of the press whose close reading of the manuscript text yielded many incisive comments and astute observations, all organized into very helpful feedback.

From Kansas City's West Bottoms to Washington, DC's Foggy Bottom, my parents, William and Dorothy Moga, sister, Catherine Moga Bryant, and brother, Erik Moga, have talked with me many times about their own experiences and perceptions of urban lowland neighborhoods. They have nourished me throughout this process, and I am particularly thankful to them. Special thanks also to Jack Graham, Julianne Graham, Susan Graham, and Stephen Larcen for your support.

The love and encouragement of family made writing this book possible. My sons, Matthew and Anders, with their curiosity, playfulness, and delightfully quirky humor, have brought me so many smiles and so much joy while writing this book. For listening and talking it through, for helping me get the time and space to write, for brainstorming and joking and laughing and strategizing and, always, for reminding me what is most important in life, I am thankful beyond words for the support of my wife, Leigh.

Notes

Introduction

1. "Negro Orphan Home," *Nashville American*, March 14, 1898, 3.

2. Sam Bass Warner Jr., *Streetcar Suburbs: The Process of Growth in Boston, 1870–1900* (Cambridge, MA: Harvard University Press and MIT Press, 1962), 15–21; see also "Life in the Walking City, 1820–1865," in *The Evolution of American Urban Society*, 7th ed., ed. Howard P. Chudacoff, Judith E. Smith, and Peter C. Baldwin (Boston: Prentice Hall, 2010), 57–75.

3. Charles Rosenberg, *The Cholera Years: The United States in 1832, 1849, and 1866* (Chicago: University of Chicago Press, 1962).

4. John S. Billings, *Report of the Social Statistics of Cities in the United States at the Eleventh Census: 1890* (Washington, DC: Government Printing Office, 1895), 4–6.

5. Nayan Shah, *Contagious Divides: Epidemics and Race in San Francisco's Chinatown* (Berkeley: University of California Press, 2001), 2.

6. Natalia Molina, *Fit to Be Citizens? Public Health and Race in Los Angeles, 1879–1939* (Berkeley: University of California Press, 2006).

7. Stanley Schultz, *Constructing Urban Culture: American Cities and City Planning, 1800–1920* (Philadelphia: Temple University Press, 1989), 112–13.

8. Jon A. Peterson, *The Birth of City Planning in the United States, 1840–1917* (Baltimore: Johns Hopkins University Press, 2003).

9. Landscape historian John Stilgoe defines the "metropolitan corridor" as "the portion of the American built environment that evolved around railroad rights-of-way" and dates it to the period 1880 to 1935. See Stilgoe, *Metropolitan Corridor: Railroads and the American Scene* (New Haven, CT: Yale University Press, 1983), 3.

10. The Mill City Museum in Minneapolis presented an exhibition on the neighborhood's history in 2015. For recent work on the history of Bohemian Flats, see "A Home Worth Fighting For: The Evictions at the Bohemian Flats," *Open Rivers Journal* 1 (Fall 2015), https://editions.lib.umn.edu/openrivers/article/a-home-worth-fighting-for-the-evictions-at-the-bohemian-flats/. The WPA monograph *The Bohemian Flats* was originally published in 1941 and republished by the Minnesota Historical Society in 1986.

11. Douglas A. Boyd, *Crawfish Bottom: Recovering a Lost Kentucky Community* (Lexington: University Press of Kentucky, 2011); "Memories from Hamblin: The Making and Unmaking of Battle Creek's African American Community," Heritage Battle Creek website, accessed June 13,

2019, http://www.heritagebattlecreek.org/index.php?option=com_content&view=article&id=155&Itemid=73.

12. Timothy W. Collins, Sara E. Grineski, and Jayajit Chakraborty, "Environmental Injustice and Flood Risk: A Conceptual Model and Case Comparison of Metropolitan Miami and Houston, USA," *Regional Environmental Change* 18, no. 2 (February 2018): 2.

13. William B. Meyer, "The Other Burgess Model," *Urban Geography* 21, no. 3 (2000): 268. Meyer has dedicated sustained attention to this topic through his career, authoring a suite of fascinating research articles exploring topography and cities beginning in 1994. See "Bringing Hypsography Back In: Altitude and Residence in American Cities," *Urban Geography* 15, no. 6 (1994): 505–13; "The Poor on the Hilltops? The Vertical Fringe of a Late Nineteenth-Century American City," *Annals of the Association of American Geographers* 95, no. 4 (2005): 773–88; "A City (Only Partly) on a Hill," in *Remaking Boston: An Environmental History of the City and Its Surroundings*, ed. Conrad E. Wright and Anthony Penna (Pittsburgh: University of Pittsburgh Press, 2009); "Hills as Resources and Resistances in Syracuse, New York," *Geographical Review* 102, no. 1 (2012): 1–16.

14. Burgess writes in "Urban Areas" (1929) that "flat" cities like Chicago should be considered separately from hilly cities like Seattle, noting that the rich were more likely to be found on the hilltops. Like land economist Homer Hoyt, Burgess shared a focus on the residential location of the upper classes, positing that the wealthy would choose the best sites first and everyone else would select from the rest. I argue that whether the city is hilly or flat makes little difference in whether or not pejoratively named and flood-prone urban lowland neighborhoods developed. The Bottoms in Columbus, Ohio, is a good example.

15. John Bodnar, *The Transplanted: A History of Immigrants in Urban America* (Bloomington: Indiana University Press, 1985), 169. In chapter 6, "Immigrants and the Promise of American Life," Bodnar cites figures by ethnic group, showing that often fewer than 30 percent achieved upward mobility in occupational status.

16. Bodnar, *The Transplanted*, 183.

17. By the late 1930s, when slum clearance became an explicit goal of federal policy, the word "slum" had an official definition. See James Ford, "What Is a Slum? Analysis of Definitions," chapter 1 in *Slums and Housing* (Cambridge, MA: Harvard University Press, 1936), 3–16; Mabel L. Walker, *Urban Blight and Slums: Economic and Legal Factors in Their Origin, Reclamation, and Prevention* (Cambridge, MA: Harvard University Press, 1938), 4.

18. Herbert Gans, "An Evaluation of the Redevelopment Plan and Process," chapter 14 in *The Urban Villagers: Group and Class in the Life of Italian-Americans* (Glencoe, IL: Free Press of Glencoe, 1962), 305–35.

19. Charles Abrams, *The Language of Cities* (New York: Avon Books, 1971), 286.

20. Alan Mayne, *Slums: The History of a Global Injustice* (London: Reaktion Books, 2017), 8–9.

Chapter One

1. Jean Louis Vignes planted a one hundred–acre vineyard in 1831; William Wolfskill planted his extensive orange groves beginning in 1838. Dolores Hayden, *The Power of Place: Urban Landscapes as Public History* (Cambridge, MA: MIT Press, 1995): 107–12. Hayden notes on page 107 that citriculture and viticulture in the region began with "Franciscans and their Native Americans workers at the San Fernando and San Gabriel missions." Blake Gumprecht, *The Los Angeles*

NOTES TO CHAPTER ONE   181

River: Its Life, Death, and Possible Rebirth (Baltimore: Johns Hopkins University Press, 1999). Gumprecht cites Father Juan Crespi, a member of the Portola expedition on behalf of the Spanish crown in 1769, on page 38, noting that he "marveled at the 'very large, very green bottomlands' that spread out on both sides of its banks as far south as he could seem 'looking from afar like nothing so much as large cornfields.'" For more on the environmental history of Los Angeles and Southern California, see William Deverell and Greg Hise, *Land of Sunshine: An Environmental History of Metropolitan Los Angeles* (Pittsburgh: University of Pittsburgh Press, 2005); Jared Orsi, *Hazardous Metropolis: Flooding and Urban Ecology in Los Angeles* (Berkeley: University of California Press, 2004).

2. The phrases "river bottoms" and "bottomlands" are quite old. In 1755, for example, Dr. Samuel Johnson defined "bottom" as "a dale; a valley; a low ground." Likewise, the *Oxford English Dictionary* states that bottom denotes "the bed or basin of a river" or "low-lying land, a valley, a dell; an alluvial hollow" and observes that the second definition is especially prevalent in the United States. As landform descriptions, the words "bottoms" and "bottomlands" came into common usage in the US in the eighteenth century. Only in the 1870s did Americans begin to use these geological terms to describe human communities within cities.

3. John W. Reps, *The Making of Urban America: A History of City Planning in the United States* (Princeton, NJ: Princeton University Press, 1965), 314; Spiro Kostof, "The Grid," in *The City Shaped: Urban Patterns and Meaning Through History* (Boston: Bulfinch Press, 1991), 95–157.

4. Americans would later call many of these places "wetlands," a term rarely used in the nineteenth century. For more on the use of the term "wetlands," see Ann Vilesis, *Discovering the Unknown Landscape: A History of America's Wetlands* (Washington, DC: Island Press, 1997).

5. Historical background on the Hansen map in figure 1.1 is from Glen Creason, *Los Angeles in Maps* (New York: Rizzoli, 2010), 38–39. Creason notes: "After statehood Los Angeles had to prove its title from the original Spanish pueblo, and after much digging by J. Lancaster Brent, an attorney hired by the City Council, the proper documents were located describing the city's lands covering four square leagues—more than seventeen thousand acres."

6. John Stilgoe, *Common Landscape of America 1580–1845* (New Haven, CT: Yale University Press, 1982), 101.

7. Jackson discusses "square" and "squareness" in the documentary film *Figure in a Landscape: Conversations with J. B. Jackson*, Claire Marino and Janet Mendelsohn, 1988.

8. Hilary Ballon, ed., *The Greatest Grid: The Master Plan of Manhattan, 1811–2011* (New York: Museum of the City of New York and Columbia University Press, 2012).

9. Grady Clay, *Close-Up: How to Read the American City* (Chicago: University of Chicago Press, 1973).

10. Warner provides an excellent description of patterns of built environment, topography, and urban growth in his analysis of Roxbury Highlands in "The Weave of Small Patterns," *Streetcar Suburbs*, 67–116.

11. Matthew Klingle, *Emerald City: An Environmental History of Seattle* (New Haven, CT: Yale University Press, 2007); Nancy Seasholes, *Gaining Ground: A History of Landmaking in Boston* (Cambridge, MA: MIT Press, 2003); Anne Whiston Spirn, *The Granite Garden: Urban Nature and Human Design* (New York: Basic Books, 1984).

12. Andrew Hurley, "Common Fields: An Introduction," in *Common Fields: An Environmental History of St. Louis*, ed. Andrew Hurley (Saint Louis: Missouri Historical Society Press, 1997), 2.

13. Some early uses of the grid were enshrined in law, such as the sixteenth-century Laws of the Indies that were implemented in many Spanish colonial settlements.

14. One exception is Franklinton, the earliest European settlement in Columbus, Ohio, founded in the Scioto River bottoms. What early boosters trumpeted as an ideal setting for urban development, economic growth, healthful living, and prosperity, later became evidence of ill-informed decisions. One observer simply claimed it was "the wrong place to put a city." Flooding and odors from industrial development had led Columbus residents to negatively reassess the city's original site. Stephen A. Fitzgerald and U. S. Morris, *History of Columbus Celebration, Franklinton Centennial* (Columbus, OH: New Franklin Publishing Company, 1897), 30.

15. The reasons for the settlement's decline continue to be debated by archeologists and historians. See William R. Iseminger, "Culture and Environment in the American Bottom: The Rise and Fall of Cahokia Mounds," in *Common Fields: An Environmental History of St. Louis*, ed. Andrew Hurley (Saint Louis: Missouri Historical Society Press, 1997), 38–57. Iseminger, an archeologist, contends that "resource overexploitation, crowded living conditions, political and economic disruptions, and climatic change all contributed to Cahokia's decline, all threads of the same tattered fabric that cloaks today's world."

16. Boosters sometimes applied the name Mill Creek proactively, rather than descriptively, as an attempt to lure development. Stanley Hedeen, *The Mill Creek: An Unnatural History of an Urban Stream* (Cincinnati: Blue Heron Press, 1994), 10.

17. Warner, *Streetcar Suburbs*, 2; Howard P. Chudacoff, Judith E. Smith, and Peter C. Baldwin, eds., *The Evolution of American Urban Society*, 7th ed. (Boston: Prentice Hall, 2010), 57–58. Chudacoff et al. describe the distance as "rarely . . . beyond two miles from the city center—the average distance a person can walk in half an hour."

18. Chudacoff et al., *The Evolution of American Urban Society*, 63–65.

19. Between 1820 and 1860, more than 1.9 million people emigrated from Ireland to the US. In Nashville, Irish immigrants lived together with Germans and free African Americans in the Sixth Ward in the 1850s and 1860s.

20. Christine Kreyling, "Nashville Past and Present," Nashville Civic Design Center, accessed June 2009, http://www.civicdesigncenter.org.

21. Trucks and automobiles would later fundamentally alter these relationships. Transportation corridors often traversed urban lowlands, but highway locations also resulted from different political and logistical considerations, including slum clearance.

22. Walter Stix Glazer, *Cincinnati in 1840* (Columbus: Ohio State University Press, 1999); Henry Louis Taylor Jr., ed., *Race and the City: Work, Community, and Protest in Cincinnati, 1820–1970* (Urbana: University of Illinois Press, 1993).

23. Kreyling, "Nashville Past and Present," 2.

24. Vilesis, *Discovering the Unknown Landscape*.

25. Some of the geological processes that formed lowlands may be inactive, such as glaciation; others continue today.

26. Carol Groneman, "Collect," in *The Encyclopedia of New York City*, 2nd ed., ed. Kenneth T. Jackson (New Haven, CT: Yale University Press, 2010), 277.

27. Joel A. Tarr, *The Search for the Ultimate Sink: Urban Pollution in Historical Perspective* (Akron, OH: University of Akron Press, 1996), 149.

28. Cities imported freshwater from long distances, with newly constructed delivery infrastructures. New York City's Croton Aqueduct, for example, was constructed between 1837 and 1842. Between the 1790s and 1860s, large cities across the US, including Philadelphia, Boston, and Chicago, all constructed major new waterworks. Carl Smith, *City Water, City Life: Water*

and the Infrastructure of Ideas in Urbanizing Philadelphia, Boston, and Chicago (Chicago: University of Chicago Press, 2013).

29. Reps, *The Making of Urban America*, 317.

30. The organism that causes the disease (*Cholera vibrio*) would be independently discovered by different scientists thirty years apart: first, Filippo Pacini in Italy in 1854, then Robert Koch in Germany in 1884. Koch won the Nobel Prize for Physiology or Medicine in 1905. "Who First Discovered Vibrio Cholera?," UCLA Epidemiology, accessed June 13, 2019, http://www.ph.ucla.edu/epi/snow/firstdiscoveredcholera.html.

31. Lewis Mumford, *The City in History: Its Origins, Its Transformation, and Its Prospects* (New York: Harcourt, Brace & World, 1961), 459–60.

32. Howard P. Chudacoff and Judith E. Smith, *The Evolution of American Urban Society*, 4th ed. (Englewood Cliffs, NJ: Prentice Hall, 1994), 70.

33. Lawrence J. Vale, *Purging the Poorest: Public Housing and the Design Politics of Twice-Cleared Communities* (Chicago: University of Chicago Press, 2013), 43–44; Harmon G. Perry, "First 'Buttermilk Bottom' Flood Victims Are Moved," *Atlanta Daily World*, July 27, 1963, 1.

34. The terms "ghetto," "floodplain," and "wetland" did not come into common use in American cities until the twentieth century. While the phrases "low-lying land" or "low-lying neighborhood" are frequently used in the early twenty-first century, the term "lowland" was more common during the period 1870–1940.

35. John Bodnar, *The Transplanted: A History of Immigrants in Urban America* (Bloomington: Indiana University Press, 1985), 177; Olivier Zunz, *The Changing Face of Inequality: Urbanization, Industrial Development, and Immigrants in Detroit, 1880–1920* (Chicago: University of Chicago Press, 1982).

36. Historians of American vernacular speech have included the terms "bottom," "hollow," and "flat" in dictionaries. Irving Allen, *The City in Slang: New York Life and Popular Speech* (New York: Oxford University Press, 1993), 230; F. G. Cassidy, "Notes on Nicknames for Places in the United States," *American Speech* 52, nos. 1–2 (Spring-Summer 1977): 19–28; F. G. Cassidy, ed., *Dictionary of American Regional English* (Cambridge, MA: Belknap Press of Harvard University Press, 1985); Clarence Major, *Juba to Jive: A Dictionary of African-American Slang* (New York: Penguin, 1994), 38, 59.

37. George Lakoff and Mark Johnson, *Metaphors We Live By* (Chicago: University of Chicago Press, 1980): 18.

38. Lakoff and Johnson, 16.

39. Major, *Juba to Jive*, 59.

40. In "The Naming of Social Differences," in a section labeled "The Wrong—and the Right—Side of the Tracks," Allen writes: "Very informal, sometimes impromptu place name-phrases for the poor sections, like those for the rich areas, also have vertical elements, such as *down by-, the lower side of-, lower-, -bottom, -hollow*, and *-flats*—all taking the perspective, whether earnest or in irony, from the higher ground and this from higher social standing." Allen, *The City in Slang*, 227.

41. Allen, 226.

42. George Edmund Haynes, "Conditions among Negroes in the Cities," *Annals of the American Academy of Political and Social Science* 49 (September 1913): 111; "White Folks Are 'Way behind' Us, Says Dr. DuBois," *Chicago Defender*, March 24, 1923, 13; Walter R. Chivers, "Do Our People Possess a Poverty-Stricken Complex?," *Atlanta Daily World*, June 2, 1940, 4.

43. Philadelphia and Detroit both had well-known Black Bottom neighborhoods. Other "black bottoms" in the North include a section of Chicago's Near West Side. See Carolyn Eastwood, *Near West Side Stories: Struggles for Community in Chicago's Maxwell Street Neighborhood* (Chicago: Lake Claremont Press, 2002).

44. Gene Frenette, "Chaney Had to Endure a Pioneer's Life," *Florida Times-Union*, accessed November 13, 2008, http://www.jacksonville.com.

45. Vivian Baulch, "Paradise Valley and Black Bottom," *Detroit News*, August 7, 1996, http://blogs.detroitnews.com/history/1996/08/06/paradise-valley-and-black-bottom/.

46. Gary White, "Residents of Historic 'Black Bottom' Lakeland Area Plan Get-Together," The Ledger, July 25, 2008, https://www.theledger.com/article/LK/20080725/news/608115174/LL/"//www.googletagmanager.com/ns.html?id=GTM-PXCWJQ".

Chapter Two

1. "A City Plague Spot," *New York Times*, June 8, 1875, 2.

2. For more on odors, see Melanie A. Kiechle, *Smell Detectives: An Olfactory History of Nineteenth-Century Urban America* (Seattle: University of Washington Press, 2017); Alain Corbin, *The Foul and the Fragrant: Odor and the French Social Imagination* (Cambridge, MA: Harvard University Press, 1986); Mark M. Smith, *How Race Is Made: Slavery, Segregation, and the Senses* (Chapel Hill: University of North Carolina Press, 2006).

3. Eric W. Sanderson and Marianne Brown, "Mannahatta: An Ecological First Look at the Manhattan Landscape Prior to Henry Hudson," *Northeastern Naturalist* 14, no. 4 (2007): 557. Sanderson and Brown report that Stuyvesant's Meadows were "the largest single wetland," while Harlem Flats was the largest wetland complex.

4. "City Health Problems," *New York Times*, June 9, 1875, 2; *New York Times*, June 9, 1875, 6.

5. Laura Wood Roper, *FLO: A Biography of Frederick Law Olmsted* (Baltimore: Johns Hopkins University Press, 1973), 127, 261; Penelope Gelwicks, "Viele, Egbert Ludoricus," in *The Encyclopedia of New York City*, 2nd ed., ed. Kenneth T. Jackson (New Haven, CT: Yale University Press, 2010), 1367.

6. The group included Hamilton Fish, August Belmont, Peter Cooper, and John Jacob Astor. Catherine McNeur, *Taming Manhattan: Environmental Battles in the Antebellum City* (Cambridge, MA: Harvard University Press, 2014), 229.

7. Harlem Flats was part of the Twenty-Ninth Sanitary Inspection District, which reached from Eighty-Sixty Street to the Harlem River (north) and from Sixth Avenue to the Harlem River (east). *Report of the Council of Hygiene and Public Health of the Citizens' Association of New York upon the Sanitary Condition of the City* (New York: D. Appleton & Co., 1865), 347.

8. "Sanitary Matters: Gen. Viele's Health Map," *New York Times*, April 9, 1874, 5.

9. *Report of the Board of Health of the Health Department of the City of New York. May 1, 1874–December 31, 1875* (New York: Martin Brown, 1878): 15. Collection of New-York Historical Society.

10. Robert Anthony Orsi, *The Madonna of 115th Street: Faith and Community in Italian Harlem, 1880–1950* (New Haven, CT: Yale University Press, 1985), 37; Robert Charles Freeman, "Exploring the Path of Community Change in East Harlem, 1870–1940: A Multifactor Approach," diss., Fordham University, 1994, 17–18.

11. Lisa Goff, *Shantytown U.S.A.: Forgotten Landscapes of the Working Poor* (Cambridge, MA: Harvard University Press, 2016), 54–84.

NOTES TO CHAPTER TWO   185

12. Richard Plunz, *A History of Housing in New York City: Dwelling Type and Social Change in the American Metropolis* (New York: Columbia University Press, 1990), 53.

13. *Report of the Council of Hygiene and Public Health of the Citizens' Association of New York upon the Sanitary Condition of the City* (New York: D. Appleton & Co., 1865), 348.

14. McNeur, *Taming Manhattan*, 184.

15. Roy Rosenzweig and Elizabeth Blackmar, *The Park and the People: A History of Central Park* (Ithaca, NY: Cornell University Press, 1992), 65–73.

16. Rosenzweig and Blackmar, 68, 77; Goff, *Shantytown U.S.A.*, 59.

17. Cited by McNeur, *Taming Manhattan*, 205. The original source is Egbert L. Viele, "Topography of New-York and Its Park System," in *The Memorial History of the City of New York*, vol. 4, ed. James Grant Wilson (New York: New-York History Company, 1893), 556–57.

18. Jeffrey Gurock, Calvin B. Holder, Durahn A. B. Taylor, and Kenneth T. Jackson, "Harlem," in *The Encyclopedia of New York City*, 573. Harlem had a population of 203 people in 1790. The greater portion of central and northern Harlem has been historically referred to as Harlem Plains.

19. John Joseph Holland, *View at Fort Clinton, McGowan's Pass*, 1814, painting, collection of the New-York Historical Society.

20. For more on the McGown house, which was located in the vicinity of 103rd Street and Fifth Avenue and owned by the Sisters of Charity in the 1840s and 1850s, see Edwin G. Burrows and Mike Wallace, *Gotham: A History of New York City to 1898* (New York: Oxford University Press, 1999), 751. McGown and Benson's son Samson B. McGown, who was born in the house in 1797, lived to the age of eighty-seven and witnessed the transformation of the flats in the 1870s.

21. The New York and Harlem Railroad was chartered in 1831 with "the right to operate a double track from City Hall to the Harlem River along Fourth Avenue." Burrows and Wallace, *Gotham*, 564.

22. Burrows and Wallace, 565.

23. Michael Lapp, "East Harlem," in *The Encyclopedia of New York City*, 391; Gurock et al., "Harlem," 573.

24. Jonathan Gill, *Harlem: The Four Hundred Year History from Dutch Village to Capital of Black America* (New York: Grove, 2011), 102, 106. After 1860 Central Harlem became the site of major land speculation and served as the "home to the most prominent members of the Tweed Ring" who built mansions there in the early 1870s.

25. Gill, *Harlem*, 109–10.

26. Initially a German neighborhood, by 1885 a third of the population was born in Ireland. Anthony Gronowicz, "Yorkville," in Jackson, *Encyclopedia of New York City*, 1428.

27. Harlem Lake is now known as Harlem Meer. The commission had "directed Olmsted to draw up a plan for the upper park making 110th Street its boundary" on August 5, 1858. Charles E. Beveridge and David Schuyler, eds., *The Papers of Frederick Law Olmsted*, vol. 3, *Creating Central Park* (Baltimore: Johns Hopkins University Press, 1983), 289.

28. Roy Rosenzweig and Elizabeth Blackmar, *The Park and the People: A History of Central Park* (Ithaca, NY: Cornell University Press, 1992), 196; "Central Park," *New York Times*, August 8, 1867.

29. The Red House Course was located just south of the creek and east of Second Avenue. See Dripps Map, 1867, collection of New York Public Library; "The Turf for 1857," *New York Times*, April 16, 1857.

30. "The Central Park," *New York Times*, November 8, 1859, 4.

31. Gill, *Harlem*, 120.

32. John W. Pirsson, *The Dutch Grants, Harlem Patents and Tidal Creeks* (New York: L. K. Strouse & Co., 1889), 107; Ted Steinberg, *Gotham Unbound: The Ecological History of Greater New York* (New York: Simon and Schuster, 2014), 48. Harlem Creek has also been known as Kill Rechawanes, Montagne's Kill, Benson's Creek, and Pension's Creek.

33. Eric W. Sanderson, *Mannahatta: A Natural History of New York City* (New York: Abrams, 2009), 95.

34. Steinberg, *Gotham Unbound*, 64–65; Nick Paumgarten, "The Mannahatta Project," *New Yorker*, October 1, 2007, http://www.newyorker.com/magazine/2007/10/01/the-mannahatta-project.

35. Marguerite Holloway, *Measure of Manhattan: The Tumultuous Career and Surprising Legacy of John Randel, Jr., Cartographer, Surveyor, Inventor* (New York: W. W. Norton, 2013); Sanderson, *Mannahatta*.

36. Laws of New York, Chapter 274, April 27, 1837; Steinberg, *Gotham Unbound*, 64–65; Ballon, *The Greatest Grid*, 70; Reuben Rose-Redwood, "Rationalizing the Landscape: Superimposing the Grid upon the Island of Manhattan," thesis, Department of Geography, Pennsylvania State University, 2002, 46–49.

37. Steinberg cites Harlem Marsh as one of the "natural features of the island [that] proved too daunting and thus escaped the commissioner's orthogonal logic," writing that it "resisted the advances of the grid." Steinberg, *Gotham Unbound*, 64–65.

38. "A Great Nuisance," *New York Times*, November 15, 1873, 5.

39. Construction of the Croton Aqueduct began in the 1830s. For a complete history, see Gerard T. Koeppel, *Water for Gotham: A History* (Princeton, NJ: Princeton University Press, 2000).

40. See, for example, Maureen Ogle, "Water Supply, Waste Disposal, and the Culture of Privatism in the Mid-Nineteenth-Century American City," *Journal of Urban History* 25 (1999): 321–47.

41. Laws of New York, Chapter 566, adopted April 19, 1871. The stated purpose was "to provide for the proper drainage of lands within the corporate limits of the city and county of New York."

42. By 1877, a second very large sewer, constructed at 106th Street, measuring five and a half feet by seven feet, began to drain an additional 286 acres. Paradoxically, however, the new sewers made drainage problems worse. The new infrastructure catalyzed a rush to fill in "sunken lots." *Sewerage and Sewage Disposal in the Metropolitan District of New York and New Jersey* (New York: Martin Brown, 1910); *Report of the Board of Health*, 1878.

43. Ocean dumping was later prohibited by the federal Marine Protection Act of 1888. Benjamin Miller, *Fat of the Land: Garbage in New York; The Last Two Hundred Years* (New York: Four Walls Eight Windows, 2000): 71.

44. Cited in Anne-Marie Cantwell and Diana diZerega Wall, *Unearthing Gotham: The Archeology of New York City* (New Haven, CT: Yale University Press, 2001): 228.

45. Tweed died in jail in 1878.

46. *Report of the Board of Health*, 1878, 15.

47. *Report of the Citizen's Committee upon the Nuisances of New York City: The Air We Breathe*, April 1878, 1.

48. *Report of the Board of Health*, 1878, 15.

49. "The Board of Health: The Harlem Flats," *New York Times*, June 7, 1873, 2.

50. "A Great Nuisance," *New York Times*, November 15, 1873, 5.

51. "Street Cleaning: Commencement of the Legislative Inquiry," *New York Times*, February, 2, 1874, 5.

52. Christopher Gray, "Streetscapes/ The Park Avenue Railroad Viaduct," *New York Times*, February 19, 1995.

53. "The Noise of the Streets," *New York Times*, July 2, 1879, 2.

54. Nels Anderson, "The Social Antecedents of the Slum: A Developmental Study of the East Harlem Area of Manhattan Island, New York City," diss., New York University, 1930, 169–70. For more on shantytowns, including the Dutch Hill settlement along the East River that preceded Harlem Flats, and a discussion of goats in the urban landscape of antebellum New York, see McNeur, *Taming Manhattan*, 185–92.

55. "Fast Time Up in the Air," *New York Times*, September 20, 1880, 2.

56. See, for example, reflections of former residents in Anderson, "The Social Antecedents of the Slum," 192–93.

57. "The Noise of the Streets," 2.

58. "Squatter Life in New York," *Harper's New Monthly Magazine*, June 1, 1880, 563.

59. The property was sold by John H. Deane to Thomas F. Treacy for $17,000. *Real Estate Record*, January 17, 1880, 60.

60. Cited by Anderson, "The Social Antecedents of the Slum," 163. The original source is *Annual Report of the Board of Health* 1875, 128.

61. Cited by Anderson, "The Social Antecedents of the Slum," 167. The original source is *New York Times*, July 19, 1885.

62. "The Harlem Flats," *Daily Graphic*, July 15, 1875, 103.

63. For example, 1,031,194 street-cleaning loads were collected in 1875.

64. *Report of the Board of Health*, 1878, 12–13.

65. *Report of the Board of Health*, 1878, 15.

66. *Report of the Board of Health*, 1878, 13.

67. *Report of the Board of Health*, 1878, 15.

68. "The Harlem Perfumery," *New York Herald*, May 25, 1875.

69. "The Foe in the Citadel—The Duty of Our Board of Health," *New York Herald*, May 24, 1875, 5.

70. *Report of the Board of Health*, 1878, 18.

71. *Report of the Board of Health*, 1878, 18–19

72. "Science on Harlem Flats," *Sun*, August 26, 1877, 5.

73. "Filling in the Harlem Flats," *New York Times*, June 20, 1878, 3; *Who's Who in New York City and State* (New York: L. R. Hamersly, 1904): 359–60.

74. "The Seven Smells of New York" and "Summer Luxuries," *Puck*, August 4, 1880, 394.

75. "The Seven Smells of New York," 1880, 394.

76. Gronowicz, "Yorkville," in Jackson, *The Encyclopedia of New York*, 1428.

77. Sanderson and Brown, "Mannahatta," 557.

78. Gronowicz writes that "the Third Avenue elevated line began service on December 30, 1878, between South Ferry and 129th Street. The Second Avenue elevated line was completed in August 1879," including stops at Ninety-Second, Ninety-Ninth, 105th, and 110th streets.

79. George E. Waring Jr., *Report on the Social Statistics of Cities* (Washington, DC: Government Printing Office, 1886), 562.

80. "The Failure of John H. Deane," *Real Estate Record and Guide*, April 26, 1884, 432.

81. Michael Lapp, "East Harlem," in Jackson, *The Encyclopedia of New York*, 391.

82. US Census of 1880.

83. Frank B. Kelley, *Historical Guide to the City of New York* (New York: Frederick A. Stokes Company, 1913), 145. McGown sold the property to Thomas B. Odell in 1845. Odell sold it to the Sisters of Charity.

84. "Destruction in the Park," *New York Times*, January 3, 1881, 8.

85. "Real Estate at Auction," *New York Times*, April 7, 1885, 7.

86. Robinson real estate atlas, 1889. Collection of New York Public Library.

87. US Census of 1900.

88. "East Harlem's History," accessed October 15, 2017, http://www.east-harlem.com/cb11 _197A_history.htm.

89. This figure was tabulated using data from the US Census of 1910 based on enumeration district boundaries and population totals.

90. *The First Report of the Tenement House Commission of the City of New York*, vol. 1 (1903), 105–6.

91. *The First Report of the Tenement House Commission*, 119.

92. Sanborn-Perris Map Company, New York, New York, volume 8, 1896; 1900 Census.

93. Decades later, in the mid-twentieth century, it would become known as Spanish Harlem.

94. The author described the neighborhood as the area east of Third Avenue between Eightieth and 125th Streets, an area larger than the boundaries of the former Harlem Flats. "New York's New East Side Explored," *New York Times*, October 9, 1904, 8.

95. Orsi, *The Madonna of 115th Street*, 37.

96. New York City Housing Authority photograph #02.003.23703, collection of LaGuardia and Wagner Archives, City University of New York.

97. "Poor Richard's Playground," NYC Parks, accessed July 26, 2018, https://www.nycgov parks.org/parks/poor-richards-playground/history.

98. Samuel Zipp, *Manhattan Projects: The Rise and Fall of Urban Renewal in Cold War New York* (Oxford: Oxford University Press, 2010), 267.

99. Zipp, 259–60.

100. Rosenberg, *The Cholera Years*, 216. The original source is cited as *Citizen* (New York), March 31, 1866.

Chapter Three

1. The land that became Black Bottom was annexed to the city by an act passed on October 14, 1824. R. B. C. Howell, "Early Corporate Limits of Nashville," *Tennessean*, November 21, 1915, 38.

2. Nashville historians Bobby Lovett, James Summerville, and Don Doyle offer three different explanations for how the neighborhood got its name. Lovett argues that the area "received the Black Bottom name because of frequent flooding and the ever-present black mud and stagnant pools of filthy water and not because of the presence of large numbers of blacks." Doyle contends the neighborhood "became 'Black Bottom' as the Negro took the place of the Irish" in the 1880s. Summerville explains that "Black Bottom's name conveyed two literal truths of physical geography: it was low alluvial land, and its soil was much darker than the clay and mineral-laden earth of surrounding middle Tennessee." Bobby L. Lovett, *The African American History of Nashville, Tennessee, 1780–1930: Elites and Dilemmas* (Fayetteville: University of Arkansas Press,

1999), 73; Don H. Doyle, *Nashville in the New South, 1880–1930* (Knoxville: University of Tennessee Press, 1985), 101; James Summerville, "The City and the Slum: 'Black Bottom' in the Development of South Nashville," *Tennessee Historical Quarterly* 40, no. 2 (1981): 182.

3. Lovett, *The African American History of Nashville*, 82.

4. See, for example, "Nashville to Be Cleansed," *New York Times*, September 16, 1886, 1.

5. By the early twentieth century, the term was also in use in northern and midwestern cities.

6. Historian Edward Baptist argues that vernacular history is "a narrative about the past constructed by laypeople in their everyday language" that "can contain the essential elements of a collected past showing who a people thought they were and how they got to be that way." See Edward E. Baptist, "'Stol' and Fetched Here': Enslaved Migration, Ex-Slave Narratives, and Vernacular History," in *New Studies in the History of American Slavery*, ed. Edward E. Baptist and Stephanie M. H. Camp (Athens: University of Georgia Press, 2006), 245.

7. Elijah Embree Hoss, "Natural Advantages," chapter 1 in *History of Nashville, Tenn.*, ed. J. Wooldridge (Nashville: Methodist Episcopal Church, South and Barber & Smith, 1890), 26–28.

8. This small spring is sometimes referred to as Hackberry Spring. See 1877 Tavel, Eastman & Howell map. One block north of Broad, another spring known as Bluff Spring could be found at the "foot of Church Street." "Map of the Original Drainage of Nashville, Tennessee by W. F. Foster," in Lizzie Porterfield Elliott, *Early History of Nashville* (Board of Education of Nashville; Nashville: Ambrose Printing Co., 1911), 16.

9. The author commented that by 1918 "the course of the Branch is concealed beneath the streets, the buildings, and the accumulated rubbish of Black Bottom." J. T. McGill, "George Wilson," *Tennessee Historical Magazine* 4, no. 3 (September 1918): 157.

10. Elliott, *Early History of Nashville*, 10.

11. Louis M. Kyriakoudes, *The Social Origins of the Urban South: Race, Gender, and Migration in Nashville and Middle Tennessee, 1890–1930* (Chapel Hill: University of North Carolina Press, 2003), 120.

12. "The Nashville Cholera: A Physician's Statement Relative to the Causes of the Disease [reprinted from the *Nashville Banner* of June 11]," *San Francisco Chronicle*, June 21, 1873, 3.

13. "The Cholera in Nashville and Memphis," *Chicago Daily Tribune*, June 13, 1873.

14. "The Cholera in Nashville," *San Francisco Chronicle*, July 7, 1873.

15. A reference to downtown sewage being dumped into Wilson's Spring Branch appears in *Horton v. Mayor and City Council*, Cases in the Supreme Court of Tennessee, *The American Reports*, ed. Isaac Grant Thompson and Irving Browne, vol. 40 (San Francisco and Rochester: Bancroft-Whitney Company, 1912), 2.

16. See, for example, "The Necropolis of the South," chapter 3 in Ari Kelman, *A River and Its City: The Nature of Landscape in New Orleans* (Berkeley: University of California Press, 2003), 87–118.

17. "The Cholera in Nashville—the Population Flying Terror-Stricken from the City," *San Francisco Chronicle*, June 27, 1873; G. Haygood, "A Few Words about Cholera in Nashville," *Atlanta Constitution*, June 25, 1873.

18. "Cholera: An Important Report," *Chicago Daily Tribune*, July 26, 1873, 2; US Surgeon General, *The Cholera Epidemic of 1873 in the United States* (Washington, DC: Government Printing Office, 1875), 141.

19. *Third Report of the Board of Health to the Honorable City Council of the City of Nashville* (Nashville: City of Nashville, 1879), 25.

20. *Third Report of the Board of Health*, 23.

21. *Third Report of the Board of Health*, 26.

22. "The Cholera in Tennessee," *New York Times*, July 11, 1873.

23. *Third Report of the Board of Health*, 34, 39, 81.

24. *Third Report of the Board of Health*, 29–30.

25. US Surgeon General, *The Cholera Epidemic of 1873*, 141.

26. *Third Report of the Board of Health*, 315.

27. Dr. J. R. Buist urged investments in sanitary infrastructure including sewers in a major address in January 1880. J. Wooldridge, ed., *History of Nashville*, 146.

28. The assistant city engineer completed plans for the Wilson Spring Branch sewer in 1884. "The Wilson Spring Sewer," *Daily American*, December 24, 1884, 8.

29. Landscape architect and planner Anne Whiston Spirn coined this term. See Anne Whiston Spirn, "Buried Floodplains: A Pervasive National Hazard," Memo to Susan Wachter, US Department of Housing and Urban Development, September 1999.

30. *Nashville Union and American*, June 2, 1874; "Almost a Riot in Nashville," *Cincinnati Daily Gazette*, August 7, 1878, 1. A few early news reports used the phrase "black bottom" to refer to an area on the north side of town, but this appears to have been a very short-lived phenomenon.

31. Hannah Rosen, *Terror in the Heart of Freedom: Citizenship, Sexual Violence, and the Meaning of Race in the Postemancipation South* (Chapel Hill: University of North Carolina Press, 2009), 15; Heather Cox Richardson, *The Death of Reconstruction: Race, Labor, and Politics in the Post-Civil War North, 1865–1901* (Cambridge, MA: Harvard University Press, 2001).

32. "A Double Crime," *Republican Banner*, May 1, 1875, 4–5.

33. "News from Nashville," *Atlanta Constitution*, September 9, 1886, 1.

34. An MEC church known as Clark Chapel was located across the street from Saint Paul's AME Church.

35. Lovett, *The African American History of Nashville, Tennessee*, 178.

36. Black persons are indicted with the abbreviation "(c)" in the 1880 Nashville City Directory.

37. Doyle, *Nashville in the New South*, 71.

38. Doyle, 71.

39. James Summerville, *Educating Black Doctors: A History of Meharry Medical College* (Tuscaloosa: University of Alabama Press, 1983), xi.

40. Lovett, *The African American History of Nashville, Tennessee*, 74.

41. Doyle, *Nashville in the New South*, 101.

42. Sanborn Fire Insurance map, Nashville, Tennessee, 1888.

43. This label appears on the Sanborn maps from 1888, 1914, and 1951.

44. Lovett, *The African American History of Nashville, Tennessee*, 74.

45. "The Flood at Nashville: Many Buildings under Water and Much Distress among the Poor," *New York Times*, March 15, 1884, 1.

46. "Floods and Fires: The Rise in the Cumberland and Elsewhere," *Washington Post*, February 20, 1880, 1; "The Rivers Rising," *Atlanta Constitution*, February 4, 1887, 5; Charles J. Burnell, *The Nashville Flood of December and January, 1926–27* (Nashville: C. J. Burnell, 1927); "1,000 Made Homeless by Nashville Flood," *New York Times*, December 26, 1926, 23.

47. "The Rivers Rising," 5.

48. "Our Sanitary Condition," *Daily American*, May 18, 1888, 5.

49. Doyle, *Nashville in the New South*, 80; "A Peep at the Future," *Daily American*, July 20, 1888, 5.

50. "Site Selected Yesterday for the Proposed Hay Market," *Daily American*, March 11, 1892, 3; Doyle, *Nashville in the New South*, 80.

51. "The City's Big Sewer," *Daily American*, October 13, 1893, 4.

52. See appendix A, Doyle, *Nashville in the New South*, 235.

53. Summerville, "The City and the Slum," 183. See appendix C for neighborhood population figures and differences in district or ward boundaries by decade.

54. Gabriel A. Briggs, *The New Negro in the Old South* (New Brunswick, NJ: Rutgers University Press, 2015), 6, 199; "Trolley Car Boycott" video, "Many Rivers to Cross in Nashville," *The African Americans: Many Rivers to Cross*.

55. "About the Nashville Globe," Chronicling America website, accessed July 13, 2017, http://chroniclingamerica.loc.gov/lccn/sn86064259/.

56. Briggs, *The New Negro in the Old South*, 115.

57. Will Allen Dromgoole, "Banner Representative Takes Slumming Tour in Black Bottom," *Nashville, Banner*, October 22, 1910, 5; Will Allen Dromgoole, "A Journey through Black Bottom," *Nashville Banner*, July 29, 1905, 5.

58. Summerville, "The City and the Slum," 182.

59. Dromgoole, "A Journey through Black Bottom," 5.

60. The quote is from Summerville, "The City and the Slum," 182. Summerville cites the original source as *Nashville American*, June 30, 1905.

61. Charles Forster Smith, "The Negro in Nashville," *Century Illustrated Magazine*, 42, no. 1 (May 1891): 154

62. Dromgoole, "Banner Representative Takes Slumming Tour in Black Bottom."

63. Dromgoole.

64. At the national level, historian Max Page argues that "the unwillingness to reward slumlords for their buildings in condemnation actions would stall slum clearance efforts in the United States for years." Max Page, *The Creative Destruction of Manhattan, 1900–1940* (Chicago: University of Chicago Press, 1999), 97.

65. Dromgoole, "A Journey through Black Bottom," 5.

66. "Cleaning Out Black Bottom," *Nashville Daily American*, December 21, 1906, 1.

67. "Cleaning Out Black Bottom," 1.

68. "Black Bottom," *Nashville Banner*, December 21, 1906, 5.

69. "Black Bottom," 5.

70. "Redemption of Black Bottom," *Nashville Daily American*, February 14, 1907, 2.

71. "Black Bottom Bond Ordinance," *Nashville Banner*, September 27, 1910.

72. Leland R. Johnson, *The Parks of Nashville: A History of the Board of Parks and Recreation* (Nashville: Metropolitan Nashville and Davidson County Board of Parks and Recreation, 1986), 74.

73. "Black Bottom Bond Campaign," *Nashville Banner*, October 19, 1910, 9.

74. Dromgoole, "Banner Representative Takes Slumming Tour in Black Bottom," 5.

75. Using this type of language, journalists reinforced the social construction of whiteness and Americanness. For more on this topic, see Matthew Frye Jacobson, *Whiteness of a Different Color: European Immigrants and the Alchemy of Race* (Cambridge, MA: Harvard University Press, 1998).

76. "Campaign for Central Park," *Nashville Banner*, November 7, 1910, 4.

77. "Campaign for Central Park," 4.

78. "Appeal from Colored People," *Nashville Banner*, November 7, 1910, 4.

79. "Two Vital Propositions," *Nashville Globe*, November 4, 1910, 2.

80. Summerville, "The City and the Slum," 186.

81. Doyle, *Nashville in the New South*, 82.

82. Louis M. Kyriakoudes, "Southern Black Rural-Urban Migration in the Era of the Great Migration: Nashville and Middle Tennessee, 1890–1930," *Agricultural History* 72, no. 2 (Spring 1998): 341–51.

83. Kyriakoudes, 348–51.

84. Don H. Doyle, "Coming in from the Country," chapter 2 in *Nashville since the 1920s* (Knoxville: University of Tennessee Press, 1985). On pages 45 and 46 Doyle explains that Kalb Hollow was located "near the Morgan and Hamilton textile mills" in North Nashville and "named for the preponderance of migrants from DeKalb County" while "Mud Flats was a pocket of white families surrounded by black residents during the 1920s and 1930s, when North Nashville became almost solidly black."

85. "Floods in Black Bottom Imperil Lives of Dozens," *Nashville Tennessean*, April 27, 1912, 1; *New York Times*, March 31, 1929, 24.

86. "Alabama Flood Loss Exceeds $10,000,000: Governor Graves Will Ask Hoover for Aid—Waters Rise at Nashville, Tenn.," *New York Times*, March 31, 1929, 24.

87. "Negro Branch of the Carnegie Library," accessed January 9, 2018, http://www.tnstate.edu/library/documents/carnegie.pdf.

88. Linda T. Wynn, "Pearl School (1883–1983)," accessed September 24, 2013, http://ww2.tnstate.edu/library/digital/pearl.htm; Lovett, *The African-American History of Nashville*, 139–40; Tommie Morton-Young, *Nashville Tennessee*, Black America series (Charleston, SC: Arcadia Publishing, 2000), 48. Young lists the date as 1916.

89. Benjamin Houston, *The Nashville Way: Racial Etiquette and the Struggle for Social Justice in a Southern City* (Athens: University of Georgia Press, 2012), 25; Lovett, *The African-American History of Nashville*, 158; "Meharry Medical College," Tennessee Encyclopedia of History and Culture, accessed August 2010, http://tennesseeencyclopedia.net; "Meharry Medical College," accessed August 2010, http://www.tnstate.edu/library/digital/meharry.htm. Nearby Rutledge Hill's white-only educational institutions also left the area during this period, and the surrounding residential neighborhood declined.

90. The city's first zoning ordinance was enacted in 1933.

91. "Our Sanitary Condition," *Nashville American*, May 18, 1888, 5.

92. *Nashville American*, November 10, 1910.

93. "Black Bottom as Warehouse Dist.," *Tennessean*, January 29, 1911, 20; "Black Bottom Problem: Real Estate Man Sees Elimination by Survival of the Fittest," *Tennessean*, December 3, 1911, 37.

94. "Statement by Mayor," *Tennessean*, August 24, 1917, 4.

95. "Improvement in Black Bottom," *Tennessean*, April 23, 1916, 7.

96. "Kerrigan Plant Wins Praise," *Nashville Tennessean*, June 10, 1945, 20.

97. The Sparkman Street Bridge was completed in 1909.

98. "Mr. Chase's Plan for Central Park Proposed to Replace Black Bottom," *Nashville American*, August 14, 1905.

99. This displacement can be seen through a comparison of the 1897 and 1914 Sanborn maps. Mapmakers labeled apartments where African Americans lived as "Negro tenements." The Sparkman Street Bridge approach extended several blocks into the Black Bottom neighborhood. It was constructed between 1907 and 1909.

100. "Negroes Making Exodus: Ex-Councilman Says 'Black Bottom' Is Changing Complexion," *Tennessean*, July 1, 1910, 10.

101. "Eye Sore of City: Black Bottom in Process of Regeneration—Some Causes," *Tennessean*, November 26, 1911, 37.

102. The text is quoted by Mason K. Christensen in "The Saloon in Nashville and the Coming of Prohibition in Tennessee," master's thesis, Middle Tennessee State University, 2013, 2. The original source is listed as James E. Caldwell, *Recollections of a Life Time* (Nashville: Baird-Ward Press, 1923), 71–72.

103. Christensen, "The Saloon in Nashville," 33.

104. Christensen, 33.

105. Doyle, *Nashville since the 1920s*, 67.

106. Christensen "The Saloon in Nashville," 43; "Official Stenographic Report by Maxson, Ford, & McSweeney," "Cooper-Sharp Trial Section," *Nashville American*, February 24, 1909, 2.

107. For more on low-as-metaphor and associations with "vice," see Luc Sante's *Low Life: Lures and Snares of Old New York* (New York: Vintage Books, 1991).

108. Doyle, *Nashville since the 1920s*, 64, 67, 68–69.

109. Zora Neale Hurston, "Characteristics of Negro Expression," in *The New Negro: Readings on Race, Representation, and African American Culture, 1892–1938*, ed. Henry Louis Gates and Gene Andrew Garret (Princeton, NJ: Princeton University Press, 2007). Lovett observes that Hurston "viewed Black Bottom in much the same view as Memphis's Beale Street, as a place where real black urban and rural life merged into colorful and folk ways." Lovett, *The African-American History of Nashville*, 74.

110. Gladys L. Knight argues that the dance originated in Nashville. See Knight, "Dance and Dance Companies," in *Encyclopedia of African American Popular Culture*, vol. 1, ed. Jessie Carney Smith (Santa Barbara, CA: Greenwood, 2011), 391. For more on the Black Bottom dance, see also Brenda Dixon Gottschild, *The Black Dancing Body: A Geography from Coon to Cool* (New York: Palgrave Macmillan, 2005); 166–67.

111. The Black Bottom achieved national publicity as part of a Broadway revue in 1925 and garnered significant media attention in the newspapers in 1927–28. Knight explains that the Black Bottom and similar dances were "appropriated by mainstream white celebrities; the dances appeared in films by both white and black filmmakers, performed by both white and black actors." Knight, "Dance and Dance Companies," 391.

112. William Barlow, *Looking Up at Down: The Emergence of Blues Culture* (Philadelphia: Temple University Press, 1989), 325.

113. Richard M. Mizelle Jr., *Backwater Blues: The Mississippi Flood of 1927 in the African American Imagination* (Minneapolis: University of Minnesota Press, 2014), 12. Mizelle cites Ralph Ellison here: "The blues is an impulse to keep the painful details and episodes of brutal experience alive in one's aching consciousness, to finger its jagged grain, and to transcend it, not by consolation of philosophy, but by squeezing from it a near-tragic, near comic lyricism."

114. *Low Standard Housing in Nashville Tennessee*, Nashville City Planning and Zoning Commission, 1937. Collection of the Tennessee State Library and Archives.

115. Bill Carey "Other Side of Revitalization," *Tennessean*, February 19, 1995, 57, E2.

116. *Nashville Tennessean*, April 21, 1946.

117. Bill Rouda, *Nashville's Lower Broad: The Street That Music Made* (Washington, DC: Smithsonian Books, 2004).

118. Bill Carey, "A City's Changing Face: Black Bottom Gone, but Memories Remain," *Nashville Tennessean*, February 9, 1995, 1B, 2B.

119. Carey, 1B; MiChelle Duke, "Blacks Strive to Restore Spirit of Lost Communities," *Nashville Banner*, February 2, 1998, A9, A11.

120. Kreyling, "Nashville Past and Present."

121. Rouda, *Nashville's Lower Broad*, 124.

122. Originally known as Nashville Arena, it would change names three times in fourteen years: first to Gaylord Arena, then Sommet Center, then Bridgestone Arena.

123. Lucinda Williams, "Foreword," in Rouda, *Nashville's Lower Broad*, xiii.

124. "Encore Opens, SoBro's First Residents Energize Emerging Neighborhood," press release, accessed August 2010, www.novaregroup.com/resources%5Cencorepressrelease.pdf.

125. Encore website, accessed September 11, 2017, http://www.encoresobro.com/neighborhood.

126. "Grand Opening for Pinnacle tower," *Nashville Business Journal*, February 11, 2010, http://nashville.bizjournals.com.

127. Music City Convention Center website, accessed September 20, 2017, https://www.nashvillemusiccitycenter.com/about/our-history.

128. John Kellogg, "Negro Urban Clusters in the Postbellum South," *Geographical Review* 67, no. 3 (July 1977): 310–21.

129. For more on race, real estate, and city planning, see N. D. B. Connolly, *A World More Concrete: Real Estate and the Remaking of Jim Crow South Florida* (Chicago: University of Chicago Press, 2014).

Chapter Four

1. *St. Paul City Directory, 1879–80* (Saint Paul, MN: R. L. Polk & Co. and A. C. Danser, 1879); US Census 1880; Sanborn map 1885; Saint Paul City Engineer's street map, 1885, collection of Saint Paul Public Library.

2. "Swede Hollow: A Capsule History of a Famous Saint Paul, Minnesota Landmark," pamphlet, prepared by the Saint Paul Garden Club, 1976. Collection of the American Swedish Institute, Minneapolis, Minnesota.

3. Skunk Hollow in Pittsburgh is one example of a similar ravine community.

4. John G. Rice, "The Swedes," chapter 12 in *They Chose Minnesota*, ed. June Drenning Holmquist (Saint Paul: Minnesota Historical Society Press, 1981), 262; David A. Lanegran, "Swedish Neighborhoods of the Twin Cities: From Swede Hollow to Arlington Hills, from Snoose Boulevard to Minnehaha Parkway," chapter 3 in *Swedes in the Twin Cities: Immigrant Life and Minnesota's Urban Frontier*, ed. Philip J. Anderson and Dag Blanck (Saint Paul: Minnesota Historical Society Press, 2001), 44; Nels M. Hokanson, "I Remember St. Paul's Swede Hollow," *Minnesota History* 41, no. 8 (1969): 363.

5. N. H. Winchell, *The Geology of Minnesota*, vol. 2, final report (Saint Paul, MN: Pioneer Press, 1888): 351. Winchell provides elevations along the length of the Saint Paul and Duluth Railway at distances north from the Saint Paul Union Depot (704), and elevations for "Mississippi river at St. Paul, ordinary low water" of 685 and "Lake Phalen" of 859 feet above sea level. See also Hokanson, "I Remember St. Paul's Swede Hollow," 366.

6. The bootlegging activities of Pierre "Pig's Eye" Parrant drew more people to the area and fostered the early development, leading one historian to quip that Saint Paul was "a town built on whiskey." Saint Paul was a fair distance from the US Army base at Fort Snelling, but it was

NOTES TO CHAPTER FOUR   195

close enough for Parrant to successfully set up illicit trade, and its limestone caves provided ample storage spaces for his supplies. Traders, soldiers, trappers, Indians, and various other river travelers made claims on the land. Parrant was quickly forced out, losing his land as a result of an unpaid debt, and relocated to the river bottom below Dayton's Bluff, an area that became known as Pig's Eye Landing. J. Fletcher Williams, *History of Ramsey County and the City of St. Paul, including the Explorers and Pioneers of Minnesota* (Minneapolis: North Star Publishing Company, 1881), 65.

7. Donald L. Empson, *The Street Where You Live: A Guide to the Place Names of St. Paul* (Minneapolis: University of Minnesota Press, 2006), 213.

8. Williams, *History of Ramsey County and the City of St. Paul*, 72.

9. Williams, 368.

10. Empson, *The Street Where You Live*, 213. Geographer David Lanegran explains that Swede Hollow was first settled "by people other than Swedes. Trappers, lumberman, and casual laborers squatted in the hollow in the 1840s. The Swedes began to occupy the shacks in the 1850s." Lanegran, "Swedish Neighborhoods," 44.

11. Incorporated as a city in March 1854, Saint Paul attracted more people, leading one observer to comment that "the city was continually full of tourists, speculators, sporting men, and even worse characters, all spending gold as though it was dross. Perhaps this 'floating population' amounted to two or three thousand persons during most of the summer, until the crash scattered them like leaves before an autumn gale." J. Fletcher Williams, *A History of the City of St. Paul and of the County of Ramsey, Minnesota* (Saint Paul: Minnesota Historical Society, 1876): 377.

12. National Register of Historic Places nomination form, Lowertown historic district, Saint Paul, Minnesota.

13. Saint Paulites began to romanticize the early history of the city, the beauty of its natural setting, and the lives of native peoples. In Williams's account, the "burning force" of industry had destroyed nature's scenery, which "must have been picturesque in the extreme," but in so doing it also aided in the creation of a "busy, populous city" and "new forms of beauty" representing civilization and progress. Williams, *A History of the City of St. Paul and of the County of Ramsey, Minnesota*, 16.

14. "Swedish Immigration to North America," Swenson Center, Augustana College, accessed June 13, 2019, https://www.augustana.edu/swenson/academic/history.

15. Williams, *A History of the City of St. Paul*.

16. Of Saint Paul's foreign born, 3,837 were from Germany, 2,662 were from Ireland, 1,850 were from Prussia, 1,437 were from Sweden, and 1,309 were from Canada. In 1880, fewer than 2,500 Swedes lived in Ramsey County. Mary Lethert Wingerd, *Claiming the City: Politics, Faith, and the Power of Place in St. Paul* (Ithaca, NY: Cornell University Press, 2001), 79.

17. Henry A. Castle, *History of St. Paul and Vicinity*, vol. 3 (Chicago: Lewis Publishing, 1914), 1070.

18. Williams, *History of Ramsey County and the City of St. Paul*, 472–73.

19. Lanegren, "Swedish Neighborhoods."

20. Williams, *History of Ramsey County and the City of St. Paul*, 473.

21. Williams, *A History of the City of St. Paul*, 435.

22. Merrill E. Jarchow, "Charles D. Gilfillan: Builder behind the Scenes," *Minnesota History* 40 (1967): 226–27.

23. Winchell, *The Geology of Minnesota*, 373. One lasting result of all the building and rebuilding at the upper end of Phalen Creek Valley was a large mill pond that became a prominent

feature of the valley, with a pathway across the top of the dam. A tunnel provided passage underneath the Saint Paul and Duluth tracks on the west slope, linking the hollow to an unpaved street. On the east side, this pathway ascended the steep eastern slope, linking to the Dayton's Bluff neighborhood. The triangle-shaped, small residential neighborhood to the west, located high above the hollow, was surrounded by railroad tracks on all sides and became known as Railroad Island. A major railroad bridge crossed over the valley at Sixth Street.

24. John T. Flanagan, *Theodore Hamm in Minnesota: His Family and Brewery* (Saint Paul, MN: Pogo Press, 1989), 11–12.

25. Flanagan, 14.

26. Flanagan, 25–27.

27. Mead & Hunt, Inc., *Saint Paul Historic Context Study: Neighborhoods at the Edge of the Walking City*, prepared for Historic Saint Paul, City of Saint Paul Heritage Preservation Commission, and Ramsey County Historical Society, 2011, 10.

28. Steve Trimble, "From the Land of Sky Blue Waters," Saint Paul Historical, accessed July 11, 2016, http://saintpaulhistorical.com/items/show/1. Flanagan reports that the brewery produced twenty-six thousand barrels a year in 1882 and thirty-five thousand barrels per year in 1893, while Trimble asserts production of forty thousand per year in 1885. I have listed production figures here as an estimate based on the discrepancy in these figures, although it is of course possible that production increased from 1882 to 1885, then declined in the early 1890s (perhaps as a result of economic downturn). Flanagan, *Theodore Hamm in Minnesota*, 14.

29. *Proceedings of Common Council of the City of St. Paul, Ramsey County, Minnesota, 1891* (Saint Paul, MN: Herald Print, 1892), 11.

30. Trimble, "From the Land of Sky Blue Waters."

31. Flanagan, *Theodore Hamm in Minnesota*, 20–21.

32. Castle, *History of St. Paul*, 1070.

33. "Minnesota's Historic Bridges, Seventh Street Improvement Arches, Historic Significance," accessed May 2010, http://www.mnhs.org.

34. "Minnesota's Historic Bridges."

35. See 1888 Sanborn fire insurance map, for example.

36. Hokanson, "I Remember St. Paul's Swede Hollow," 369n9; James P. Shannon, "Bishop Ireland's Connemara Experiment," *Minnesota History* 35 (March 1957): 212.

37. "Three of a Kind: A Triplet of Small Blazes during the Past Twenty-Four Hours," *Saint Paul Daily Globe*, March 1, 1884, 8. The reporter refers to "the ravine known as Swede hollow [with] a nest of fifteen quite comfortable cottages." See also "The Squatter's Home," *Saint Paul Daily Globe*, March 21, 1886, 13.

38. One of the residents listed in the 1879 city directory worked for the Saint Paul Water Company. Hokanson reports that plat, title, tax, and land commissioner records are somewhat murky on landownership in the valley, but that owners included Sheriff John Wagener, who acquired land between 1887 and 1903; Edward H. Cutler; and Hamm's Realty Company. Hokanson, "I Remember," 3633.

39. Jarchow, "Charles D. Gilfillan," 221, 228.

40. "To the Honorable, the Mayor and the Common Council of the City of St. Paul," letter published in the *Saint Paul Daily Globe*, December 5, 1884, 6.

41. "The Squatter's Home"; "A Plague Spot," *Saint Paul Daily Globe*, February 27, 1885, 2.

42. "To the Honorable, the Mayor and the Common Council of the City of St. Paul," 6.

43. "To the Honorable, the Mayor and the Common Council of the City of St. Paul," 6.

NOTES TO CHAPTER FOUR

44. "To the Honorable, the Mayor and the Common Council of the City of St. Paul," 6.

45. "A Plague Spot," 2.

46. "Swedish American Newspaper Publishing," Minnesota Historical Society, accessed January 11, 2018, http://www.mnhs.org/newspapers/swedishamerican/publishing.

47. *Skaffaren och Minnesota Stats Tidning*, August 6, 1884, 8.

48. "Talking about Parks. Discussion in the Chamber of Commerce on Como Park and Swede Hollow," *Saint Paul Daily Globe*, March 17, 1885, 2.

49. "Talking about Parks," 2.

50. "Talking about Parks," 2.

51. For more on Phalen Creek as the source of the city's original water supply, see Jarchow, "Charles D. Gilfillan," 226.

52. *Annual Reports of City Officers and City Boards of the City of St. Paul for the Fiscal Year Ending October 31, 1886* (Saint Paul, MN: D. Ramaley and Son, 1887), 279.

53. This figure was calculated by comparing the structures identified on the 1892 Donnelley real estate atlas (approximately 115 are shown) in the area labeled "Swede Hollow" with the thirty-nine households listed with the address "Phalen Creek" in Polk's city directory of 1879. Donnelley atlas, 1892, collection of Minnesota Historical Society; *St. Paul City Directory, 1879–80* (Saint Paul, MN: R. L. Polk and A. C. Danser, 1879).

54. 1892 Donnelley atlas.

55. "A City's Sad Charge," *Saint Paul Daily Globe*, September 23, 1888, 1.

56. "A City's Sad Charge," 1.

57. "A City's Sad Charge," 1.

58. "Down in the Hollow," *Saint Paul Daily Globe*, December 24, 1894, 8; "Summit to Swede Hollow, Extremes of Social Life in St. Paul," *Saint Paul Daily Globe*, May 29, 1898, 6.

59. "Summit to Swede Hollow," 8.

60. *Skaffaren och Minnesota Stats Tidning*, December 26, 1883.

61. "Reports from Kindergarten Clubs," *Kindergarten*, monthly magazine (Chicago: Alice B. Stockham and Co., 1890), 416.

62. Hokanson, "I Remember Swede Hollow."

63. Hokanson, 363.

64. Hokanson, 365.

65. Hokanson, 367.

66. A highly detailed map of the area prepared by the Sanborn Fire Insurance Company in 1903 documented eighty-nine dwellings, five outbuildings, and three shanties in the area between East Seventh Street and Minnehaha Avenue The old mill building is labeled as vacant. At the north end of the hollow, the creek is shown emerging above ground just below Hamm's Brewery.

67. R. L. Polk and Co., *St. Paul City Directory* (Saint Paul, MN: R. L. Polk & Co. Publishers, 1914), 157–58.

68. Gentille Yarusso, "Swede Hollow, Then Up on the Street," historical booklet published through the courtesy of Mueller Mortuary, Carlson Funeral Home, Phalen Park Funeral Home, Saint Paul (September 1968). Collection of the American Swedish Institute, Minneapolis, Minnesota.

69. Rudolph J. Vecoli, "The Italians," chapter 24 in *They Chose Minnesota*, ed. June Drenning Holmquist (Saint Paul: Minnesota Historical Society Press, 1981), 449.

70. Wingerd, *Claiming the City*, 79.

71. Vecoli, "The Italians," 450, 453, table 24.2.

72. Vecoli, 452. He writes: "A 1905 survey reported that the approximately 60,000 track laborers in Illinois, Wisconsin, Minnesota, and Iowa were mainly Italian and Slavs. A cryptic message from the Great Northern Railroad in 1897 reflected the invidious distinctions made by railroad management between 'dagoes' (Italians) and 'white men' (Americans and Northern Europeans): 'White men coming to Duluth will not work. Dagoes only men who will work,' it read. 'Send more dagoes and shut off white men.'"

73. National Park Service, "Little Italy: A Floodplain Neighborhood," brochure produced in association with the Mississippi National River and Recreation Area, accessed July 14, 2016, https://www.nps.gov/miss/learn/education/upload/LittleItaly_30x40.pdf.

74. Vecoli, "The Italians," 453.

75. National Park Service, "Little Italy: A Floodplain Neighborhood."

76. Carol Aronovici, *Housing Conditions in the City of Saint Paul: Report Presented to the Housing Commission of the St. Paul Association* (Saint Paul, MN: Amherst H. Wilder Charity, 1917).

77. Aronovici, 7.

78. Aronovici, 11.

79. Aronovici, 74–75.

80. "Housing Conditions in the City of Saint Paul," Wilder Foundation website, accessed January 11, 2018, http://www.wilder.org/Wilder-Research/Publications/Studies/Forms/Study/.

81. *Plan of Saint Paul*, 1922, 12.

82. Dewey Albinson, "Swede Hollow, St. Paul," Bulletin of the American Swedish Institute (Winter 1962–63), 10. Collection of the American Swedish Institute.

83. Robert L. Crump, *Minnesota Prints and Printmakers, 1900–1945* (Saint Paul: Minnesota Historical Society Press, 2009), 53.

84. Albinson, "Swede Hollow, St. Paul," 10.

85. Thomas O'Sullivan, "Shaping the Land: Minnesota Landscapes 1840s to the Present," University Museum of Art, University of Minnesota, Minneapolis, 1985, 10.

86. Moira F. Harris, *Minnesota Modern: Four Artists of the Twentieth Century* (Afton, MN: Afton Historical Society Press, 2015), 33, 42–43.

87. Mary Towley Swanson, "The Artist as Chronicler," *Minnesota History* 52, no. 7 (Fall 1991): 274.

88. Albinson, "Swede Hollow, St. Paul" 10.

89. Crump, *Minnesota Prints and Printmakers, 1900–1945*, 54, 104, 164. These artists' works are in the collection of the Minnesota Historical Society.

90. J. B. Jackson, *Discovering the Vernacular Landscape* (New Haven, CT: Yale University Press, 1984), 3.

91. O'Sullivan, "Shaping the Land."

92. George Nasen, "Visiting around St. Paul Parks," *Saint Paul Dispatch*, November 25, 1932.

93. Transition to Phalen Creek Sewer North of Fourth Street, Drawing No. 629, Saint Paul, Minnesota, 1936, records of the Sewer Utility Division, Saint Paul Public Works, received by author, correspondence with Donovan O'Connor, August 5, 2016.

94. "City Acts to Get New Park Site," *Saint Paul Dispatch*, January 13, 1945. Clipping in Swede Hollow vertical file, Saint Paul Public Library.

95. *Lost Twin Cities 2*, television documentary produced by Twin Cities Public Television, text of narration accessed April 4, 2010, http://www.tpt.org/lostcity/swede.html.

96. "Swede Hollows Goes Up in Smoke as Shacks Burn," *Saint Paul Dispatch*, December 11, 1956, 1.

97. "Swede Hollows Goes Up in Smoke as Shacks Burn," 1.

98. Lanegren, "Swedish Neighborhoods in the Twin Cities," 44.

99. Rudolph Vecoli, "Immigrants and the Twin Cities: Melting Pot or Mosaic?," chapter 1 in Anderson and Blanck, *Swedes in the Twin Cities*, 21.

Chapter Five

1. *Los Angeles City Directory* 1890; Sanborn map 1888.

2. Leonard Pitt and Dale Pitt, *Los Angeles A to Z* (Berkeley: University of California Press, 1997), 416.

3. Dolores Hayden, *The Power of Place: Urban Landscapes as Public History* (Cambridge, MA: MIT Press, 1995), 111.

4. The *Los Angeles Times* published a three-part report on the challenges of modifying the riverbed and building up the city in 1882. See "Los Angeles River," *Los Angeles Times*, November 14, 1882, 4.

5. For a discussion of the zanjas, see Gumprecht, *The Los Angeles River*, 69–78.

6. "They'll View Ugly Slums," *Los Angeles Times*, February 25, 1906.

7. Kevin Starr, *Inventing the Dream: California through the Progressive Era* (New York: Oxford University Press, 1985), 54.

8. Natalia Molina, *Fit to Be Citizens? Public Health and Race in Los Angeles, 1879–1939* (Berkeley: University of California Press, 2006), 18; William Deverell, *Whitewashed Adobe: The Rise of Los Angeles and the Remaking of Its Mexican Past* (Berkeley: University of California Press, 2004), 28; Mike Davis, *City of Quartz: Excavating the Future in Los Angeles* (New York: Vintage Books, 1992), 26; Starr, *Inventing the Dream*, 54.

9. Molina, *Fit to Be Citizens?*, 19.

10. Eric Hobsbawm, "Introduction: Inventing Traditions," chapter 1 in *The Invention of Tradition* (Cambridge: Cambridge University Press, 1983), 1–14.

11. Richard Griswold del Castillo, *The Los Angeles Barrio, 1850–1890: A Social History* (Berkeley: University of California Press, 1979), 148–49.

12. Ricardo Romo, *East Los Angeles: History of a Barrio* (Austin: University of Texas Press, 1983), 29.

13. For Los Angeles city population data by race from 1880 to 1940, see table 1 in Molina, *Fit to Be Citizens?*, 7. Molina notes that "from 1890–1920 Mexicans were legally considered white," and her calculation of the Mexican population for these years is based on the number of foreign-born Mexicans, not people of Mexican origin.

14. Romo, *East Los Angeles*, 29.

15. Mark Wild, *Street Meeting: Multiethnic Neighborhoods in Early Twentieth-Century Los Angeles* (Berkeley: University of California Press, 2005), 29; Molina, *Fit to Be Citizens?*, 7.

16. Romo, *East Los Angeles*, 31.

17. Romo, 32.

18. Wild, *Street Meeting*, 19.

19. Wild, 19.

20. Molina, *Fit to Be Citizens?*, 6.

21. Molina, 8.

22. Molina, 5.

23. Diego Vigil, "Barrio Geneology," *City & Community* 7, no. 4 (December 2008): 368–69.

24. Wild, *Street Meeting*, 27.

25. "Still Improving: How the City Grows in All Quarters," *Los Angeles Times*, May 20, 1889, 4.

26. See "Remembering a River," chapter 3 in Deverell, *Whitewashed Adobe*, 91–128.

27. "They Build Nests in the River Bed," *Los Angeles Times*, January 6, 1901, C4.

28. Deverell, *Whitewashed Adobe*, 108.

29. "The New Railway Project—Through to Salt Lake," *Los Angeles Times*, November 27, 1888, 4. Floods threatened homes and railways facilities. In a news article on the history of Los Angeles River floods, the *Times* noted that "in one small section between First and Aliso streets in the 1884 flood, at least thirty-five homes were carried away and so severe was the railroad damage that Los Angeles was without communication with the north or east for two weeks. In the flood two years later, although that same section had been presumably protected by a levee, again a number of houses were swept away, only one bridge across the river remained standing and this could be negotiated only by brave foot travelers. Again the city was marooned, even wire communication being cut off almost two days." "Old Timers Recollect Floods of Past Years," *Los Angeles Times*, January 3. 1934, 7.

30. "Tie and Track: Getting Nervous about the Salt Lake Project," *Los Angeles Times*, May 25, 1889, 3; "The Salt Lake Railroad," *Los Angeles Times*, February 19, 1889, 4.

31. Pitt and Pitt, *Los Angeles A to Z*, 416; Charles Dwight Willard, *The Herald's History of Los Angeles* (Los Angeles: Kingsley-Barnes and Neuner Co., 1901): 338; "W. A. Clark's Big Deal," *Los Angeles Times*, August 21, 1900, 2, 3.

32. John R. Signor, *The Los Angeles and Salt Lake Railroad Company: Union Pacific's Historic Salt Lake Route* (San Marino, CA: Golden West Books, 1988): 18.

33. "Spanning History: The Bridges of the Los Angeles River," Los Angeles Conservancy, 2008.

34. "The City Council," *Los Angeles Times*, November 7, 1890, 2.

35. "Boyle Heights," *Los Angeles Times*, August 4, 1889, 10.

36. Wild, *Street Meeting*, 37; Official Map Number 2 of Los Angeles City, approved November 17, 1868 in Creason, *Los Angeles in Maps*.

37. "Andrew Boyle . . . paid $3,000 for an acre . . . for a plot of riverfront land east of the river. He paid just 25 cents an acre for unirrigated hill land nearby, which would become Boyle Heights." Gumprecht, *The Los Angeles River*, 78. A 1906 article in the *Herald* noted that while lowland real estate was expensive at between "$100 and $200 per acre while the highland . . . sold for as low as $5 per acre." "Boyle Heights in Early Days," *Los Angeles Herald*, June 3, 1906, 2.

38. Pitt and Pitt, *Los Angeles A to Z*, 56.

39. Rockwell D. Hunt, "William Henry Workman," *California and Californians* 3 (1930): 9–10, copy obtained from the vertical file "East Los Angeles—Boyle Heights," Los Angeles Public Library. From the same vertical file, see also William A. Spalding, *History of Los Angeles City and County* 2 (1929): 76–80; "Boyle Heights," *Los Angeles City Directory*, 1886–87, 304–8; "Boyle Heights in Early Days," 2. Workman was elected to eight terms on the city council (1872–87), one term as mayor (1887–88), and three terms as city treasurer (1901–7), as well as serving at various times as a park commissioner and a member of the board of education. Pitt and Pitt, *Los Angeles A to Z*, 56–57, 557.

40. "Public Improvement, Publicly Ratified," *Los Angeles Times*, November 9, 1901, 7. Arroyo de las Posas is an alternate spelling that appears in some newspaper reports.

NOTES TO CHAPTER FIVE

41. "A Vital Question. A Sanitary Sewer Needed for the County Hospital," *Los Angeles Times*, May 6, 1895, 10; "Sewage versus Storm Water," *Los Angeles Times*, January 25, 1895, 8; "Board of Public Works. County Hospital Sewage in Arroyo de Los Posas," *Los Angeles Times*, January 26, 1895, 8.

42. "Los Posos Gets Modern Bridge," *Los Angeles Herald*, October 30, 1906, 5.

43. Gumprecht, *The Los Angeles River*; Jared Orsi, *Hazardous Metropolis: Flooding and Urban Ecology in Los Angeles* (Berkeley: University of California Press, 2004); J. J. Warner, "Los Angeles River," *Los Angeles Times*, November 14, 1882, 4; "The Storm," *Los Angeles Times*, February 15, 1887, 1; George H. Cecil, "The Flood Control Problem," *Los Angeles Times*, January 12, 1932, A4; "Rainfall Record Broken in City with 5.32 Inches," *Los Angeles Times*, January 1, 1934, 1; "The Storm and Flood," *Los Angeles Times*, January 3, 1934, 4; "Old Timers Recollect Floods of Past Years."

44. Orsi, *Hazardous Metropolis*.

45. Norman Klein, *The History of Forgetting: Los Angeles and the Erasure of Memory* (London: Verso, 1997), 33.

46. Anna Sklar, *Brown Acres: An Intimate History of the Los Angeles Sewers* (Santa Monica, CA: Angel City Press, 2008).

47. Sklar.

48. Wild, *Street Meeting*, 28; Lillian Sokoloff, "The Russians in Los Angeles," *Studies in Sociology*, Sociological Monograph no. 11, 2, no 3 (March 1918): 1.

49. "Modern Ways Leave No Mark on Molokanes," *Los Angeles Herald*, April 21, 1907, 3.

50. Sokoloff, "The Russians in Los Angeles," 11–12.

51. Sokoloff explains on pages 2 and 3: "This name was applied because of the fact that the Molokans drink milk every day in the week, while the Greek Catholics abstain from it on Wednesdays and Fridays, which are fast days for them."

52. "Peter Demens," Saint Petersburg, Florida, webpage, accessed November 18, 2017, http://www.saint-petersburg.com/famous-people/peter-demens/.

53. Sophie Spalding, "The Myth of the Classic Slum: Contradictory Perceptions of Boyle Heights Flats, 1900–1991," *Journal of Architectural Education* 45, no. 2 (February 1992): 109.

54. Romo, *East Los Angeles*, 67.

55. "Fresh Batch of Molokans," *Los Angeles Times*, February 5, 1905, 12.

56. "Clever Fist Beats Chair," *Los Angeles Times*, May 19, 1907, V14.

57. Spalding, "The Myth of the Classic Slum," 109.

58. "Clever Fist Beats Chair," V14.

59. "Clever Fist Beats Chair," V14.

60. "Ninth Ward Gets Miles of Sewer," *Los Angeles Herald*, November 21, 1906, 12.

61. These lots appear to be approximately twenty to forty feet wide and seventy to one hundred feet long. See 1906 Sanborn.

62. "Clever Fist Beats Chair," V14.

63. "Clever Fist Beats Chair," V14.

64. Kevin Starr, *Inventing the Dream: California through the Progressive Era* (New York: Oxford University Press, 1985), 246.

65. Jennifer Lisa Koslow, *Cultivating Health: Los Angeles Women and Public Health Reform* (New Brunswick, NJ: Rutgers University Press, 2009), 54–55. Koslow describes Chicago-based social settlement leader Graham Taylor's visit to Los Angeles and the Bethlehem Institution.

66. "D. W. Bartlett Friend of Poor," *Los Angeles Herald*, September 17, 1905, 4; Kevin Starr, *Inventing the Dream*, 246.

67. Dana Bartlett, *A Better City: A Sociological Study of a Modern City* (Los Angeles: Neuner Press, 1907), 72.

68. Bartlett, 72.

69. "D. W. Bartlett Friend of Poor," 4.

70. "D. W. Bartlett Friend of Poor," 4.

71. "A Woman Worker in the Tenements," *Los Angeles Times*, May 18, 1902, C7.

72. "A Woman Worker in the Tenements," C7.

73. "Woman Comes to Aid Poor," *Los Angeles Times*, December 13, 1908, V, 18.

74. Starr, *Inventing the Dream*, 248.

75. Koslow, *Cultivating Health*, 44.

76. Koslow, 47–48.

77. Bessie Stoddart, "Courts of Sonoratown: The Housing Problem as It Is to Be Found in Los Angeles, *Charities and Commons* (December 1905): 296.

78. Stoddart, 295–99; Koslow, *Cultivating Health*, 57; Douglas Monroy, *Rebirth: Mexican Los Angeles from the Great Migration to the Great Depression* (Berkeley: University of California Press, 1999), 7–33; Stephanie Lewthwaite, *Race, Place, and Reform in Mexican Los Angeles: A Transnational Perspective, 1890–1940* (Tucson: University of Arizona Press, 2009), 39.

79. Koslow, *Cultivating Health*, 58; "Fight the 'Slums,'" *Los Angeles Times*, February 14, 1906, sec. 2, 2.

80. "'Housing Committee,'" *Los Angeles Times*, February 15, 1906, sec. 2, 2. Koslow lists the original members as Coffey, Kenney, Veeder, Day, and architect George E. Bergstrom. Day took the place of Dr. Richard Malony on the commission when he refused to serve. The architect Bergstrom replaced building superintendent Backus by September 1906.

81. Koslow, *Cultivating Health*, 59.

82. "War on the Slums Now to Be Pressed," *Los Angeles Times*, September 7, 1906, sec. 2, 1; note the *Times* spells his name Howton. See Koslow, *Cultivating Health*, 62 for more on Houghton.

83. "They'll View Ugly Slums," *Los Angeles Times*, February 25, 1906, sec. 2, 6.

84. "War on the Slums Now to Be Pressed," sec. 2, 1.

85. The theme has been repeatedly deployed and reinterpreted by Angelenos, historians, urban critics, and writers. To cite just two examples, editor Charles Fletcher Lummis used the phrase "land of sunshine" as the title of his journal and Mike Davis's first chapter in his classic *City of Quartz* is "Sunshine or Noir?"

86. Stoddart, "Courts of Sonoratown," 298.

87. Molina, *Fit to Be Citizens?*, 6.

88. Molina, 1.

89. "The Candidates and the Sordid Meddlers," *Los Angeles Times*, November 11, 1906, sec. 2, 4. For more on Harper's reputation for corruption, see, for example, Glen Creason, "This 1909 Map Is a Throwback to the Time of One of L.A.'s Most Corrupt Mayors," *Los Angeles Magazine*, published to web on July 13, 2016, accessed August 10, 2017, http://www.lamag.com/citythinkblog/l-s-26th-mayor-excellent-mustache-also-wildly-corrupt/.

90. "To Eradicate Slums, Mayor as Inspector," *Los Angeles Times*, August 8, 1907, sec. 2, 2.

91. Koslow, *Cultivating Health*, 62.

92. Los Angeles Housing Commission, *Report of the Housing Commission of the City of Los Angeles, 1908* (Los Angeles: City of Los Angeles), 3.

93. Koslow, *Cultivating Health*, 68.

94. Koslow, 75.

95. Los Angeles Housing Commission, *Report of the Housing Commission of the City of Los Angeles*, 1906–8 (Los Angeles: City of Los Angeles): 3.

96. Los Angeles Housing Commission, 6–7.

97. Koslow, *Cultivating Health*, 63–64. Koslow cites the board of health minutes from November 22, 1906, and a *Times* article. Interestingly, the *Times* article refers to "maps showing the Utah-street district." "Housing Ordinance," *Los Angeles Times*, November 23, 1906, sec. 2, 2.

98. Los Angeles Housing Commission, *Report of the Housing Commission*, 7.

99. City of Los Angeles, Ordinance No. 14,113, approved February 5, 1907; text of the ordinance is included in the *Report of the Housing Commission*, February 20, 1906, to June 30, 1908.

100. Bartlett, *A Better City*, 72.

101. Los Angeles Housing Commission, *Report of the Housing Commission*, 7–8.

102. Dana Cuff, *The Provisional City: Los Angeles Stories of Architecture and Urbanism* (Cambridge, MA: MIT Press, 2000), 131.

103. The housing commission report noted: "As soon as notice was served on the land owners after the passage of the ordinance governing house courts, the Utah street court, the Aliso street, the Seaton street, and other smaller courts, to a total of twelve, were entirely demolished." Los Angeles Housing Commission, *Report of the Housing Commission of the City of Los Angeles*, 1906–8, 12.

104. Bartlett, *A Better City*, 74.

105. See, for example, "Capital for House Court," *Los Angeles Times*, September 6, 1908, sec. 2, 1.

106. Los Angeles Housing Commission, *Report of the Housing Commission*, 4.

107. Los Angeles Housing Commission, 10.

108. "Some of the Mexican laborers have constructed small houses on leased ground and pay $2.50 per month for ground rent and water, which is cheaper than renting a two room shack for perhaps $6 or $7. . . . Let us raise the standard of living and help the workingman to his just pay, better homes and health will be the result which will pay ten-fold the small investment any city makes in establishing such work. Wretched habilitations of the Chinese have made it possible for them to pursue their opium habit. Do away with these and substitute cleaner, lighter, habilitations and regular inspection, and conditions in Chinatown will improve (1909: 14)."

109. Los Angeles Housing Commission, *Report of the Housing Commission*, 4.

110. The house court issue continued to attract local and national attention in the 1910s. In 1916, for example, USC sociologist Emory Bogardus reported on the continuing relevance of the problem in the *American Journal of Sociology*.

111. Wild, *Street Meeting*, 10–11; Pitt and Pitt, *Los Angeles A to Z*, 537.

112. W. W. McEuen, thesis, USC, 1914, accessed via Hathi Trust, September 5, 2017, 39.

113. Sokoloff, "The Russians in Los Angeles," 5–6.

114. Sokoloff, 6.

115. Sokoloff, 10.

116. M. C. Kennedy, *History of the California Congress of Mothers* (Pomona, CA: Pomona Progress Print, 1913), 99.

117. Kennedy, *History of the California Congress of Mothers*, 100.

118. Sokoloff, "The Russians in Los Angeles," 11. "New Home for Melting Pot," *Los Angeles Times*, December 20, 1915, sec. 2, 5.

119. Sokoloff, "The Russians in Los Angeles," 12.

120. Sokoloff, 12.

121. US Department of Commerce, Bureau of the Census, Fourteenth Census of the United States 1920—Population, California, Los Angeles County, Los Angeles City, District 8, Enumeration District 234, Sheet number 9585.

122. Stevenson map, 1884. Collection of Los Angeles Public Library.

123. Architectural historian Sophie Spalding cites Young's positive portrayal of the community as "poor but functioning" as a "contrasting view" in opposition to the dominant characterization of the neighborhood as a slum.

124. Pauline V. Young, *The Pilgrims of Russian Town: The Community of Spiritual Christian Jumpers in America* (Chicago: University of Chicago Press, 1932), 17–18.

125. Young.

126. Barbara Miller, "Cosmorama on the East Side," *Los Angeles Times*, February 17, 1935, J6.

127. Wild, *Street Meeting*, 29.

128. Wild, 30.

129. "Spanning History: The Bridges of the Los Angeles River."

130. Gumprecht, *The Los Angeles River*, 222.

131. Gumprecht, 227.

132. Young, *The Pilgrims of Russian Town*, 17.

133. Cuff, *The Provisional City*, 132.

134. Cuff, 158. Cuff notes that "Wright visited Washington in secrecy and with great political machinations to obtain a PWA project for Los Angeles and the commission to design it for his team. The same group, under the name Housing Architects Associated, worked together to design the first of the ten early LA housing developments, Ramona Gardens [and later] Rancho San Pedro."

135. Cuff, 149.

136. Cuff, 111.

137. Steven T. Moga, "Projects and Slums: A Context Statement Describing the Photographs of the Housing Authority of the City of Los Angeles Subcollection of the Los Angeles Public Library," University of California Los Angeles, 1999, appendix 3.

138. The figure $15 million is from "Council Approves Housing Project," *Los Angeles Times*, June 4, 1941, 1A. The figure 3,748 units is from "Housing Project Agreements Signed," *Los Angeles Times*, November 1, 1941, 16. The as-built total of units constructed at the original ten developments was 3,162 (Moga, "Projects and Slums," appendix 3). A 1945 HACLA report cites a figure of 3,468 homes constructed. Housing Authority of the City of Los Angeles, *A Decent Home an American Right*, 1945, 25.

139. "Council Approves Housing Change," *Los Angeles Times*, May 17, 1941, 2.

140. "Council Approves Housing Change," 2; "Council Approves Housing Project," *Los Angeles Times*, June 4, 1941, 1A.

141. HACLA, *A Decent Home an American Right*, 1945, 28.

142. Cuff, *The Provisional City*, 141.

143. The 1945 HACLA report includes slightly different unit numbers, perhaps citing planned construction rather than as-built numbers: 260 units at Pico Gardens, 802 units at Aliso Village.

144. HACLA, *A Decent Home an American Right*, 1945, 28.

145. Planning historians have characterized this era as the peak of public housing construction in the United States, a period that has begun to look shorter in duration and more like an "experiment" than an ongoing policy commitment (or significant component of American

social policy) over time. See Joseph Heathcott, "The Strange Career of Public Housing: Policy, Planning, and the American Metropolis in the Twentieth Century," and Lawrence J. Vale and Yonah Freemark, "From Public Housing to Public-Private Housing: 75 Years of American Social Experimentation," *Journal of the American Planning Association* 78, no. 4 (2012): 360–75, 379–402.

146. The name Flats did not disappear. Sociologist James Diego Vigil writes that "in the mid-1930s, the Cuatro Flats gang emerged here, beginning as a group of youth claiming Fourth Street as its domain. Like the rest of East Los Angeles residents, the group had as its activities mostly just hanging around together and partying. Early in the 1940s, the area became known as Tortilla Flats, and later in the decade the *placa* (graffiti logo) 'Cuatro Flats' came into extensive use." James Diego Vigil, *The Projects: Gang and Non-Gang Families in East Los Angeles* (Austin: University of Texas Press, 2007), 40. The name was also used by young men around First Street who adopted the term Primavera Flats.

147. Cuff, *The Provisional City*.

148. See "Hispanic Trends," Pew Research Center, accessed November 18, 2017, http://www.pewhispanic.org/2012/06/27/regional-distribution-of-hispanic-origin-groups/.

149. "Pueblo del Sol," McCormack Baron architects, accessed September 21, 2017, http://www.mccormackbaron.com/community-profiles/pueblo-del-sol.

Chapter Six

1. *Third Report of the Nashville Board of Health*, 1879, 32.

2. *Report of the Metropolitan Board of Health*, New York City, 1866, 109.

3. "The Cholera and Fever Nests of New York," *Frank Leslie's Illustrated Newspaper*, September 15, 1866.

4. William Deverell, *Whitewashed Adobe: The Rise of Los Angeles and the Remaking of Its Mexican Past* (Berkeley: University of California Press, 2004), 188. Deverell examines the plague in chapter 5, "Ethnic Quarantine."

5. Lewthwaite, *Race, Place, and Reform in Mexican Los Angeles: A Transnational Perspective, 1890–1940* (Tucson: University of Arizona Press), 120. Lewthwaite discusses the plague outbreak and its consequences in chapter 5, "The Iconography of the 'Mexican' Slum": Plague, Housing, and Documentary Photography."

6. "Our Own Little Playground, Swede Hollow," typed recollections of life in Swede Hollow in the 1920s and 1930s, vertical files "St. Paul—Descriptions—Districts and Areas," collection of the Minnesota Historical Society.

7. Records of the Saint Paul Public Works Department; *Sewerage and Sewage Disposal in the Metropolitan District of New York and New Jersey* (New York: Martin Brown, 1910); *Report of the Board of Health of the Health Department of the City of New York. May 1, 1874–December 31, 1875* (New York: Martin Brown, 1878), collection of New-York Historical Society.

8. Anne Whiston Spirn, "Buried Floodplains: A Pervasive National Hazard," Memo to Susan Wachter, US Department of Housing and Urban Development, September 1999. Spirn argues that the dynamics of floodplains, particularly storm water runoff problems, persist even when a polluted waterway is removed from view. Nineteenth-century systems of engineered drainage and sanitation interact with natural processes to create hybrid landscape in urban neighborhoods. Spirn's analysis of landscape change in the Dudley Street neighborhood in the Roxbury section of Boston and Mill Creek in West Philadelphia powerfully demonstrates how building

on the valley bottoms led poorly constructed houses and apartment buildings to subside, flood, or collapse and how vacant lowlands represent a potential resource to address environmental problems. Spirn, *The West Philadelphia Landscape Plan: A Framework for Action* (Philadelphia: Department of Landscape Architecture and Regional Planning, University of Pennsylvania, 1991); Spirn, *The Language of Landscape* (New Haven, CT: Yale University Press, 1998); Spirn, "Reclaiming Common Ground: Water, Neighborhoods, and Public Places," in *The American Planning Tradition: Culture and Policy*, ed. Robert Fishman (Washington DC: Woodrow Wilson Center Press, 2000), 297–313; Spirn, "Restoring Natural Resources and Rebuilding Urban Communities," in *Planning for a New Century: The Regional Agenda*, ed. Jonathan Barnett (Washington DC: Island Press, 2001): 167–68; Spirn, "Urban Ecosystems, City Planning, and Environmental Education: Literature, Precedents, Key Concepts, and Prospects," in *Understanding Urban Ecosystems: A New Frontier for Science and Education*, ed. Alan R. Berkowitz, Charles H. Nilon, and Karen S. Hollweg (New York: Springer-Verlag, 2003), 204.

9. The Cumberland River flooded Nashville in 1884, 1887, 1926–27, 1929, and 2010. "The Flood at Nashville. Many Buildings under Water and Much Distress among the Poor," *New York Times*, March 15, 1884, 1. See, for example, "Floods and Fires: The Rise in the Cumberland and Elsewhere—Work of the Flames," *Washington Post*, February 20, 1880, 1; Charles J. Burnell, *The Nashville Flood of December and January 1926–27* (Nashville: C. J. Burnell, 1927); "1,000 Made Homeless by Nashville Flood," *New York Times*, December 26, 1926, 23; "The Rivers Rising," *Atlanta Constitution*, February 4, 1887, 5; "Alabama Flood Loss Exceeds $10,000,000: Governor Graves Will Ask Hoover for Aid—Waters Rise at Nashville, Tenn.," *New York Times*, March 31, 1929, 24; Summerville, "The City and the Slum," 182–83.

10. "The Rivers Rising," 5.

11. "1,000 Made Homeless by Nashville Flood: They Are Driven Out in Lower Part of City as River Goes 9 Feet above Flood Line," *New York Times*, December 26, 1926, 23.

12. The Los Angeles river flooded in 1884, 1886, 1889, 1914, 1934, and 1938.

13. Gumprecht, *The Los Angeles River*, 173.

14. Gumprecht, 217.

15. Joseph L. Arnold, "The Evolution of the 1936 Flood Control Act, Office of History," US Army Corps of Engineers, printed by the US Government Printing Office, Washington DC, 1988, accessed June 7, 2017, http://www.publications.usace.army.mil/Portals/76/Publications/EngineerPamphlets/EP_870-1-29.pdf.

16. The *Oxford English Dictionary* and *Merriam-Webster Dictionary* date the first use of the term to 1873, but it was not until the 1930s that the phrase began to be widely used (and spelled as "floodplain" rather than "flood plain") in the United States; Gilbert F. White, *Human Adjustment to Floods: A Geographical Approach to the Flood Problem in the United States*, Research Paper No. 29 (Chicago: University of Chicago, 1945): 44–45.

17. "Stormwater and Your Community," accessed August 2010, http://ohioline.osu.edu/aex-fact/0442.html.

18. Matthew Klingle, *Emerald City: An Environmental History of Seattle* (New Haven, CT: Yale University Press, 2007), 180.

19. This problem is particularly acute in an era of extreme weather and climate change.

20. For a discussion of the "railroad slum" and the destructive power of railroad development on American city form, see Mumford, "Factory, Railroad, and Slum" in *The City in History*, 458–65.

21. As historian Paige Glotzer notes, four of the most well-known suburban communities of the early twentieth century, including Roland Park in Baltimore, Palos Verdes Estates

in Southern California, Forest Hills Gardens in New York, and Kansas City's Country Club District, all used racial covenants to exclude nonwhites. Glotzer, "Exclusion in Arcadia," 479. For more on covenants, see Charles S. Johnson, *Patterns of Negro Segregation* (New York: Harper & Brothers, 1943), 177; Mitchell Duneier, *Ghetto: The Invention of a Place, the History of an Idea* (New York: Farrar, Straus and Giroux, 2016), 29; Yale Rabin, "Expulsive Zoning: The Inequitable Legacy of Euclid," in *Zoning and the American Dream: Promises to Keep* (Chicago: American Planning Association, 1989): 106–7.

22. Steven T. Moga, "The Zoning Map and American City Form," *Journal of Planning Education and Research* 37, no. 3 (September 2017): 271–85.

23. The light industry zone placed over this residential area allowed all uses except for twenty-six explicitly prohibited activities or "similar obnoxious purposes" detailed in the ordinance.

24. The portion of the block fronting Broad Street, between Fifth and Sixth Avenues, Broad Street and the back alley was designated commercial. The southern portion of that block was zoned industrial as was the block to the south bounded by McGavock, Fifth, Demonbreun, and Sixth. Further south, in the center of the Black Bottom neighborhood, the boundary line between the industrial and commercial zones ran along the alley between Fifth and Sixth Avenues from Demonbreun to Peabody.

25. For more on expulsive zoning and a review of the literature on zoning, race, and ethnicity, see Andrew Whittemore, "The Experience of Racial and Ethnic Minorities with Zoning in the United States," *Journal of Planning Literature* 32, no. 1 (2017): 16–27.

26. Seymour Toll, *Zoned American* (New York: Grossman Publishers, 1969); Marina Moskowitz, *Standard of Living: The Measure of the Middle Class in Modern America* (Baltimore: Johns Hopkins University Press, 2004).

27. Hirt describes how the purely single-family residential district of detached homes, a pattern that was in comparative perspective "not only spatially but also *legally exceptional*" compared to other nations (Sonia Hirt, "Home, Sweet Home: American Residential Zoning in Comparative Perspective," *Journal of Planning Education and Research* 33, no. 3 (2013): 293, emphasis in original).

28. Moskowitz, *Standard of Living*.

29. Shaun McGann and Jack Dougherty, "Federal Lending and Redlining," from the webpage On The Line, accessed February 15, 2017, http://ontheline.trincoll.edu/book/chapter/federal-lending-and-redlining/, 1; Kenneth T. Jackson, *Crabgrass Frontier: The Suburbanization of the United States* (New York: Oxford University Press, 1985), 197; Gwendolyn Wright, *Building the Dream: A Social History of Housing in America* (Cambridge, MA: MIT Press, 1981), 247; McGann and Dougherty, "Federal Lending and Redlining."

30. Eric Avila, *Popular Culture in the Age of White Flight: Fear and Fantasy in Suburban Los Angeles* (Berkeley: University of California Press, 2004), 35. A slighter longer version of the same text is cited by Woods, "The Federal Home Loan Bank Board," 1047. Woods lists the original source as "Area Description of Metropolitan Los Angeles, California, Housing Survey," 1, folder: Metropolitan Los Angeles, California, Security Map and Area Description vol. 1 (2), box 78, New York California, Records Relating to the City Survey File, 1935–40, Homer Owners' Loan Corporation, RG195, Records of the FHLBB, National Archives II, College Park, MD (see 1058n69 and 1058n76).

31. Woods, "The Federal Home Loan Bank Board," 1044–45.

32. Jackson, *Crabgrass Frontier*, 198.

33. HOLC report for Chicopee, MA, "Undesign the Redline" exhibit, Neilson Library, Smith College, 2017.

34. For more on the mortgage interest deduction and its relationship to economic polarization and income inequality, see Matthew Desmond, "How Homeownership Became the Engine of American Inequality," *New York Times Magazine*, May 9, 2017.

35. "U.S. Railroad Route Miles and Revenue," RailServe, accessed June 9, 2017, http://www.railserve.com/stats_records/railroad_route_miles.html.

36. "U.S. Railroad Route Miles and Revenue," RailServe.

37. Raymond A. Mohl, "Planned Destruction: The Interstates and Central City Housing," in *From Tenements to the Taylor Homes: In Search of an Urban Housing Policy* (University Park: Pennsylvania State Press University Press, 2000); Eric Avila, "The Sutured City," chapter 6 in *Popular Culture in the Age of White Flight: Fear and Fantasy in Suburban Los Angeles* (Berkeley: University of California Press, 2004), 185–223; Karilyn Crockett, "Introduction," in *People before Highways: Boston Activists, Urban Planners, and a New Movement for City Making* (Amherst: University of Massachusetts Press, 2018), 1–18.

38. Cliff Ellis, "Professional Conflict over Urban Form: The Case of Urban Freeway," chapter 11 in *Planning the Twentieth-Century American City*, ed. Mary Corbin Sies and Christopher Silver (Baltimore: Johns Hopkins University Press, 1996), 267.

39. Chudacoff et al. identify steel frame construction and electric elevators as key technological advancements that made skyscraper development possible; Chudacoff et al., *The Evolution of American Urban Society*, 59.

40. Yi-Fu Tuan, *Space and Place: The Perspective of Experience* (Minneapolis: University of Minnesota Press, 1977).

41. Irving Allen, *The City in Slang: New York Life and Popular Speech* (New York: Oxford University Press, 1993), 230.

42. David Ward, *Poverty, Ethnicity, and the American City: Changing Conceptions of the Slum and the Ghetto* (Cambridge: Cambridge University Press, 1989): 19.

43. Alan Mayne, *Slums: The History of a Global Injustice* (London: Reaktion Books, 2017), 41.

44. "Urges Battle with Slums," *Los Angeles Times*, March 11, 1911, sec. 2, 2.

45. The author wishes to thank Larry Vale for this insight regarding not just the "peculiarity" of these activities, but their negative social implications with regard to the proper use of the bathtub or parlor as domestic spaces. Aronovici, *Housing Conditions in the City of Saint Paul*, 11–14.

46. Dromgoole, "A Journey through Black Bottom," 5.

47. For example, the Pittsburgh Survey identified, labeled, and documented slums. The description of Skunk Hollow is an excellent example of the analysis of conditions in an urban lowland during this period.

48. *Los Angeles Times*, February 14, 1906.

49. McKenzie wanted to know the extent to which environment influenced juvenile delinquency versus variables such as culture or previous environments where individuals had lived (especially rural places). McKenzie's thesis was published in a series of articles in the *American Journal of Sociology* and as a scholarly monograph entitled *The Neighborhood: A Study of Local Life in the City of Columbus, Ohio.*

50. Cited in Klingle, *Emerald City*, 186–87, 307n14, as: R. D. McKenzie, "The Ecological Approach to the Study of Human Community," *American Journal of Sociology* 30 (November 1924): 301.

51. Nels Anderson, "The Slum: A Project for Study," *Social Forces* 7, no. 1 (September 1928): 87–90.

52. The use of ecological terminology as metaphor in the writing of these scholars, without any reference to concerns of environmental justice or attention to the interaction of natural processes within urban environments, is sometimes uncanny, giving the writing an odd quality.

53. Alexander von Hoffman, "The Origins of American Housing Reform," Joint Center for Housing Studies, Harvard University, working paper W98-2 (August 1998).

54. Duneier, *Ghetto*, 45.

55. Mabel L. Walker, *Urban Blight and Slums: Economic and Legal Factors in Their Origin, Reclamation, and Prevention* (Cambridge, MA: Harvard University Press, 1938), 4.

56. In contrast, advocates for public housing like Catherine Bauer critiqued market failures under capitalism and "the incapacity of private enterprise to meet the great need for new housing in the future" as the main problem. Gail Radford, *Modern Housing for America: Policy Struggles in the New Deal Era* (Chicago: University of Chicago Press, 1996), 186–87.

57. Robert Fogelson, *Downtown: Its Rise and Fall, 1880–1950* (New Haven, CT: Yale University Press, 2001), 319–20.

58. Mindy Thompson Fullilove, *Urban Alchemy: Restoring Joy in America's Sorted-Out Cities* (New York: New Village Press, 2013).

59. Zora Neale Hurston, "Characteristics of Negro Expression," in *The New Negro: Readings on Race, Representation, and African American Culture, 1892–1938*, ed. Henry Louis Gates and Gene Andrew Garret (Princeton, NJ: Princeton University Press, 2007), 361–62.

60. Duneier, *Ghetto*, 24. Duneier describes the importance of African Americans' experience in the military during World War II, especially related to the Nazi's use of the term of "ghetto" and the ideology of Aryan supremacy in comparison with the US.

61. Duneier, 24.

Epilogue

1. Mike Harden, "'End,' 'Side' as Different as North and—Uh—West," *Columbus Dispatch*, November 21, 1994, 1E.

2. Kevin Lynch, *The Image of the City* (Cambridge, MA: MIT Press, 1960), 110.

3. Jeff Ueland and Barney Warf, "Racialized Topographies: Altitude and Race in Southern Cities," *Geographical Review* 96, no. 1 (January 2006): 50.

4. Timothy W. Collins, Sara E. Grineski, and Jayajit Chakraborty, "Environmental Injustice and Flood Risk: A Conceptual Model and Case Comparison of Metropolitan Miami and Houston, USA," *Regional Environmental Change* 18, no. 2 (February 2018).

5. Linda Villarosa, "America's Hidden H.I.V. Epidemic," *New York Times*, June 6, 2017.

6. Evelyn Nieves, "Skid Row Makeover," *Salon*, August 8, 2006, accessed August 2010, http://www.salon.com/news/feature/2006/08/08/skid_row.

7. John Futty and Alayna DeMartini, "Driven to Addiction: Street Prostitutes Trapped in Desperate Tangle of Abuse," *Columbus Dispatch*, December 17, 2001, A1.

Index

Pages in italics refer to images.

Abrams, Charles, 8
African Americans, 1–9, 23, 26–27, 55, 67, 69, 71, 75, 77–78, 153, 158, 163, 173, 209n60; "black bottom" term, 28–30, 57, 164; black crime, white fears of, 29; black spaces, racializing of, 30, 56–57; blaming of, 72; and cholera, 60; disease risk, 57, 148–49; and ghetto, 169; housing markets, prejudice against, 156; low value land, 83–84; marginalizing of, 29; and morality, 74; quarantine, attempts to, 66; and racialized poor whites, 74; racialized violence, threat of, 149; red light districts, 68; urban lowland neighborhoods, community formation in, 84; urban migration of, 70; white abuse of, 64–65
African Methodist Episcopal (AME) church, 56
agency, 112
ague, 22
Albinson, Dewey, 105–6, 108, 110, 164–65
Allen, Irving, 163, 183n40
American Dream, 7, 111
American Federation of the Arts, 106
Americanization, 88, 138
American-Scandinavian Foundation, 106
Amherst H. Wilder Charity, 103, 165
Anderson, Nels, 166
Andrus, Vera, 106
architecture, 1, 173
Aronovici, Carol, 103–4, 108, 164–65
Aryan supremacy, 169, 209n60. *See also* white supremacy
Asia, 2, 163
assimilation, 2–3, 88, 111–12, 118, 140, 165

Astor, John Jacob, 184n6
Atlanta, GA, 83–84; Buttermilk Bottom, 26; Tanyard Flats, 26

Backus, J. J., 130, 202n80
Backwater Blues (Mizelle), 80
Baltimore, MD, 11, 23; Roland Park, 206–7n21
Baptist, Edward, 189n6
Barlow, William, 80
Bartlett, Dana W., 127–29, 134–35
Baton Rouge, LA, 17
Battle Creek, MI, 6
Bauer, Catherine, 209n56
Bayley, Richard, 41
Belmont, August, 184n6
Bennett, Edward H., 104
Benson, Margaret, 35, 38
Bergstrom, George E., 202n80
Betancourt, Alvaro, 50
Bethlehem Institute, 125, 127–28, 201n65
Better City, The (Bartlett), 127, 134
Billings, John S., 4
Bishop, General, 97
Black Bottom, 5–9, 29–30, 56, 59, 60, 66–67, 79, 146–51, 158, 170, 173, 188n1, 189n9, 192n99, 207n24; African Americans in, 163, 188–89n2, 192n99, 193n109; alcohol, shaping of, 78, 80; beautiful city, as menace to, 72; as black cat, 72, 73; black life, as symbol of, 27; Bucket of Blood saloon, 78; cholera in, 84; as dance craze, 80, 169, 193n111; disappearance of, 82–83; first appearance in print, 60, 64; flooding of, 1, 55, 69, 76, 153–54; goats in, 164; Hay Market, 59, 69,

Black Bottom (*cont.*)
74, 77; highway construction, 160; industrial designation in, 77, 155–56, 157; Irish in, 188–89n2; name, origins of, 188–89n2; negative reputation of, 70, 83; newspaper coverage of, 71–72; population decline, 76, 80–81, 172; public park, 73–75; public scrutiny of, 71; racialized space of, 57; and redlining, 159; reformers, reaction to, 73–74; renaming of, 173; sacred and profane space in, 68; sewer project, and displacement, 4; slum, as racially coded synonym for, 55; slum, reputation of, 162; slum clearance, 74–75; as SoBro, 173; streetcar conflict, link with, 70; targeting of, by whites, 65; tenement buildings, demolition of, 77–78; as term, 169; white vigilantes in, 55; Wilson's Spring Branch, pollution of, 57–64, 69; and zoning, 160. *See also* Nashville, TN
Black Hand, 51
blackness, 72
blues, 80, 193n113
Bodnar, John, 180n15
Bogardus, Emory, 203n110
Bohemian Flats (monograph), 6
Boston, MA, 17, 23, 182–83n28; Roxbury, 205–6n8
"bottoms," 5, 168; as defined, 181n2; as derogatory, 169, 174; as despised urban districts, 75; as generic descriptor, 57; as landscape term, 28–29; as pejorative, 28, 56–57, 64, 163; as phrase, 190n30; racializing of, 29–30, 56–57; as stigmatized, 76; as term, 28, 146, 162, 164, 169
bottoms, hollows, and flats, 7, 9, 13, 26–30, 76, 146–47, 152, 158, 162, 168–74; as term, 183n36
Boyd, Henry A., 70
Boyd, Richard Henry, 70
Boyle, Andrew, 122, 200n37
Boyle, Maria Elizabeth, 122
Brainard Flouring Mills, 90, 92
Brent, J. Lancaster, 181n5
Brettheimer, Emil, 50
Britain, 163
Brooklyn, NY, 23
Brown, Robert (Bob), 106
bubonic plague, 149, 150
built environment, 157
Burrell, Charles A., 70

Cahokia, IL, 15–16, 182n15
California, 11, 88, 113, 116
California Real Estate Association, 143
Camareno, Frances, 141
Canada, 195n16
canal building, 23
Cantal-Dupart, Michel, 168
capitalism: industrial, 2, 9, 12–13; laissez-faire, 3
Carmack, Edward Ward, 78
Carnegie Library, 77

Casoto, Paolo, 51
Central Park, 32–35, 38–39, 50, 54, 148, 158
Central Tennessee University, 67
Charleston, SC, 17
Charlick, Oliver, 43
Chicago, IL, 23, 89, 180n14, 182–83n28; Black Bottom, 184n43
Chicago school of sociology, 140, 165–66, 169; critique of, 167
Chicopee, MA, 158
Chivers, Walter, 28
cholera, 4, 21–22, 41, 45, 52–53, 59–60, 63–64, 83–84, 95–98, 101, 148–50, 183n30
cholo, 133; cholo courts, 163
Cincinnati, OH, 17–18, 23
Citizens' Association, 33, 35, 39, 41, 51, 149
City Beautiful movement, 127
city planning, 1, 4–5, 8, 171, 174; gridiron plan, 13–16; maps, reliance on, 168; public health, 62; sanitary systems, 170; uniformity of, 13; urban parks, 170
Civil War, 12, 17, 23, 29, 55–56, 58, 84, 112
Clark, Emmons, 42
Clark, William Andrews, 120
class, 165; and ethnicity, 151; and land, 167; and morality, 9; and race, 83, 151; and segregation, 157; and space, 170; and topography, 83
Clay, Grady, 14–15
Cleveland, OH, 6; the Flats, 17; Irishtown Bend, 17
climate change, 54
Coffey, Titan, 130, 133, 202n80
Cohn, Sol, 78, 80
Columbus, OH, 26, 182n14; Bottoms, 165, 173–74, 180n14
Colvin, George, 50–52
company towns, 13
Connemara Patch, 95
containment, 3–4, 75, 97, 165, 174; vs. dispersal, 151; and segregation, 57
Cooper, Duncan, 78
Cooper, Peter, 184n6
Country Music Hall of Fame, 82
Creason, Glen, 181n5
Crespi, Juan, 180–81n1
Croton Aqueduct project, 39
Cuff, Dana, 142–44, 204n134
Cumberland Lumber Company, 68–69

Daniel, William, 81
Davis, James A., 1
Davis, Mike, 202n85
Day, William Horace, 130, 202n80
decentralization, 160–61
Demens, P. A., 125
demography, 158; demographic change, 172
Detroit, MI, 29; Black Bottom, 184n43
Deverell, William, 150

INDEX   213

Dickens, Charles, 163
disease, 20, 34, 59–60, 148–49, 151, 167, 174; and diet, 62; disease theory, and lowlands, 145; fear of, 146, 169–70; miasmatic theory, 63–64; and race, 61, 165; and topography, 61. *See also individual diseases*
displacement, 3–5, 30, 112, 144
Dolores Mission Church, 138
"Down in Black Bottom" (Evans), 80
Doyle, Don, 66, 188–89n2, 192n84
Dromgoole, Will Allen, 72
DuBois, W. E. B., 28
Duluth, MN, 89, 102
Duluth and Saint Paul Railroad, 94, 155
Duneier, Mitchell, 169, 209n60
Durham, NC, 83–84

Early, Jordan W., 66
earthmoving practices, 173
ecosystems, 166
Ellison, Ralph, 193n113
emancipation, 17, 57, 83–84, 163
Emigrant and Refuge Hospital, 39
engineering, 1, 15, 33; civil, 22, 98, 173; public health, 22; sanitary, 4
environmental determinism, 170
environmental justice: social equity, 9–10; and sustainability, 174
ethnicity, 2, 7–8, 10, 26–27, 104, 111, 119, 125–26, 155, 158, 163, 168, 170
Europe, 2
Evans, Joe, 80
eviction, 112
Ewing, Charles, 138
Ewing, Robert, 77
Excelsior Brewery, 85–86, 92–93, *93*, 94. *See also* Hamm's Brewery
Exhibition of American Art, 106

fair housing, 9–10
Farrington, Joseph O., 33, 167
Fish, Hamilton, 184n6
Fisk University, 76, 80, 158
Flanagan, John T., 196n28
Flats, 8–9, 11, 30, 113–14, *115*, 118–22, *128*, 131–32, *139*, 146–51, 153, 158, 163, 165, 172; Aliso Village, 142–43, *143*, 144–45, 173; as Cuatro Flats, 205n146; demolition in, 142–43; and dumping, 152; as failure, 115–16; flooding of, 123, 141; foreignness, association with, 125–26; growth of, 126; highway construction, 160; light industry designation of, 156, *157*; Mexican community in, 134, 145; Molokans in, 124, 126–27, 134, 137–38, 140, 145; multiculturalism of, 125; overcrowding in, 134; Pico-Aliso, 173; Pico Gardens, 142–43, *143*, 144; Pueblo del Sol, 145, 173; rail yards, proximity to, 155; and redlining, *159*; renaming of, 173; sense of place, 141–42; as slum, reputation of, 136, 162; superblocks, 143; as thriving urban neighborhood, 141; Tortilla Flats, 205n146; urban reformers, interest in, 127; Utah Street housing project, 142; as zone of transition, 140. *See also* Los Angeles, CA
Flood Control Act (1936), 154
floodplain, 173, 205–6n8; as term, 154, 183n34, 206n16
floods: in Los Angeles, 113–14, 123, 137, 141, 151, 153, 200n29, 206n12; of lowland neighborhoods, 20–21, 153–54, 158–59; in Nashville, 1, 55, 63, 69, 76, 82, 151, 153–54, 206n9; in New York City, 154; place, negative images of, 154; sewer construction, 153
Ford, James, 167–68
Fort Snelling, 88, 194–95n6
Frankfort, KY, 6
Frazier, Robert, 65
Friday Morning Club, 129
Friends of Swede Hollow, 110

Gans, Herbert, 8
Gauger, Augustus F., 92
Gazzola, Alexander, 51–52
genocide, 169
George Washington University, 173
Germany, 5–6, 92, 195n16
germ theory, 22, 83, 149, 151
ghetto: Nazi use of, 154, 209n60; as term, 169, 183n34
Ghetto (Duneier), 169
Gilded Age, 170
Gill, Jonathan, 39
glaciation, 182n25
Glendale, CA, 120
Globe (newspaper), 70, 75
Globe Publishing Company, 70
Glotzer, Paige, 206–7n21
Gold Coast and the Slum, The (Zorbaugh), 167
Great Depression, 108, 142, 153, 159–60
Great Migration, 76
Great Northern and Northern Pacific Railways, 89, 102–3
Great Northern Railroad, 198n72
Griswold del Castillo, Richard, 117
Gumprecht, Blake, 153, 180–81n1
Guthrie, Woody, 141

Hamm, Louise, 92
Hamm, Theodore, 85, 90, *91*, 94, 147; mansion of, *91*, 92–93, *93*, 109
Hamm, William, 25, 92, 108
Hamm Park, 108
Hamm's Brewery, 101, 109–11, 152, 196n28, 197n66. *See also* Excelsior Brewery; Stroh's

Hamm's Brewery and Swede Hollow (Albinson), 106
Hancock, Henry, 14
Hansen, George, 14
Harlem Flats, 8–9, 19, 22, 30–31, 32, 38, 38, 39, 46, 49, 146–47, 150–51, 163, 166, 184n7, 188n94; controversy over, 34, 42, 44; and disease, 148, 167; flooding of, 154; as Goat Town, 44, 164; industrial development, 155, 157; landfilling, 33, 40–41, 43–49, 52–53; as New East Side, 51; newspaper coverage of, 45, 48, 148; odors in, complaints about, 44, 48–49; and redlining, 159; sewer construction, 152; and shantytowns, 35, 53, 148; slum, reputation of, 33, 162; superblocks, 52; tenement construction, 50–51; as wetland complex, 151. *See also* New York City
Harper, Arthur C., 132
Harriman, Edward, 120
Harris, Charles, 66
Hart, Dock A., 70
Hausener, Wilby, 106
Hayden, Dolores, 180–81n1
Hayes, George Edmund, 28
Herrold, George H., 104, 109
heterogeneity, 2–3
highway construction, 161, 172; and suburbanization, 160–61
Hill, James J., 89
Hirt, Sonia, 207n27
Historical Society of Southern California, 116
Hokanson, Nels, 100, 102, 109, 196n38
Holland, John Joseph, 35, 37
homeownership-as-citizenship, 157
Home Owners Loan Corporation (HOLC), 143, 158
Hoovervilles, 160
HOPE VI redevelopment program, 145, 173
Houghton, Arthur D., 130–31
house courts, 126, 129, 134, 137, 145, 165, 203n103, 203n110; as "dark spots," 131–32; legal definition of, 133; as notorious, 130; and sanitation, 136
housing, 84; highway construction, 160; housing demolition, 158, 172; housing reform, 170; housing shortages, 8; substandard housing, 4
Housing Act (1937), 142, 167; equivalent elimination clause, 168; slum clearance, 168
Housing Act (1949), 144
Housing Architects Associated, 204n134
Housing Authority of the City of Los Angeles (HACLA), 142, 144–45, 204n138
Housing Conditions in the City of St. Paul (Aronovici), 103
Howse, Hillary, 78, 80
Hoyt, Henry F., 96–98, 149
Hoyt, Homer, 180n14
Hunt, Rockwell D., 122
Hurricane Sandy, 54, 154
Hurston, Zora Neale, 80, 169, 193n109

Illinois, 15, 198n72
immigration, 2–3, 5, 7–9, 17, 23, 26–27, 34, 53, 112, 160, 172; class differences within, 111; heritage museums, 6
Indian lands: building over, 16; private property turn into, 15
industrialization, 12–13, 112
International Institute, 140–41
Iowa, 198n72
Ireland, 5–6, 49, 95, 182n19, 185n26, 195n16
Ireland, John, 95
Irish, 68; squatters, 38
Iron Range, 102
Iseminger, William R., 182n15
Italy, 102–3

Jackson, Helen Hunt, 116
Jackson, J. B., 13–14
Jackson, MS, 174
Jacksonville, FL, 29
Jaeger, Louis, 50
Jakobson, Bengt, 85
Japan, 124
jazz, 80
Jefferson, Thomas, 22
Jim Crow, 2, 70, 76, 84
Joaquino, Moisado, 113
Johnson, Mark, 28
Johnson, Samuel, 181n2
Jones, Talbert, 98
Juba to Jive (Major), 28
juvenile delinquency, and environment, 208n49

Kansas City, MO: Country Club District, 206–7n21; Quality Hill, 2; West Bottoms, 2
Keller, Andrew F., 92
Kenney, Elizabeth L., 130, 202n80
kindergarten movement, 100
Kinney, Abbot, 116
Klein, Norman, 123
Klingle, Matthew, 154
Koch, Robert, 183n30
Koslow, Jennifer Lisa, 201n65, 202n80
Kowalczyk, Stefanie, 110
Kreyling, Christine, 17
Krom, Jacob, 113
Krom, Moses, 113
Kyriakoudes, Louis M., 76

Lakeland, FL, 29
Lake Superior and Mississippi Railroad, 25, 89. *See also* Saint Paul and Duluth Railroad
Lakoff, George, 28
landfilling, 22, 31–34, 40–41, 43–49, 51–53, 170
Landmarks Club, 116
Land Ordinance (1785), 13

INDEX

land organization: grid plans, 14; land use planning, 5; popular appeal of, 13–14
landscape, 1, 110–11, 161–62; as horizontal, 7, 147; landscape painting, tied to, 108; power in, 154
Landscape [Swede Hollow] (Hausener), 106
Lanegran, David, 110–12, 195n10
Language of Cities, The (Abrams), 8
Larsmo, Ola, 110
Latin America, 2
Lawrence, Abraham R., 48
Laws of the Indies, 181n13
Levee neighborhoods, 165
levees, 17, 24, 113–14, 119–20, 121, 123, 134, 153–54, 200n29
Lewthwaite, Stephanie, 150
Lexington, KY, 83–84
Lindsley, John Berrien, 148, 149
Looking Up at Down (Barlow), 80
Los Angeles, CA, 8–9, 11, 15, 23–24, 27, 30, 152–53, 172, 181n5, 201n65; African Americans in, 163; anti-Chinese prejudice in, 118–19; Boyle Heights, 113, 117, 121–23, 125, 138, 140–41, 144–45, 160, 173, 200n37; Bunker Hill, 122; Chinatown, 116; cholera, as nonfactor, 149; city boosterism, 116, 123–24; containment, as strategy, 165; "dark spots" in, 149; East Los Angeles, 120, 122–23, 142, 205n146; Fickett Hollow, 137, 142; flooding in, 123, 137, 151; founding of, 14, 113–14; as future city, 129; highway construction, 160; housing developments in, 204n134; image of, 124, 145; immigrant communities in, 135–36, 149; in-migration to, 118; invented tradition, 116; Jewish community in, 141, 144, 158; land use zoning, 138, 140; Macy Street Bridge, 141; Mexican Americans and Mexicans in, 4, 133, 137, 140–41, 144–45, 158, 163, 199n13; Mexican emigrants, "reconquest" of, 117; Molokans in, 124–25, 144, 158; multiple identities of, 116–18, 131–33, 136, 140, 144; overcrowding in, 135, 149; as paradise, 124; Progressives in, 127–32; public housing in, 142–44; race, notion of in, 163; real estate market boom, 113; Russian Town, 137, 145; Salt Lake and Los Angeles Railroad, 24; San Pedro, 120; as segregated, 118; sewer construction, 152; Skid Row, 174; slum clearance, 160; slums in, 133; Sonoratown, 116, 129–31; Spanish Fantasy Past of, 116; sunshine, as metaphor for, 131, 202n85; Terminal Railway, 24; Utah Street School, 135, 137–38, 141; Venice, 116; white racial character of, at risk, 136; white supremacy, 116, 118, 136; zoning ordinances, 156. *See also* Flats; Los Angeles River
Los Angeles and Salt Lake Railroad, 119
Los Angeles Aqueduct, 124
Los Angeles College Settlement Association (LACSA), 129–30, 132
Los Angeles County, 144, 153

Los Angeles County Hospital, 152
Los Angeles Federation of the California Congress of Mothers, 137–38
"Los Angeles New Year's Flood" (Guthrie), 141
Los Angeles River, 11, 14, 24, 114, 118, 121, 122, 124, 137, 139, 151; bubonic plague, 149–50, 150; as concrete, image of, 153; flooding of, 113–14, 141, 153, 200n29, 206n12; Mexican residents, 150; as urban swampland, 119
Louisiana, 50, 163
Louisiana Purchase, 88
Lovett, Bobby, 188–89n2, 193n109
Lummis, Charles Fletcher, 116, 202n85
Lundberg, Caroline, 113
Lundberg, Ludwig, 113
Lynchburg, VA, 17
lynching, 65

Madison Real Estate Company, 81
Madonna of 115th Street, The (Orsi), 51
Mairche, Guiseppina, 51
Mairche, Santi, 51
Major, Clarence, 28
malaria, 4, 21–22, 64
Malony, Richard, 202n80
Manhattan, 33–35, 38–39, 50; landfilling project, 31–32; street plan of, 14, 19, 20, 20, 21; wetland area, erasure of, 49. *See also* New York City
Mapel, E. B., 137–38
Marine Protection Act (1888), 186n43
Martin, Charles A., 74
Mayne, Alan, 8, 163
McAleer, Owen C., 130, 132
McGown, Andrew, 35, 38
McGown, Samson B., 50, 185n20
McKenzie, Roderick, 165–66, 208n49
McNeur, Catherine, 35
McWilliams, Carey, 116
Meharry Medical College, 67, 77, 84
Memphis, TN, Beale Street, 193n109
Methodist Episcopal Church (MEC), 66
Metropolitan Board of Health, 41
Mexican-American War, 116
Mexican International Railroad, 117
Mexico, 116–17, 133, 138
Meyer, William B., 7, 180n13
miasmatic diseases, 4, 22; disease theory of, 63–64, 83, 150–51, 166, 170
Mill City Museum, 179n10
Milwaukee, WI, 17, 89
Minneapolis, MN, 6, 27, 90–91, 102; Bohemian Flats, 106, 108
Minnesota, 85–86, 88–89, 95, 100, 102, 108, 198n72
Minnesota Territory, 88
Mizelle, Richard M., Jr., 80, 193n113
Mobile, AL, 17

Model Winery and Distillery, 121
Mohl, Raymond, 160
Molina, Natalia, 131–32, 199n13
Molloy, Thomas, 18
Molokans (Spiritual Christians), 124–27, 134, 137–38, 140, 144–45, 158, 201n51
morality, 22, 29, 57, 74, 131; and class, 9; and disease, 84; environment, and behavior, 170
Morgan, J. P., 120
Morris, John J., 44
Morris, Moreau, 42
Morris, Thomas, 72–74
Morton, Jelly Roll, 80
Mumford, Lewis, 23, 155
Municipal League of Los Angeles, 129–30
Music City Convention Center, 82–83

Napa, CA, 11
Napier, James C., 55, 70
Nasen, George, 108
Nashville, TN, 1–2, 5, 7–8, 11, 16, 23–24, 30, 57–58, 60–61, 64, 77, 151, 160, 163, 172–73, 192n84, 192n89, 194n122; African Americans, and cholera outbreak, 4; African Americans in, 4, 27, 29, 55–56, 65–72, 75–76, 78, 80–81, 158, 182n19; animals in, 63; antiblack violence in, 65; Broad Street, as urban boundary, 83; changing downtown of, 81–82; disease crisis in, 62, 148–49; flooding problems, 63, 69, 82, 151, 153–54, 206n9; Freedman Flats, 69; Germans in, 55, 182n19; Greek Revival architectural style in, 17; Hell's Half Acre, 9, 27, 69; highway construction, 160; Irish in, 55, 182n19; Jewish population in, 55; Jook section of, 169; Kalb Hollow, 9, 76; Little Ireland, 68; lowland neighborhoods in, 9; Mud Flats, 9, 76; "night soil" men, 63; original plot for, 18; park project, 74; population growth, 70, 76; poor sanitation in, 59; race-restrictive covenants in, 81; removal projects, 69; sanitation in, 62; segregation of, 81; sewer construction, 63–64, 152; shanties in, 69; South Nashville, 169; Trimble Bottom, 9, 27, 80–81; urban lowland neighborhoods, 84; urban redevelopment in, 82–83; as walking city, 66; zoning ordinances, 156. *See also* Black Bottom
Nashville Board of Health, 62
Nashville Civic Design Center, 82
Nashville Predators, 82
National Association of Real Estate Boards, 143
National Park Service, 6
nativism, 170
neighborhood demolition, 3
Nevada, 119
New Deal, 3, 5, 108, 144, 153, 166; and segregation, 158
New Orleans, LA, 7, 11–12, 18, 22–23, 117; Hurricane Katrina, 6; Lower Ninth Ward, 174

New York and Harlem Railroad, 38, 185n21
New York City, 8, 17, 22–23, 27, 30–31, 33, 41, 49–50, 61, 127, 133, 151, 162, 182–83n28, 186n41; cholera outbreaks, 148; disease in, 149; East Harlem, 34, 52–54, 156, 158, 160, 166, 172–74; flooding in, 154; Forest Hills Gardens, 206-7n21; grid plan of, 39; Harlem, 34–35, 38, 48, 51–52, 185n18, 185n24; Italians in, 51–52; landfilling, 34, 40; Lower East Side, 174; public housing, 52, 174; Rockaway, 174; Seneca Village, 35; sewer construction, 152, 186n42; slum clearance, 160; Spanish Harlem, 173, 188n93; Yorkville, 32, 34, 38; zoning ordinances, 156. *See also* Harlem Flats; Manhattan
New York City Housing Authority (NYCHA), 52
Northwest Territory, 88

Olmsted, Frederick Law, Sr., 33, 38, 185n27
Ord, Edward O. C., 14
Orsi, Robert, 51–52
O'Sullivan, Thomas, 108
"Other Burgess Model, The" (Meyer), 7
Other Side of the Tracks, The (Brown), 106
Owens Valley, 124

Pacific Coast Biscuit Company, 126
Pacini, Filippo, 183n30
Page, Max, 191n64
Park, Robert, 140, 166
Parrant, Pierre "Pig's Eye," 194-95n6
Parsons, William E., 104
Pasadena, CA, 120
Pearl School, 67–68, 84
Pesca, Patsy, 52
Peters, John C., 61
Petterson, Paul, 100
Phelan, Edward, 88
Philadelphia, PA, 11, 23, 182–83n28; Black Bottom, 184n43; Mill Creek, 205-6n8
Pilgrims of Russian Town, The (Young), 140
Pittsburgh, PA, 26; Skunk Hollow, 194n3, 208n47
place names, 173, 183n40; demeaning of black life, by whites, 57
Poland, 5–6
poverty, 2, 62, 115–16, 124, 127, 154, 164–67, 169; and dependency, 99; and disease, 34; and environment, 3, 6–7, 8–10, 12, 30, 53, 145, 147, 150, 153, 168, 174; low ground, connection between, 1, 174; as persistent, 170; and power, 174; and race, 64–65; urban, 4, 10; and water, 63
Princeville, NC, 83
Progressive Era, 3–4, 146–47, 163–64, 170
Progressives, 127, 129, 131–32, 167. *See also* urban reformers
Prohibition, 78
Protestant work ethic, 127

INDEX   217

Provisional City, The (Cuff), 143
Prussia, 49, 195n16
public health, 1, 62, 101, 108, 150–51
public housing, 1, 52–54, 81, 142–44, 172, 174, 204–5n145, 209n56; stigmatizing of, 145
public hygiene, 63
public space, 51
Public Works Administration (PWA), 80, 142, 204n134
Puck (magazine), 48

Quierolo, Nicholas, 132

race, 2, 10, 59, 83, 155, 169–70; and altitude, 173; and disease, 61, 165; and ethnicity, 158, 163; as miasma, 145; race-restrictive covenants, 81, 84, 156, 158, 160, 206–7n21; and racism, 149; and segregation, 157; in urban landscape, 57
racism, 81, 146–48, 163, 169, 174; and race, 149
ragpickers, 40, 45, 71
ragtime, 80
railroads, 23–24, 112; boundaries, reinforcing of, 155; decline of, 160; railroad slums, 155. *See also individual railroads*
Rainey, Ma, 80
Ramona (Jackson), 116
Ramsey County, 100, 102, 195n16
Ramsey County Medical Society, 96
Randel, John, 39
Reconstruction, 5, 29, 56–57, 70, 163
red light districts, 68
redlining, 81, 146, 156, *159*, 160, 171
Reed, Jo, 65
Report of the Metropolitan Board of Health (report), 148
Reps, John, 13
Resler, George, 106, *107*
Revolutionary War, 35
Richmond, VA, 17, 83–84
Riis, Jacob, 129, 133, 163
Rogers, Mary Elizabeth, 80–81
Romo, Ricardo, 117, 125
Rosenberg, Charles, 4
Russia, 5–6, 124, 125, 158
Ryman Auditorium, 81, 153

Saint Louis, MO, 23, 127
Saint Paul, MN, 5, 8, 16, 23–24, 27, 30, 86–88, 92, 95–96, 101, 106, 109, 147, 151, 158, 160, 163, 165, 172–73, 195n13; bootlegging in, 194–95n6; cholera epidemic, avoidance of, 149; floating population of, 195n11; immigrant population in, 89–90, 102–4, 195n16; immigrants, as threats, 4; Little Italy, 6; rapid growth of, 89–90; Seventh Street Improvement Arches, 155; sewer construction, 152–53; Swedish population in, 98, 100; Upper Levee, 103, 165; zoning ordinances, 156. *See also* Swede Hollow
Saint Paul and Duluth Railroad, 24, 85, 89, 101, 194n5, 195–96n23. *See also* Lake Superior and Mississippi Railroad
Saint Paul Board of Health, 96
Saint Paul Department of Public Works, 108
Saint Paul Mills, 90
Saint Paul Railroad, 89
Saint Paul's AME Church, 1, 66, *67*, 68, 83–84
Saint Paul Water Company, 85, 91–92, 95, 196n38
Salt Lake and Los Angeles Railroad, *24*
Salt Lake City, UT, 127
Salt Lake Railroad, 131
Sanborn Fire Insurance Company, 104, 109, 197n66
Sanchelli, Michael, 152
San Francisco, CA, 26; Chinese residents, demonization of, 4
sanitary geology, 62
sanitation, 4, 20, 34, 39, 52–54, 62–63, 136, 169–70; water problems, 151
Schermerhorn Symphony Center, 82
Seattle, WA, 26, 166, 180n14
segregation, 7, 27, 70–71, 76–77, 81, 84, 118, 158, 169; by class, 147, 157; and containment, 57; by race, 157
Shacks and Snow (Albinson), 106
shantytowns, 34, *36*, 44, 52–53, 160; cholera outbreak in, 45; spatial arrangements in, 35
Shattuck, Charles, 143
Sidewalk Law, 63
skyscrapers, 208n39
slavery, 2, 17, 56 *58*, 84
slum clearance, 3, 52, 72, 74–76, 160, 172, 180n17, 182n21, 191n64; and housing, 168
Slum Clearance Committee, 52
slums, 6, 28, 33, 53, 55, 71, 131, 133, 136, 146, 169, 180n17; abhorrence of, 8; attraction of repulsion, 163; concept of, 8; definitions of, 162, 167; as diseased environment, 150; documenting of, 103; and housing, 166–67; as imagined places, 163; and journalists, 165; and maps, 168; origin of, 163; policy and planning debates about, 9; as problematic term, 8; railroad slums, 155; slum clearance, 3, 52, 72, 74–76, 142; slum housing campaigns, and sunshine, 145; social cohesion, lacking in, 167; social disorganization, 166–67; social scientists, 165–66; stigmatization of, 2; as term, 26, 163, 165; urban spatial structure, 166
Slums (Mayne), 8
Slums and Housing (Ford), 167
Snow, John, 148
social mobility, 2, 7, 165, 168–69
Sohner, Theodore, 108
Sokoloff, Lillian, 137–38, 201n51
Sonoma, CA, 11

Southern California, 144; Palos Verdes Estates, 206–7n21
Southern California Packing Company, 121
Southern Pacific and Santa Fe Railroads, 113
Southern Pacific Railroad, 117
space, and place, 162
Spalding, Sophie, 125, 204n123
spatialization, 28; spatial arrangement, 88; spatial organization, 155, 170; spatial patterns, 173; spatial practices, 9, 84; spatial segregation, 70; spatial sense, 162
Spirn, Anne Whiston, 190n29, 205–6n8
squatters, 35
Stern, Charles, 121
Stilgoe, John, 13; metropolitan corridor, 179n9
Stoddart, Bessie, 130–31
Stroh's, 110. *See also* Hamm's Brewery
substandard housing, 4
suburban housing construction, 158
suburbanization, 147; highway construction, 160–61
Summerville, James, 71, 188–89n2
Swanson, Albert, 108
Swede Hollow, 5, 8, 24, 25, 27, 30, 85, 86, 86, 87, 90, 91, 92–93, 105, 146–51, 158, 160, 163, 170, 172, 197n53; artistic depictions of, 105–6, 107, 108; cholera risk, 95–98, 101; as city park, 109–10; decline of, 104; demographics of, 87; as denigrated, 88; description of, in heroic terms, 110; and dumping, 152; as engineered landscape, 111; fire in, 109; forced removal, debates over, 96–98, 101, 108; as "foreign colony," 88; goats in, 164; growth of, 101; heavy industry designation, 156, 157; as imageable urban landscape, 110; Italian immigrants in, 102–4, 111, 164–65; "legend" of, 105; name of, 87; as paradoxical urban landscape, 111; park proposal, 108–9; as picturesque, 164–65; as "plague spot," 95, 98; professions in, 101–2; rail yards, proximity to, 155; and redlining, 159; as refuge, 112; renaming of, 173; romanticized view of, 88, 98–100, 164; Seventh Street Improvement Arches, 94–95, 101; as slum, reputation of, 111–12, 162, 165; as stepping-stone, 98, 111–12; Swede Hollow Park, 173; Swedish population in, 98–99, 111, 164–65, 195n10; walking tours of, 110. *See also* Saint Paul, MN
Swede Hollow (Andrus), 106
Swede Hollow (Brown), 106
Swede Hollow (Larsmo), 110
Swede Hollow (Resler), 106, 107
Swede Hollow (etching; Sohner), 106, 108
Swede Hollow (painting; Sohner), 106, 108
Swede Hollow Park, 165
Sweden, 85, 89, 100, 110, 195n16

Tammany Hall, 41, 48
Tatom, Eric, 81
Taylor, Graham, 201n65
Tennessee, 5–6, 76, 78
Terminal Railway, 120–21
Texas, 163
Thilo, Mae, 139
Thoen, Phillip, 90
topography, 7, 53, 59, 155; city planning, 104; and class, 2, 83, 144; flood risk, 6; and nationality, 145; and race, 83, 144–45; urban landscape, 4, 112
Treaty of Guadalupe Hidalgo, 116
Trimble, Steve, 196n28
Truesdell, William Albert, 94
Tuan, Yi-Fu, 162
Turnblad, Swan, 102
Tweed, William M. "Boss," 41, 185n24, 186n45
Twin Cities, Swedish Americans in, 164. *See also* Minneapolis, MN; Saint Paul, MN
two birds theory, 160
typhoid, 4, 21–22
Tyree, Evans, 70

Ueland, Jeffrey, 173
Union Transportation Company, 70
United States, 1, 4, 7, 13, 50, 61, 67, 88, 101, 106, 112, 116, 118, 125–26, 141, 163, 172, 174, 181n2, 182n19, 182–83n28, 206n16, 209n60; Italian immigration to, 102; public housing construction in, 204–5n145; Swedish immigration to, 89; town settlements, 16; urban population, growth in, 23
upward mobility, 111–12
urban form, 53
urbanization, 112
urban landscape, 2–3, 8–9, 11, 18, 26, 29–30, 51, 174; gridiron plan, 13, 34–35; as hierarchical, 170; physical alterations to, 4, 35; and race, 57; and railroads, 155; reshaping of, 12; sociospatial structure of, 173; superblocks, 173; and topography, 112; transformation of, 52; urban lowland neighborhoods, 154
urban land use, 84; contests over, 83
urban lowland neighborhoods, 10, 18, 34, 53–55, 83–84, 86, 88, 103, 111, 125–26, 146–47, 166, 171; agency, exercising of, 112; animals in, 164; automobile, ascendance of, 161; bottom of social hierarchy, 1–2; class-based segregation, 7; as clearly bounded, 27; and containment, 174; creation of, by structural forces, 112; cultural stigmatism against, 57; as dangerous, 174; demonizing of, 30; disease, fear of, 4, 21–22; dismantling of, 5; and displacement, 112; and eviction, 112; flooding in, 20–21, 153–54, 158–59; foreign people, occupied by, 163–64; goat, as symbol of, 164; highway construction, and housing demolition, 160; immigration history as part of, 8; industrial use, zoning for, 5, 156;

industry, dominated by, 16; as intentionally built, 13; landfilling, 170; landscape element, and social construction, 170; legacies of, 174; local histories of, 6; low position and low status, as intertwined, 28; low-quality housing in, 26–27; as maligned, 154; manufacturing and warehousing, as sites for, 156–58; marginalization of, 2; migrants in, 12; moral behavior in, 6; motley character of, 12; names of, 26–28; negative reputation of, 151; as neglected, 154; neighborhood identity, and geographical language usage, 26; newspaper coverage of, 27, 30, 164; others, as places for, 170; and overcrowding, 26; pejorative place names of, 1, 3, 6; as plague spots, 3; population decline, 160; as potential redevelopment sites, 5; railroad-industrial neighborhoods, morphing into, 11, 23–24, 26, 170; redevelopment of, 159; renaming of, 172–73; sanitary problems, 26; segregation of, 27; sewer construction, 152, 170; as slums, 2, 165; as stepping-stones, 7; and stigmatization, 174; as term, 183n34; as threat, 149, 167–68; transportation corridors, 182n21; as undesirable, 26; urban landscape, familiar aspect of, 154; urban landscape, sociospatial structure of, 173; as urban problems, 29–30; as urban spaces, reimagining of, 20; and waterfronts, 16–17; water problems of, 152. *See also* Black Bottom; Flats; Harlem Flats; Swede Hollow

urban morbidity, 4

urban planning, 3, 7, 84

urban reformers, 1, 3, 5, 8, 22, 103, 124, 127, 136, 159. *See also* Progressives

urban renewal, 1, 9, 144, 150, 172; and dislocation, 174; mass demolition, 174

urban sociology, borrowing from plant ecology, 166

urban space, 17, 173; class, ethnicity, and race, 168; racialized view of, 163; vertical classifications of, 28

urban spatial relationships, highway construction, 160

urban spatial structure, 168; and slums, 166; vertical hypothesis, 7

urban topography, association with disease, 4

Urban Villagers, The (Gans), 8

US Army Corps of Engineers, 154

Utah, 119–20

Utah Street Architects Association, 142

Vale, Lawrence, 208n45

Van Nort, George M., 43

Vaux, Calvert, 38

Vecoli, Rudolph, 112

Veeder, Mary Adair, 130, 202n80

Viele, Egbert, 19, 20, 34–35, 44, 47, 148; maps of, 33

View at Fort Clinton, McGown's Pass, New York City (Holland), 35, *37*

Vigil, Diego, 118, 205n146

Vignes, Jean Louis, 113, 180–81n1

von Wagner, Johanna, 127–28, *128*, 129, 132–33

Wagener, Jacob, 95

Wagener, John, 109, 196n38

Ward, David, 163

Wards Island, 39

Warf, Barney, 173

War of 1812, 35

Washington, DC, 17; Foggy Bottom, 173

Washington Territory, 50

waste, 40–41, 46, 84

Watergate hotel, 173

Watkins, J. L., 66

wetlands, 32, 44, 49, 53, 151, 181n4, 184n3; as term, 183n34

whiteness, 145; and Americanness, 191n75

white supremacy, 116, 118, 136, 164, 170. *See also* Aryan supremacy

Wickham, William H., 47

Wild, Mark, 118

Willard, Charles Dwight, 129

Williams, Lucinda, 82, 195n13

Wilson, George, 58

Winchell, N. H., 92, 194n5

Winter (Swanson), 108

Winter Scene, Swede Hollow (Albinson), 106

Wisconsin, 198n72

Wolfskill, William, 113, 180–81n1

Woman's Civic League, 128

Women's Civic Federation, 131

Workman, William, 122

Workman, William H., 122–23, 200n39

Works Progress Administration (WPA) Writers' Project, 6

World War II, 108, 144, 173, 209n60

Wright, Lloyd, 142, 204n134

xenophobia, 146–48, 165, 174

Yarusso, Gentille, 102

Yarusso, Joseph, 102

yellow fever, 4, 21–22

Young, Pauline V., 140, 204n123

Young Women's Christian Association (YWCA), 129

zanjas, 114, 123–24

Zipp, Samuel, 52

zoning, 1, 5, 9–10, 81, 138, 140, 146, 156–57, 160, 168, 171; as exclusionary, 158; industrial, 172

Zorbaugh, Harvey, 167

zymotic diseases, 53

www.ingramcontent.com/pod-product-compliance
Lightning Source LLC
Chambersburg PA
CBHW022053290426
44109CB00014B/1085